Health and Class:
The Early Years

Health and Class: The Early Years

Chris Power, Orly Manor and John Fox

Based on research carried out at the Social Statistics Research Unit, City University, London

CHAPMAN & HALL

London · New York · Tokyo · Melbourne · Madras

UK	Chapman & Hall, 2–6 Boundary Row, London SE1 8HN
USA	Chapman & Hall, 29 West 35th Street, New York NY10001
JAPAN	Chapman & Hall Japan, Thomson Publishing Japan, Hirakawacho Nemoto Building, 7F, 1–7–11 Hirakawa-cho, Chiyoda-ku, Tokyo 102
AUSTRALIA	Chapman & Hall Australia, Thomas Nelson Australia, 102 Dodds Street, South Melbourne, Victoria 3205
INDIA	Chapman & Hall India, R. Seshadri, 32 Second Main Road, CIT East, Madras 600 035

First edition 1991

© 1991 Chapman & Hall

Phototypeset in 10/12pt Palatino by Intype, London
Printed in Great Britain by St Edmundsbury Press Ltd,
Bury St Edmunds, Suffolk

ISBN 0 412 41570 4

British Library Cataloguing in Publication Data
Power, C.
    Health and class: the early years
    I. Title II. Manor, O. III. Fox, J.
    614.4

ISBN 0 412 41570 4

Library of Congress Cataloging-in-Publication Data
Power, Chris, 1951–
    Health and class : The Early Years / Chris Power, Orly Manor, and John Fox. – 1st ed.
        p.   cm.
    Includes bibliographical references and index.
    ISBN 0–412–41570–4
    1. Social medicine—Great Britain.   2. Social classes–Great Britain.   I. Manor, Orly, 1952–.   II. Fox, John, 1946, April 25–.   III. Title.
    [DNLM: 1. Health Status.   2. Longitudinal Studies—Great Britain.   3. Socioeconomic Factors.   WA 900 FA1 P8h]
    RA418.3.G7P68   1991
    362.1'0941–dc20
    DNLM/DLC
    for Library of Congress   91–15998
                                                                  CIP

Contents

Contents

Acknowledgements

This book has developed from a project on Health and Social Mobility among Young Adults which began in 1985 and was funded by the Department of Health and Social Security. Ken Fogelman was closely involved with the work until the original project was completed in 1988. Although, since his move to Leicester, he has not been able to contribute to the preparation of the book, the majority of the ideas presented derive from the four of us, as is reflected in publications from the original project.

We are also indebted to a number of professional colleagues who read earlier manuscripts of the book and gave very valuable advice. Particular thanks are expressed to Abe Adelstein, Eva Alberman, Mel Bartley, Mildred Blaxter and Peter Goldblatt.

Researchers using longitudinal data sets such as the National Child Development Study must always acknowledge the debt that they owe those who have invested in the collection, documentation and organization of earlier data. The National Birthday Trust supported the initial sweep and the National Children's Bureau has been responsible for the next three. We should acknowledge, in particular, the work of Peter Shepherd at City University, who, with colleagues funded by the Economic and Social Research Council, provided considerable assistance in the early period of the project.

Other colleagues at City have contributed to the project in a variety of ways, primarily through discussions about methods and interpretation. Special thanks are due to Sharon Clarke who patiently helped prepare the manuscript for publication.

The book would never have been completed without the financial support provided to Chris Power by City University after the end of the Department of Health grant. Thanks are due to Professor John Bynner, Director of the Social Statistics Research Unit.

1

The health inequalities debate

1.1 Introduction

In England and Wales in the 1970s it was estimated that children born to professional families outlived – by as much as seven years or more – their peers born to parents who were skilled and in manual jobs. Babies surviving the first month of life had more than four times the risk of death before reaching their first birthday when born to families of unskilled, compared to professional, parents. Young men entering employment as unskilled labourers had only two-thirds the chance of drawing their retirement pensions at age 65 as did young men entering a profession. These patterns are typical of those seen in other developed countries.

In the post-war era it was assumed that such health inequalities would have diminished, if not disappeared, as a result of the development of the Welfare State. This belief was supported by the rapid decline in mortality rates and the consequential increase in life expectancy. However, it is now recognized in many countries that differences between social groups have in fact been increasing since the 1930s. Inequalities widened as the major diseases of poverty, tuberculosis and infectious diseases were in decline. But the demise of these diseases was offset by new epidemics, including those of cancer, circulatory disease, accidents and violence.

The new epidemics have not affected all sections of society equally. Proportionately, more early deaths have occurred due to each of these causes among unskilled than professional workers. Young men, aged 25–44, in unskilled occupations have four times the risk of dying from lung cancer, stomach cancer, ischaemic heart disease and stroke than young men in professional occupations. For accidents, the relative risk is threefold. In childhood an overall relative risk of three for accidents and violence conceals differences of tenfold or more for deaths from falls, fires and drowning.

Differences are observed in stillbirths, and in deaths during infancy through adulthood to old age. They tend to be greatest among children and young adults.

Mortality gives only one view of the health of a nation – it does not necessarily reflect the pattern of disease or disability, nor does it indicate quality of life. However, morbidity data are much more difficult to obtain. They derive mainly from interview and examination surveys, from reports of service use – hospital inpatient and outpatient attendances and general practitioner consultations – and from registers of medically confirmed diseases, such as population cancer registers. Despite limitations of these data sources, social patterns are similar to, but not always consistent with, those described above for mortality. Social differences are even evident from people's perceptions of their own health.

Diverse explanations have been put forward for differences observed and widening inequalities over time. Some suggest that the differences are not real but reflect an artefact of the way statistics are obtained. Others see them as resulting from a social Darwinistic selection process by which those in better health are more able to climb the social hierarchy and the least healthy drift downwards. It has also been argued that they reflect genetic endowment or, alternatively, the circumstances and way of life of different social groups. This book explores these explanations.

It is only by developing an understanding of the factors responsible for social differences in health that policies can be promoted which encourage a healthy life across the whole population. However, information on health inequalities has several other purposes. It is used to monitor public health; to plan and target services and distribute resources; to identify new and emerging problems and to assist in discovering causes, so that remedial action can be taken; to assist in formulating and evaluating health service policy; and as inputs to estimates of funding requirements of pensions, health insurance and even housing need.

Farr (1839), in the first annual report of the Registrar General, made the following comment:

> 'One of the many applications of the facts will be the promotion of practical medicine. The extent to which epidemics vary in different localities, seasons and classes of society, will be indicated by the registered diseases; and the experienced practitioner, wherever he may be placed, will learn to administer remedies with discrimination, and with due reference to the circumstances of the population.'

Farr's primary concern was to identify aspects of the circumstances in which people lived which might explain the differences in mortality between different communities. Since then the emphasis appears to have moved to the use of these data and data on the social circumstances in different localities regionally in assessing need for services and ways of allocating resources.

Health policy since the Second World War has often been framed in terms of differences between sections of the community. The World Health Organization has added to this tendency by promoting workshops, bringing together researchers in this field particularly under the umbrella of its initiative 'Health for all in the year 2000' which sets particular targets, including targets for a reduction in differences in health within countries.

It has been suggested that little is to be gained from further arguments about explanations for health inequalities; the policy implications are already clear (Carr-Hill, 1987). However, that can never be the case as long as the pathways are not known. Without some understanding of the series of chains through which health inequalities develop, there is a weak basis for directing most effectively the resources needed to address the problems. This is not to deny that grounds already exist for some decisions (Chalmers, 1985) but even in these cases a better understanding of the processes involved would be of considerable value. Society would be neglecting its responsibilities if it chose to do nothing on the grounds that little would be achieved without radical changes to social organization.

The primary objective of this book is to examine the relative merits of different explanations for social differences in health. In order to accomplish this, a framework for investigating health differences is suggested – a framework which brings together different explanatory factors, allowing each to compete with others, and, at the same time, acknowledging that differences in health are contingent upon previous experiences as well as those currently prevailing. Following this, the suggested framework will be used to examine differences in health that are observed among young adults.

One might ask why we have chosen to study explanations in early adulthood? It is after all a stage of life when serious conditions are relatively uncommon. However, it is also a stage when factors in infancy interact with socio-economic circumstances in childhood; when differences in health behaviour such as smoking and drinking may be seen; and when people start to establish their own social positions. It is consequently a stage when competing explanations might all be expected to contribute to differences in health between social groups. This age is consequently of particular interest if one wishes to investigate different explanations.

The young adults studied are subjects in the 1958 birth cohort (National Child Development Study). Details of this sample follow in

Chapter 2. Meanwhile, further background to the inequalities debate is provided as introduction to the conceptual framework adopted for the study.

1.2 Literature review

To do justice to recent research into this subject considerable space would have to be devoted to a review. Fortunately, in the past few years a number of books have been published on the subject. The reader is referred to *Cycles of Disadvantage* (Rutter and Madge, 1976) and *Despite the Welfare State* (Brown and Madge, 1982) both of which came out of the DHSS and ESRC series of studies in disadvantage and deprivation; to *Inequalities in Health* (Townsend and Davidson, 1982) and *The Health Divide* (Whitehead, 1988) which followed Lord Ennals' initiative led by the Health Education Council. The ESRC also sponsored work which led to *Class and Health* (Wilkinson, 1986) and, with the European Science Foundation, to *Health Inequalities in European Countries* (Fox, 1989).

Since the main aim of this book is to describe new analyses bringing together a range of explanations, the literature presented here is selected to put this evidence into context. The emphasis is on data collected at the national level, or at least studies which are representative of the national picture; limitations of space do not allow a fully comprehensive account of the wide range of smaller studies. However, it is important to outline the historical and international setting of the research, recent findings and data limitations, explanations and how they have been compared.

Whereas the primary concern here is with inequalities in health – usually measured by ill-health – until recently the main data relate to mortality not 'health'. National mortality statistics provide a rich source of data from the middle of the last century. However, these data are limited in several respects. Apart from well-recognized weaknesses arising from the way in which the figures are compiled (discussed on page 17) there is an extensive literature on the limitations of statistics from deaths to indicate morbidity, let alone health. In addition, it is now being recognized that, as a consequence of increased life expectancy, 'health' and morbidity should assume more prominence in the investigation of health inequalities (Carr-Hill, 1987; Blaxter, 1989).

The growth in interest in quality of life and 'disease free' life gives rise to pressure to strengthen the national armoury through the introduction of new data sources such as *The Health and Lifestyle Survey* (Cox *et al.*, 1987) and the continuous health surveys planned by OPCS (1990). Despite signs that more data will be available for future generations the reader should appreciate that a review which draws on published material and its interpretation, such as this, will still appear to give too much emphasis to mortality.

1.2.1 Historical background

a) Mortality
Farr's early work (Farr, 1860) on mortality of health districts was undertaken in an attempt to assess how far people in less healthy circumstances might avoid ill health in the same way as those in more advantaged circumstances.

'With the growing knowledge that the greatest gaps between the mortality of the upper classes and that of the general population occurred in infancy and childhood, there was strong concern within the statistical movement to obtain statistics on childhood mortality of the poorer classes. This concern was heightened when, with the marked improvements in adult mortality from 1840 onwards, there was virtually no change in infant mortality, which was annually responsible for the loss of 15 per cent of births. Mr Humphries, the Assistant Registrar General, addressed the Royal Statistical Society in 1887 and stated that it was "urgently desirable that we should know more of the rates of mortality prevailing in the different strata of society".'

Although Farr in his analysis of mortality for England for the period 1861–70 combined occupations into categories which corresponded to a loosely defined ordering of early industrial society (industrial workers, agricultural workers, domestic workers, etc.) in order to distinguish the social and biological influences from the direct hazards of specific occupations, this sort of grouping was not regularly repeated until Stevenson (1923, 1928) developed the first classification of social classes in the 1920s. The link between these two classifications is described by Szreter (1984, 1986) and by Goldblatt (1990a).

The social class distribution of mortality in men shown in the 1921 decennial supplement is reproduced in Figure 1.1 (Stevenson, 1927). Standardized death rates for all causes combined increased with decreasing social class. The class gradient was especially pronounced for specific causes of death, notably respiratory diseases and bronchitis, and less marked for others, such as peptic ulcer. There were variations, however, such that classes I and II had the highest rates of mortality for some conditions, and for appendicitis and diabetes the gradient was reversed.

Early analyses, such as those by Farr, were derived from the routine vital registration data and were of necessity based on information

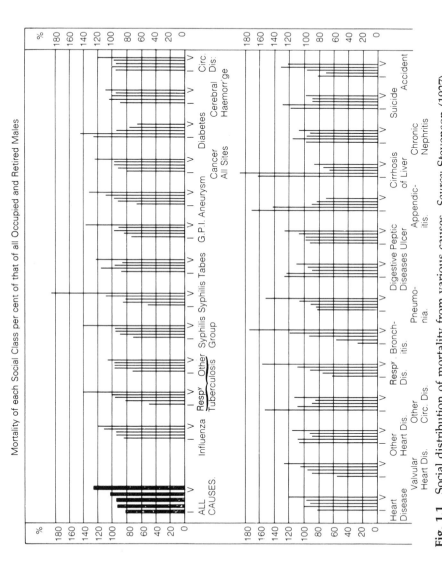

Fig. 1.1 Social distribution of mortality from various causes. *Source:* Stevenson (1927).

recorded on the death certificate. Of these characteristics only address and occupation could reasonably be used to indicate socio-economic circumstances and in consequence these provided the principal means of distinguishing between different social groups.

It is interesting to note, however, that when Stevenson used the 1911 Census to investigate differences in fertility and child mortality he experimented with housing circumstances as an indicator of socio-economic conditions (Fox and Goldblatt, 1982). Farr, in the latter part of his reign in the General Registrar Office, also used the fact that at marriage registration the parties marrying signed their names (as opposed to putting a cross) as an index of social position (Registrar General, 1857). Clearly this was designed to reflect educational attainment.

Since the Second World War changes to the social class allocations of individual occupations have been largely based on the education and skill requirements of the occupation, thus reflecting the importance of education to social stratification (Halsey *et al.*, 1980).

While the early analyses of occupational mortality were primarily directed at men of working age, there was substantial interest in peri-natal and infant mortality (see the above quote concerning Humphries' paper to the Royal Statistical Society in 1887) and some attempts were made to look at the occupational mortality of women (Tatham, 1908).

b) Morbidity
Reliance on mortality as an indicator of health has been unavoidable since no national data on morbidity or health and their relationships with occupation or other measures of social position were systematically collected before the Second World War. The lack of data was addressed by *The Survey of Sickness 1943 to 1952* (Logan and Brooke, 1957). The extent of social differences found in this survey are illustrated by Table 1.1, using the income group of the chief wage earner as an indicator of social position. Mean monthly sickness, prevalence, incapacity and medical consultation rates (defined in the table) all varied by income: the highest rates were consistently found in the lowest income group and decreased with increasing income.

The Survey of Sickness was followed by the first National Morbidity Survey (Logan, 1960) which collected morbidity statistics on the basis of consultations with general practitioners in the year 1955/6. These studies provide the earliest morbidity data for England and Wales for which repeat surveys have been conducted. In each case an attempt was made to assess the pattern of disease and service demands by socio-economic factors. Relevant findings from the most recent survey, and limitations of such studies, are mentioned later in this chapter.

The 1970s saw the introduction of the General Household Survey –

Table 1.1 Mean monthly sickness, prevalence, incapacity and medical consultation rates per 100 persons interviewed, by sex and income group of chief wage earner, 1947, 1949, and of 'head of household', 1951

	Sickness*		Prevalence†		Incapacity‡		Consultations§	
	M	F	M	F	M	F	M	F
INCOME GROUP OF CHIEF WAGE-EARNER, 1947								
Under £3	79	80	184	201	200	136	68	55
£3 and under £5.10	61	70	112	156	110	95	38	38
£5.10 and under £10	57	69	102	151	85	90	34	42
£10 and over	61	67	108	140	71	108	39	49
Not known	58	70	104	152	88	92	29	44
Total	61	71	114	160	106	100	39	42
INCOME GROUP OF CHIEF WAGE-EARNER, 1949								
Under £3	82	83	198	214	261	159	89	63
£3 and under £5 or £5.10.0	63	74	121	169	113	111	45	49
£5 or £5.10.0 and under £7.10.0 } $7.10 and under £10	61	73	112	161	84	92	34	44
£10 and over	59	71	110	158	66	85	36	47
Not known	59	73	109	164	69	94	33	48
Total	63	74	121	171	104	107	41	49
INCOME GROUP OF 'HEAD OF HOUSEHOLD', 1951								
Up to £3	77	82	171	202	198	139	77	62
Over £3 and up to £5	71	76	151	176	179	133	59	56
Over £5 and up to £7.10.0	65	73	119	162	112	100	41	47
Over £7.10 and up to £10	63	71	112	153	76	97	36	44
Over £10	63	71	113	145	72	91	34	39
Not known	62	72	111	156	92	97	45	46
Total	67	75	127	170	119	111	47	51

* Number of people (per 100 interviewed) reporting some illness or injury in a month regardless of when they began to be ill.
† Number of illnesses and injuries reported in a month (per 100 people interviewed).
‡ Number of days away from work during the month or, for people not usually employed, the number of days confined to the home (per 100 people interviewed).
§ Number of visits in the month made to or by a medical practitioner (per 100 people interviewed).

Source: Logan and Brooke (1957).

an annual national survey of some ten thousand private households sampled from the electoral register – which collects information for government departments including health indicators such as longstanding illness* and visits to the general practitioner (OPCS, 1973). This was

* Informants are asked whether they have any longstanding illness, disability or infirmity. Those who report a longstanding illness are then asked whether this limits their activities in any way. Thus, a two-stage measure is available: (i) all longstanding illness and (ii) limiting longstanding illness.

an important development because the survey attempts to be nationally representative. GHS data, as GP morbidity surveys, can now be used to monitor trends in differences between socio-economic groups (Balarajan *et al.*, 1987), although for a shorter time period.

The first of three national birth cohort studies (Douglas and Blomfield, 1958; Butler and Bonham, 1963; Chamberlain *et al.*, 1975) was started shortly after the Second World War. Since each study commenced at birth they allowed an assessment of the importance of social factors in the outcome of pregnancy. Striking socio-economic differences were found for both mortality and low birthweight and the latter differences can now be explored across generations (Alberman *et al.*, 1991). The richness of data contained in these studies allows a detailed examination of the social circumstances surrounding birth.

The birth surveys developed into longitudinal studies which follow the health and educational development of children born in one week in March 1946, March 1958 and April 1970. A common theme has been to shed light on socio-economic and other factors influencing subsequent health and development (Douglas, 1964; Davie *et al.*, 1972; Butler and Golding, 1986). The studies have shown a general pattern of poorer health among people living in poorer socio-economic circumstances, but there are exceptions to this overall trend depending on the particular illness being considered. For example, lower respiratory tract illness was more prevalent among young children with manual backgrounds compared with those with non-manual backgrounds, irrespective of whether they were born in 1946 or 1970 (Douglas and Waller, 1966; Butler and Golding, 1986); eczema, on the other hand, was reported more often in children from non-manual classes born in 1958 and 1970, although in the 1946 study rates were lower for classes I and II (Taylor *et al.*, 1984).

After the introduction of the birth cohorts, interest in the growth of children in England and Scotland led, in 1972, to the National Study of Health and Growth (Holland *et al.*, 1981). Social differences in growth were demonstrated and further analyses may reveal secular trends in such differences.

More recently there have been several national studies which improve knowledge of the social patterns in such measures as height, weight and disability and also in health-related behaviours such as smoking, drinking and diet. Further discussion of these will be given later in this chapter.

1.2.2 International evidence

Although no other country has as long a history of conducting such analyses as those published regularly in the decennial supplements on occupational mortality, interest in this topic has not been restricted to England and Wales. During the past thirty years national studies of differences in mortality between socio-economic groups have been undertaken in the Nordic countries (Norway [Kristofersen, 1979], Denmark [Lynge, 1979], Finland [Marin, 1986], Sweden [Central Statistics Office, 1981] and Iceland [Nordic Statistical Secretariat, 1988]), in various Commonwealth countries (including New Zealand [Pearce *et al.*, 1983], Canada (Howe and Lindsay, 1983), Australia, Scotland [General Register Office, 1981] and Northern Ireland [Park, 1966]), in central and south European countries (including Hungary [Central Statistical Office, 1988], France [Desplanques, 1979], Italy [Pagnanelli, 1986] and Switzerland [Minder, 1986]) and also in the USA (Kitagawa and Hauser, 1973) and Japan (Ministry of Health and Welfare, 1973). A number of countries, for example, Sweden and the USA, also collect routine health survey data which are used to study socio-economic differences and their trends over time.

In each of these countries the least advantaged sections of the different communities suffer the highest mortality rates. There have been a number of initiatives by international organizations to promote comparative work (e.g. WHO, 1978 and UN/WHO, 1980; Preston, 1980). However, it is only as more international data accumulate that comparisons can be made between countries. Since 1980 the international committee for coordination of research in economics and demography has organized a series of meetings with the aim of promoting the collection of suitable data and the development of methods of comparison (CICRED, 1982, 1984, 1985). Participation has in the main been from industrialized countries.

The attempts to compare countries have highlighted the problems of such comparisons (Fox, 1989). Even if similar schemes of classification are used in the different countries, the industrial, occupational and social structures vary greatly. Some attempts have been made to overcome these problems: for example, by ranking occupations on the basis of mortality as an indicator of socio-economic circumstances (Kagamimori *et al.*, 1983) or by using alternative indicators of social group (Valkonen, 1987, 1989). Such studies are, however, as yet largely inconclusive.

1.2.3 Recent findings

These latest international developments coincide with further studies in Britain; this section describes the main findings that emerged. Again emphasis is given to the larger, usually national, studies mentioned above.

The decennial report of mortality for the years 1970–72 gave an estimate of a difference of over seven years of life expectancy from birth between social classes I and V (OPCS, 1978). This is confirmed by data from the most recent decennial supplement on occupational mortality and the OPCS Longitudinal Study (Haberman and Bloomfield, 1988).

Although the decennial supplements have been, to a large extent, restricted to differences in mortality between men in different occupations and social classes at working ages, they indicate that differences exist for men and women at all ages. Figure 1.2 is included here to illustrate class differences for specific causes of death, using mortality data for 1970–72 (OPCS, 1978). While a clear class gradient can be seen for most causes, the trend does vary: for example, mortality resulting from mental disorders is higher in women from social classes I and II than from classes IV and V, which is the reverse of the pattern for most diseases.

The variation in the extent of class differences in mortality is also apparent early in life. Figure 1.3 shows that infant mortality from accidents, bronchopneumonia and acute bronchitis is more sharply differentiated by social class than conditions associated with perinatal mortality and congenital anomalies. In general, the decennial reports suggest that differences in mortality are evident at all ages and, in recent years, evident for most causes.

The main extensions to this which have come from the Longitudinal Study, apart from confirmation that the figures included in the decennial supplement are broadly speaking correct, have been those relating to differences at older ages (Fox *et al.*, 1985), differences among women (Moser *et al.*, 1988) and changes over time (Goldblatt, 1989). The Longitudinal Study has also been used to show that there are other, sometimes better, ways of characterizing social differences in mortality; particularly in groups defined in terms of their housing circumstances or access to cars (Fox and Goldblatt, 1982). In each case the group that is least well-off in terms of a variety of socio-economic indicators has the highest mortality. Alternative characteristics that have been considered include education (Valkonen, 1987), unemployment (Moser *et al.*, 1987), country of birth (Raftery *et al.*, 1990) and type of neighbourhood (Fox *et al.*, 1984). The study has also been used to establish how the overlap of measures influences differences that are found (Goldblatt, 1987).

Through linkage to the national cancer registration scheme the OPCS Longitudinal Study has also been used to study socio-economic differences in incidence (Leon, 1988) and in survival from cancer (Kogevinas, 1990). These analyses indicate that while social class V generally has poorer survival, class differences in mortality from cancer primarily reflect differences in cancer incidence rather than in survival. Similar analyses and results have been produced from the Swedish Cancer Registry (Vagero and Persson, 1987) but do not appear to be readily

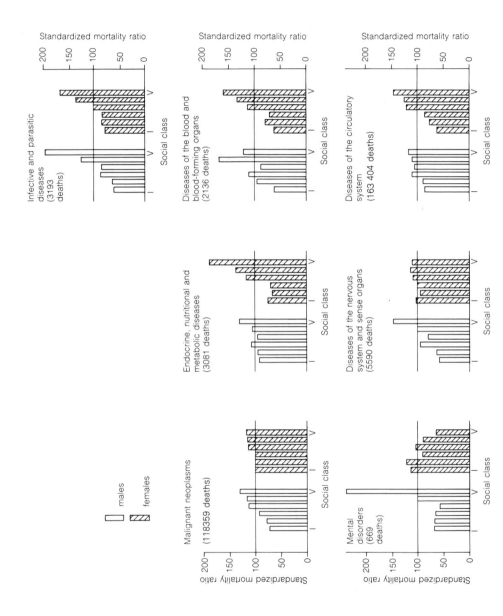

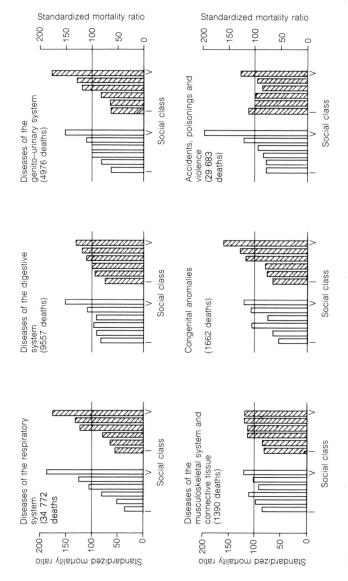

Fig. 1.2 Mortality by social class and cause of death: standardized mortality ratios for men and married women (by husband's occupation) aged 15–64. *Source:* OPCS (1978).

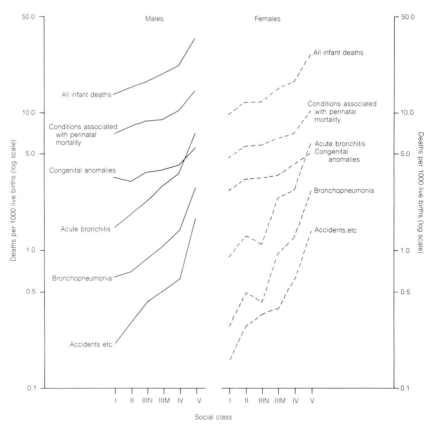

Fig. 1.3 Infant mortality by sex, social class and cause of death.
Source: OPCS (1978).

available from other countries. There are exceptional causes of death for which the socio-economic gradient may be absent or even reversed, however: for example, data for the UK show that the gradient for breast cancer, while not pronounced, is the reverse of the overall trend (Kogevinas, 1990).

While the OPCS Longitudinal Study has been a major source of information in respect of socio-economic differences in health, other studies have made important contributions. The British Regional Heart Study collected data on cardiovascular risk factors in 7735 men aged 40–59, selected randomly from general practices in England, Scotland and Wales (Shaper *et al.*, 1981). At the initial screening the prevalence rate of ischaemic heart disease was higher in manual workers, and six years later the attack rate of major IHD events was 44% higher in manual workers (Pocock *et al.*, 1987).

Other studies based on specific populations also provide important evidence. For example, the 'Whitehall' Study compared mortality rates across civil service employment grades and found a steep inverse relationship (Marmot *et al.*, 1984). The differential in this study was greater than that found when using the Registrar General's occupational class as a measure, and in view of reservations about the latter it may well be the case that the extent of social inequalities are underestimated when using the conventional RG classification.

Linking of the second and third GP morbidity surveys to the census meant that several social measures could be explored: not just social class but housing tenure, economic status and ethnic origin, for example. The latest study (McCormick and Rosenbaum, 1990) found that – for all diseases and conditions taken as a group – differences were evident for most of the social measures examined. The pattern varied according to the severity of the condition but for 'serious' conditions differences were such that, in general, the better off had fewer consultations. Thus, social classes I and II were less likely to consult than other classes. Consultations increased between 1970/1 and 1981/2 among women in all social classes. Among men an increase was shown for manual classes and this applied to both 'serious' and 'trivial' conditions.

Group differences in limiting longstanding illness or disability* found in the annual General Household Survey include: women have higher rates than men; social class differences are similar to those for mortality (Arber, 1989). Differences for limiting illness were also found according to housing tenure, car access and education, and again these are similar to those for mortality.

Other national surveys conducted on an *ad hoc* basis are a major source of data on the extent of social differences in health and illness. Between 1985 and 1988 OPCS conducted a major national survey of disability across all age groups and found that, as a consequence of being less likely than the population as a whole to have earned income, disabled adults had on average lower incomes than the rest of the population (Martin and White, 1988). State benefits compensated to some extent but, overall, disabled adults were likely to have lower standards of living.

A broader range of health measures and socio-economic circumstances was included in *The Health and Lifestyle Survey* (Cox *et al.*, 1987). This study collected information from a sample of approximately 9000 adults aged 18 years and over, during 1984–85. The dimensions of health included were self-reported symptoms and disease, psychosocial well-being, mental health, cognitive status and physiological measures such as height, weight, blood pressure and lung function. Analyses of these data have shown consistent differences across a range of health

---

* See page 8 for definition.

and socio-economic measures, such that the poorest health was generally found in the most disadvantaged groups (Blaxter, 1987; Cox *et al.*, 1987).

Some of these trends had been found in earlier surveys. In particular those for height and weight had been reported by an OPCS study conducted in 1980 (Knight, 1984); further, the measurements available from the 16 to 64-year-olds included in the survey have been used to examine time trends in height. It was found that the shorter average stature of the unskilled manual classes relative to the professional classes had existed since 1940 (Carr-Hill, 1988). Information about social class differences in height is indeed becoming richer; for example, the British Regional Heart Study also shows a class difference in mean height among men born between 1919 and 1939, and this persisted for the period under observation (Walker *et al.*, 1988).

For height during childhood, other data sources have been available. The national birth cohorts mentioned previously included measurements of height and weight at several stages during childhood, and consistent social gradients were observed in the 1946 and 1958 studies (Douglas and Simpson, 1964; Goldstein, 1971). These findings, together with those from the National Study of Health and Growth (Rona *et al.*, 1978) and Nine Towns Study (Whincup *et al.*, 1988) suggest that differences in adulthood height are likely to persist into the near future.

Obesity is recognized as a risk factor for several diseases (Royal College of Physicians, 1983) but until the OPCS survey of heights and weights of adults in Great Britain (Knight, 1984) information on the prevalence of overweight and obesity was limited. It is now known, however, that manual classes are heavier for their height on average than non-manual classes and this applies across most age groups. This was confirmed subsequently for middle-aged men in the British Regional Heart Study (Weatherall and Shaper, 1988). Social differences are not apparent at younger ages (Rona and Chinn, 1982; Peckham *et al.*, 1983).

There are many other studies which attempt to measure health and morbidity, but it is necessary to limit the details described here. Some of the studies not mentioned will be relevant later, especially in Chapter 3, and the accounts given will rectify, in part, the omissions apparent in the above.

A general theme that emerges, however, from mortality data and numerous measures of health and ill-health, is that social differences are evident across an extensive range of measures: the gradient is almost always in favour of the richer classes.

1.2.4 Strengths and weaknesses of different studies

In order to interpret the findings from different sources one must appreciate their strengths and limitations.

a) Mortality
A criticism of studies based on mortality is that they do not necessarily indicate 'healthiness' among the living. The background to the *Survey of Sickness* conducted shortly after the Second World War (Logan and Brooke, 1957) illustrates the point:

'The year 1942 was one of record breaking vital statistics, the maternal and infant mortality rates, the proportion of stillbirths and the standardised death rate among civilians being the lowest ever recorded in England and Wales. The incidence of infectious diseases was also remarkably low. Such statistics, however, did not reveal the details of the national well- or ill-being, since minor ailments and the "below-par" feeling did not come within their scope.'

However, even accepting this criticism, it remains reasonable that life is 'better' than death. Mortality has been well documented and analysed and the limitations of traditional mortality statistics have been regularly rehearsed (OPCS, 1978). The main weakness arises from occupational descriptions for numerators and denominators being taken from two sources and being recorded in quite different circumstances. Widely recognized biases exist between census and death registration, and at regular intervals these doubts have called into question the value of this analysis. The analysis is also limited by the quality, scope and relevance of socio-economic information collected when deaths are registered – in particular for women, children and the retired.

Some of these limitations have been overcome through studies such as the OPCS Longitudinal Study (Fox, 1980) which link census and death records for each individual. This overcomes potential biases between the sources that provide the numerator and denominator, and at the same time produces statistics according to a wider range of socio-economic characteristics and indicates how differences change over time. Inclusion of records from successive censuses can reveal the experiences of successive generations. The longitudinal detail also facilitates investigation of different explanations, providing a stronger basis for statistical inference than cross-sectional data.

The Longitudinal Study confirmed that the traditional cross-sectional statistics were not generally misleading but national record linkage studies are limited, first by their size and, at this stage, by their short history. This means that less common causes of death cannot be investigated using this approach.

Other longitudinal studies such as the Regional Heart Study (Shaper *et al.*, 1981) and the Whitehall Study (Marmot *et al.*, 1984) followed samples of men after obtaining socio-demographic information and measures of risk factors considered to be most relevant, in particular for heart and respiratory disease. These studies indicated the distributions of risk factors and behaviours in social and geographic groups. However, they are limited by size to the main diseases they are designed to investigate.

b) Morbidity
Studies based on morbidity data also have strengths and limitations. In particular, if the purpose is to examine social differences in health then clearly measures of morbidity do not indicate 'healthiness'. Quantification of the latter is problematic and so most studies rely on information about ill-health, its converse. Even then, it is difficult to obtain meaningful data. For example, in the three surveys of morbidity in general practice, statistics were obtained by recording all the contacts and consultations for all patients in samples of practices over twelve-month periods. These statistics do not necessarily measure incidence or prevalence of morbidity because they are affected by decisions on whether or not to consult and, if so, whom to consult – the general practitioner, the local hospital or non-conventional advice. This is especially important when considering social differences since consultation behaviour is to a large extent socially, occupationally and culturally determined (Blane *et al.*, 1990).

The difficulty of obtaining good quality socio-economic data from the GP Morbidity Survey detracts further from the usefulness of the study. In the first survey general practitioners volunteered to collect details of their patients' occupations, and some did so better than others. In the second and third surveys this and other information was obtained by complex links to census records, but this may not be possible for the most recent survey. In addition, general doubts remain about the representativeness of the practices included in the survey.

Socio-economic data and representativeness of the sample are less of a problem for the General Household Survey but the limited information on health imposes a considerable restriction on any analyses of social differences.

The three national birth cohort studies have better measures of morbidity and socio-economic circumstances, since they have collected information about health in childhood (and the first two, health in early adulthood) from physical examinations and measurements, questionnaires and structured tests. They cover a range of problems from particular physical and mental diseases and handicaps, to accidents, service use and perceptions of health. These studies provide a basis for considering changes in the importance of different factors between the generations. The strengths of the birth cohort approach are widely appreciated (Mednick and Baert, 1981) in particular in relation to health inequalities (Blaxter, 1986). The limitations arise mainly from the time and cost of following a sample over a long period and because the cohort is not under continuous surveillance. Given the age of the subjects in the three studies, the information available so far has meant that they have emphasized differences in health at younger ages only.

Despite these limitations the three cohorts have provided information about changing health patterns and powerful data on causal processes. The data offer a unique opportunity for addressing questions within a generation about the importance of different explanations at different stages of people's lives.

1.2.5 What are the main explanations?

The patterns of health observed in social groups can be explained at different levels. For example, cigarette smoking is recognized as a cause of lung cancer. There are also social class differences in cigarette smoking and social class differences in the same direction in the risk of developing lung cancer. Inevitably, therefore, one could speculate that the social class differences in lung cancer are a consequence, at least in part, of the differences in cigarette smoking. At this level, explanation for the health pattern lies in differences in behaviour; some would deem that the lower social groups are responsible for their higher lung cancer mortality.

At another level one might question why people in manual classes smoke more than people in non-manual social classes. After all, the reverse pattern is thought to have existed prior to the Second World War. Does the pattern reflect the social distribution of knowledge about the adverse effects of smoking and social influences on smoking behaviour? Is it a result of free choices individuals have made or is it, for example, a result of it being more difficult for people under 'duress' to stop smoking, with less skilled people more likely to find themselves in this category? Such 'explanations' address issues at a macro or sociological level. An example of this can be seen in work on women's smoking habits. Graham (1989) describes the paradox in which smoking can be viewed as a strategy enabling women to cope with stress and therefore support those they care for, while at the same time undermining their own health and that of their children.

Extending the macro or sociological approach, one might look at the effects of attempts to persuade people to stop smoking in different social groups and the peer group factors that may have influenced the behaviours of subsequent generations.

While the study of individual health outcomes, such as lung cancer, sheds some important light on relevant processes it has been argued that much more is to be learned by reviewing the general pattern observed across a range of conditions. For example, Marmot *et al.* (1984) observed as clear differences in mortality for diseases that are not related to cigarette smoking in the Whitehall Study as for smoking-related diseases. The decennial supplement suggested that the consistency in class gradients may be a recent phenomenon; whereas in the 1920s and 1930s different patterns were observed for different diseases, most diseases now show greater mortality among lower social classes. It has been proposed that there are 'general explanations' for the general patterns. These include: general susceptibility and host resistance – a biological explanation (Berkman and Syme, 1979); locus of control (Antonovsky, 1987); sense of coherence – psychological explanations (Antonovsky, 1989); and a range of other explanations of a more sociological type covered by recent research into social networks, social support, isolation and social integration, which some have termed 'social network interaction' (Fox, 1988).

The social class pattern of mortality has probably become more consistent in recent years and there may well be some general explanations for this. However, it is important to resist oversimplification of this issue since, as noted already, there are variations in the patterns observed for mortality at different ages and also for different health indicators.

A framework for most recent discussion about explanations was put forward at the beginning of the 1980s in the Black Report and the follow-up review for the Health Education Council (see Townsend and Davidson, 1982; Whitehead, 1988). They consider four broad areas of explanation, namely: artefact, selection, material circumstances and behavioural patterns.

According to the artefact explanation, health inequalities are largely a product of the method used to derive the statistics. There are two reasons why this explanation has been given some credence recently. As mentioned above, there are potential numerator–denominator biases in the decennial supplement on occupational mortality which could influence the figures. At the same time the decline in size of social class V could explain the widening difference observed between classes I and V.

These arguments are generally given more weight than they merit. In the 1970s the decennial supplement provided the principal source of data on this topic and doubts about its validity were justified. Today there are a range of different studies which support the principal findings, and some suggest that the decennial supplement underestimates the differences. The OPCS Longitudinal Study (Fox, 1980; Fox and Goldblatt, 1982; Goldblatt, 1989), the Whitehall Study of civil servants

(Marmot *et al.*, 1984) and the British Regional Heart Study (Pocock *et al.*, 1987) all support the conclusions drawn from the decennial supplements. Differences in infant mortality, based on linked data for the past fifteen years and in morbidity as recorded in a variety of surveys, also suggested that the findings from the decennial supplement were real. However, since debate, particularly in the last few years, was centred on data from the latest decennial supplement it is not surprising that weaknesses in the method again affected the tone of discussion.

The second of the artefact explanations focuses on changing class sizes over time. This is a more complex argument. It proposes that as class V declines in size it becomes a more extreme group and its mortality a less significant social indicator. A rise in mortality relative to that of other classes is not necessarily an indication of greater social inequality but a result of characterizing a smaller group of individuals. Such an argument ignores what has happened to the mortality of men in other social classes that have also changed in size. In particular it does not take account of what has happened to social class I. As social class V has declined, so social class I has grown. The argument that attributes the worsening of the position for men in social class V to the decline in the class size should simultaneously predict a reduction in the advantage enjoyed by men in the growing social class I. However, quite the opposite has occurred with men in social class I being at even more advantage than they were in the 1930s when they comprised a substantially smaller proportion of the population.

Also, to promote the argument about changing class size is to ignore the recent work of Preston *et al.* (1981) and Koskinen (1985) who used measures of inequality not affected by class size. Goldblatt (1990b) presents evidence from the OPCS Longitudinal Study which suggests that groups at the extremes of the spectrum of socio-economic circumstances are larger than those indicated by social classes I and V and that these larger groups have different mortality rates. According to this argument, even though the proportions in classes I and V changed over time, they can be regarded as samples from the underlying larger groups whose mortality rates they still reflect.

The second main explanation for social differences in health resembles a social Darwinist view, suggesting that health inequalities result from a continuous process of social mobility, with those moving up being healthier than those moving down the social scale. Strong evidence for this argument was provided by Illsley (1955) in a study of infant mortality according to class of father and class of husband. The study showed that women marrying up were on the whole taller than those marrying down and that they had heavier babies and lower infant mortality. Illsley (1986) shows that this is still the case today. Stern (1983) also showed mathematically the effect that such processes might

21

have. However, Fox *et al.* (1984) showed that differences in mortality are as wide at ages over 65 as they are at younger ages, and since it is unlikely that social mobility is a significant factor at these ages it was concluded that selection would not play a significant role in explaining the differences observed.

This is not to say that at a stage in life when social mobility is more common such a process could not be operating, although Wilkinson (1986) argued on the basis of data provided by Illsley that even at younger ages this was unlikely to be a sufficient explanation.

The behaviourist and materialist explanations distinguish between lifestyle and socio-economic circumstances. As illustrated above for class differences in lung cancer, there is an extent to which these explanations are interwoven, in that the social and economic circumstances of a group might influence behaviour in that group. Not surprisingly the distinction drawn between them has been criticized (Blaxter, 1983; Blane, 1985). It might still be argued, however, that different levels of explanations need to be explored, even though they can attract a different emphasis in terms of the perceived responsibility for inequalities. While some see behaviour as influenced by social and cultural forces of a particular group, others place the onus on the individual to 'choose' his or her own lifestyle and to a large extent blame the individuals for not choosing correctly. Materialist explanations locate the responsibility for inequalities in health in the social structure governing the distribution of resources towards different groups of people.

Since the Black Report, the debate on health inequalities has centred on macro issues. Prior to the report, authors considered at a less general level the influences of inheritance, socio-economic circumstances, education and attitudes, health behaviour, and early health as well as parental influences. The framework that is described below attempts to revert to these explanations and to investigate them empirically. This reflects our concern to identify those aspects of people's circumstances or behaviours that most strongly influence their life chances in health terms and the stages when these operate. We ignore questions of 'blame' or how such attitudes come about.

The focus at this stage is almost entirely with individual level explanations within a particular generation since the individuals studied here were all born in 1958. There are no attempts as yet to compare explanations between generations, so data on societal level factors are not included.

1.3 Theoretical approach

In Figure 1.4 the wide range of explanations suggested in the previous section have been brought together under five main headings. These are socio-economic circumstances, behaviour, education and attitudes, 'inheritance' at birth, and health. The approach is similar to that taken by Carr-Hill (1985) but since his model focuses on the specific relationship between health and income, Figure 1.4 provides a more general model.

The five categories used in Figure 1.4 may each be related to one (or more) of the Black Report categories, although we attempt to combine them rather than isolate them. Family and household structure and domestic organization, housing, economic activity, income, wealth and local environment are all characteristics reflecting aspects of (and influencing) socio-economic circumstances; tying most closely to 'materialist'

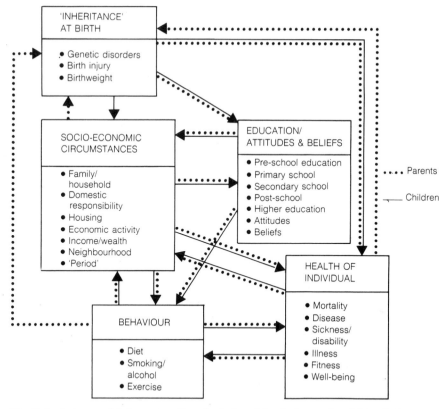

Fig. 1.4 Inter- and intragenerational relationships between health and circumstances.

factors in the Black Report. The characteristics considered under 'inheritance' are not directly equivalent to any of the categories used in the Black Report although they are in some sense related to the selection argument; while those grouped under behaviour relate to the third explanation considered by the report. Education and attitudes have been grouped together, but separated from other explanations because of their role in determining the extent and direction of ties between the material circumstances, experiences and behaviour of the parents and children (Halsey *et al.*, 1980). Each of the five main areas is represented in Figure 1.4 by a box containing some of the main characteristics covered by the heading.

It is important to recognize the interrelationships between the possible influences identified in the figure. Causal paths can operate in opposite directions or can become cyclical. For example, individuals' socio-economic circumstances, such as whether or not they are unemployed, can be shown to influence their health, which itself can be shown to influence their likelihood of being unemployed at some future date (see, for example, Moser *et al.*, 1984; Fox and Shewry, 1988). Similarly, individuals' socio-economic circumstances have been found to influence their education and training, which in turn influences subsequent socio-economic circumstances (Fogelman, 1985; Fogelman and Richardson, 1974; Hibbett and Fogelman, 1990). In the figure lines connecting different boxes indicate suggested causal paths.

Parental characteristics may also influence those of the individual. These are represented in the figure in two ways. Pathways from parents to children are indicated by dotted as opposed to continuous lines; while the box labelled ' "inheritance" at birth' separates those characteristics present at birth from those occurring throughout childhood. For the purposes of the framework outlined in the figure 'inheritance' includes genetic inheritance, socio-economic circumstances at or prior to birth, and parental health behaviour such as smoking during pregnancy. In a broader use of the term Rutter and Madge (1977: 322) refer to the 'hereditary element' of mental illnesses or disorders as including marital discord and interfamilial relationships after birth. In Figure 1.4 these would not be included in the ' "inheritance" at birth' box but depicted by dotted lines from the box labelled 'socio-economic circumstances' to that labelled 'health of the individual'.

Even though Figure 1.4 may appear complex, it is a gross oversimplification. First, it does not represent adequately the extent of relationships between possible influences that are grouped together (i.e. in a box) – particularly the relationships that exist between different aspects of an individual's socio-economic circumstances. Second, the specific characteristics listed in each box are not exhaustive. Third, the suggested relationships are between the areas represented by the boxes

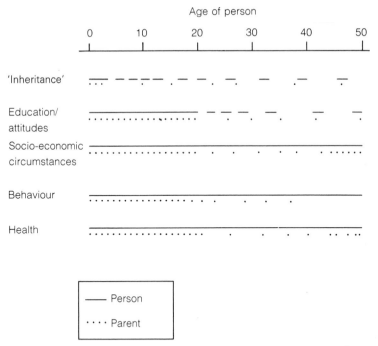

Fig. 1.5 Hypothetical weighting of inter- and intragenerational influences on health at different ages (spacing widens as influences decrease).

and do not necessarily imply relationships between all specific characteristics. Fourth, it only provides a static representation: most of these characteristics change over time, as the individual ages and passes through various stages of domestic/family and economic life cycles and as the macro environment or socio-economic climate (which we have labelled 'period') changes. Finally, the figure shows only limited suggestions of the range of health outcomes that might be considered.

Figure 1.5 suggests what might be found if a time dimension were imposed on Figure 1.4. The result would be a relative weighting of explanations at each age. One way of addressing the questions of relative importance overall, as attempted in the Black Report, would be to summate such weightings over ages.

Figure 1.5 is a first step towards this. Against each of the headings from Figure 1.4 lines or dots represent possible contributions to the individual's health at a particular age. The presence or absence of a particular dot or line indicates that certain characteristics of the parent or individual are salient at a particular age, whereas gaps indicate that they are of diminished importance.

For example, the line for individual's 'inheritance' at birth is continuous during the early period of childhood and then becomes broken.

This suggests that an individual's 'inheritance' influences health at the earliest stages of life, but that the influence diminishes with increasing age of the individual. Similarly, the line for the influence of parents' education is shown to be continuous during childhood, up to early adulthood, and then to be broken. Again, this is a factor that might be important with respect to the health of children, but is likely to be less important with respect to the health of adults.

It is important to stress that, while Figure 1.5 attempts to take account of a wide range of research findings, it is a *subjective* assessment and has *no* scientific or empirical foundation, especially in respect of the weights shown. In some circumstances it may well be the case that the effect of some potential influences appears to wear off, only to re-emerge at a later age. Also, genetic influences may not always emerge early in life, but later on. However, Figure 1.5 is meant to convey three important points. First, the weighting to be attached to different explanations probably varies with age. (The weightings will also vary with health measure, but this is not shown in the figure.) Second, most potential explanations identified in Figures 1.4 and 1.5 might be expected to contribute to health inequalities during childhood and early adulthood. It is not surprising, therefore, that support for some of the arguments about particular explanations for health inequalities is frequently drawn from this end of the age spectrum. Third, both these points suggest that extrapolation from the relative balance of explanations for health inequalities in childhood and early adulthood may be misleading if applied to those anticipated at older ages.

The analyses required to test Figure 1.5 would be extensive since the importance of different explanations would need to be assessed over the life course. This is not the purpose of this book, but Figure 1.5 has been presented to convey how different explanations are likely to have varying relevance at different stages of life. The figure therefore provides the context in which the framework given in Figure 1.4 should be regarded.

It should be stated at the outset that while attempting to incorporate a greater degree of complexity into a framework for examining health inequalities, it is still not possible to overcome all limitations (as will be discussed in Chapter 5). Even so, it offers an improvement upon the unidimensional explanations that have been examined to date. This will become evident when, after considering each of the areas of the framework in detail, an attempt to integrate the explanations is presented.

Before embarking on this, the next chapter describes the data that will be used for the study. Differences in health evident by early adulthood are described in Chapter 3 and this is followed by a consideration of whether social mobility could account for such differences (Chapter

4). As mentioned above, methods and constraints of the framework and data are discussed in Chapter 5 and it is following this that areas of the framework are investigated separately (in Chapters 6 to 10) and together (Chapter 11). The final chapter discusses the strengths and weaknesses of the work and summarizes the main findings.

1.4 Conclusions

Differences in health between people in different socio-economic groups have been reported regularly since the beginning of the last century and can be traced back almost 2000 years (Antonovsky, 1967). Although the earliest reports were based on analyses of mortality, there is a growing body of evidence from morbidity and health surveys. The main explanations for differences are generally grouped under the headings: artefact, selection, behavioural and material. Longitudinal data are essential if these explanations are to be disentangled. A framework has been put forward to investigate explanations for health inequalities; it is intended that this incorporates a longitudinal dimension. This will be used in an examination of origins of class differences in health among young adults.

Longitudinal data: the 1958 birth cohort

The large, national sample of young adults included in the 1958 birth cohort study (National Child Development Study (NCDS)) offers a unique opportunity to investigate explanations for health inequalities using the framework outlined in Chapter 1. The breadth of data available and longitudinal dimension are especially important for this purpose. This chapter describes the aims and background of the NCDS, the response of the study sample and the information collected at successive sweeps.

2.1 Origins and aims

The NCDS originated in the Perinatal Mortality Survey (PMS) which included virtually all babies born in the week 3–9 March 1958. The study was sponsored by the National Birthday Trust with the aim of determining the social and obstetric factors associated with stillbirth and death in early infancy. Information was obtained on 98% of births – numbering over 17 000 babies – to parents resident in Great Britain (Butler and Bonham, 1963; Butler and Alberman, 1969).

The initial survey formed the basis of a continuing longitudinal study (the NCDS) designed to monitor social, educational and physical development from birth onwards. Subsequently, the cohort was contacted by the National Children's Bureau, principally in 1964 when the children were 7 years of age, in 1969 at age 11, in 1974 at age 16 and most recently in 1981 when the subjects had become young adults of 23 years. Immigrants to Britain born during the same week in 1958 were incorporated into the survey at each sweep except at age 23. A further follow-up is planned for age 33.

As illustrated in Figure 2.1, information was collected from a variety of sources, which varied between sweeps. The 1981 survey differed from earlier follow-ups in that it consisted exclusively of an interview with the individual subject, whereas data were gathered previously

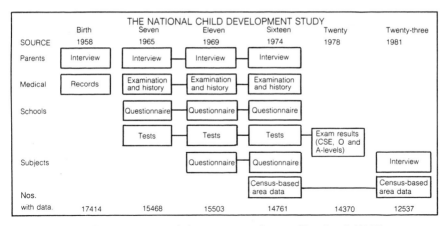

Fig. 2.1 NCDS: a summary of data sources. *Source*: Shepherd (1985).

from parents and schools (teachers and doctors) as well as from the individuals.

Given the volume of data that has accumulated, only an outline can be presented here, although more detail will be given for measures relevant to health inequalities. Figure 2.2 summarizes the type of information available. These data have been the subject of numerous publications: for example, Davie *et al.* (1972) gave an overview of the period between birth and age 7 and Fogelman (1983) extended this to age 16. Many other books and articles examine aspects of development of these young people. An important focus of this work has been the relationship between health and social and environmental factors; although there has been little systematic attempt to explain social differences in health, some related research has already been conducted. For example, Goldstein (1971) assessed the contribution of birth factors to height at age 7 and Tibbenham *et al.* (1983) looked at whether family size affected the social class differences in height that were apparent throughout childhood.

2.2 Tracing and response

Research based on the NCDS depends upon the continued representativeness of the original sample, so tracing and response of the sample are important.

The 1958 birth survey relied upon the National Health Service to identify births in the appropriate week. Subsequently, the cohort had to be retraced for each follow-up. For the 7-, 11- and 16-year sweeps the majority of children were contacted through their school. A variety

SOURCE	PMS:1958	NCDS1:1965	NCDS2:1969	NCDS3:1974	NCDS4:1981
Parents	Social and Family background Obstetric history Antenatal care Abnormalities during pregnancy Length and abnormalities of labour Analgesia and anaesthesia Sex, weight, progress, management and outcome of infant Mother's smoking during pregnancy	Family size Parental situation Father's occupation Father's education Mother's work Type of accommodation Tenure Number of rooms Household amenities Periods "In Care" Hospital admissions Clinic attendance Medical history Behaviour Physical coordination Adjustment to school Separation from mother Pre-school experience Infant welfare clinic attendance	As NCDS1 Financial situation Housing satisfaction Satisfaction with neighbourhood	AS NCDS1 and 2 Child's future education and employment	
Medical		Height Weight Head circumference Tests and clinical assessments of motor coordination and laterality Full clinical examination	As NCDS1 Pubertal development	As NCDS1 and 2	
School		School size and organization School and parents Teacher's assessment of child's abilities, attainment and behaviour	As NCDS1	As NCDS1 and 2 Child's future education and employment	[EXAMS: Details of entry and performance in public examinations were obtained from schools in 1978]
Subject		Southgate Reading test Copying Designs test Good enough Draw-a-man test Problem Arithmetic test	Reading Comprehension test Mathematics Comprehension test General Ability test Copying-designs test Short questionnaire on interest out of schools and educational aspiration Essay describing their life at age 25	AS NCDS2 Questionnaire covering: School Education Further and higher education Future employment Relationships with the family Marriage and family plans Leisure activities	Employment and unemployment Apprenticeship and training Education and qualifications since school Literacy and numeracy Periods out of the labour force Attitudes to school and work Number, age and sex of all natural children Children's health Marriage and cohabitation Characteristics of partners Marriage, family plans Contraceptive use Housing Family income and savings Health, accidents and hospital admissions Height and weight Leisure and voluntary activities Economic status of parents Experience of Care as a child 'Malaise Index [AREA DATA*]

Fig. 2.2 Summary of the information collected during the Perinatal Mortality Survey (PMS) and the National Child Development Study (NCDS) 1958–1981. *Source*: NCDS (1988).

Note: (*) AREA DATA: These data provide details of the location and characteristics of the area in which the subject was living at NCDS4 and NCDS3. They are based on the Small Area Statistics of the 1971 and 1981 Census.

Table 2.1 Response to NCDS follow-ups

Cohort age (years)	Target* sample ($n = 100\%$)	Some data (%)	Refused (%)	Others without data (%)
Birth	17 733	98	–	2
7	16 883	91	1	8
11	16 835	91	5	4
16	16 915	87	7	6
23	16 457	76	7	17

* Number from previous stage plus known immigrants, less known deaths
and emigrations.
Source: Shepherd (1985).

of other sources – local authorities, health authorities and social services
– were used to locate the remainder.

Tracing for the 23-year interview was based primarily on the latest
recorded addresses (usually at age 16) and a series of requests for
forwarding addresses. As in previous sweeps it was necessary to contact
many organizations – the armed services, local housing departments,
Family Practitioner Committees – to trace the cohort members.

Table 2.1 shows that the response at each stage of the study remained
high, although declining from 98% of subjects in 1958 to 76% in 1981.
Refusals increased during this period, but the lower response at the
latest sweep was largely attributed to difficulties in tracing the young
people.

Goldstein (1983) analysed the sample remaining in the study for
representativeness by age 16. While his findings were generally reassuring, Table 2.1 shows that the greatest reduction in sample numbers
occurred after age 16. Further analyses were necessary, therefore, and
details of these are available in Appendix D. In summary, few serious
biases existed, although the previously reported under-representation
of certain disadvantaged groups was also observed for the sample at
age 23. Comparisons designed to examine the particular relationships
relevant to the present investigation of social differences in health,
suggest that, in general, sample attrition would not bias the results
(Power *et al.*, 1990; Appendix D).

2.3 Measures relevant to social differences in health

These can be examined in three main categories, namely:

1. measures of health at age 23;
2. measures of social position at age 23; and

3. measures of earlier characteristics (such as health and behaviour) and circumstances (e.g. socio-economic).

1. The measures of health at age 23 are the health 'outcomes' that will be compared in different social groups. Information was elicited from the replies by individual cohort members to the questionnaire in Appendix A. This includes reports of self-rated health, longstanding illness or disability, limitation of function, height, weight, sight, migraine, fits, asthma, wheezy bronchitis, cough and phlegm, any other condition with regular medical supervision, disability hindering employment, accidents since age 16, hospitalizations, specialist consultation for psychological problems and the malaise inventory (defined on page 50). In another part of the questionnaire (not shown in the appendix) respondents reported miscarriages and abortions; birthweights of children and infant deaths.

2. Measures of social position, also collected from the individuals at age 23, are detailed but the measures mentioned here will be restricted to characteristics traditionally used to indicate inequality – namely, occupational class, housing tenure, education and income.

3. As shown in Figure 2.2, measures of earlier characteristics and circumstances are also comprehensive and are relevant to areas identified in the framework for the present enquiry. It is in this context (i.e. of the five headings given in Figure 1.4) that the earlier information will be viewed.

Measures of *'inheritance' at birth* are available mainly from the Perinatal Mortality Study (PMS). These data include some physical indicators for parents (such as height) and for the child (such as length of gestation and birthweight); socio-economic circumstances at birth (such as father's occupation and level of education); and health-related behaviour (notably mother's smoking during pregnancy).

Socio-economic circumstances during childhood are well represented. For example, father's occupation and economic activity, housing tenure, family composition and financial position were collected from an interview with the parents at each of the three follow-ups after the Perinatal Mortality Survey.

Educational achievement was assessed at ages 7, 11 and 16 by a series of specially designed tests in reading, mathematical and general ability. Latterly, the schools provided information on qualifications gained by each of the study subjects through national examinations. However, before the 23-year interview only limited information was available on individual attitudes and beliefs.

So far, health has been considered (in (1) above) as an outcome measure, but Figure 1.4 and accompanying text suggests that earlier measures of health could be viewed as 'explanatory'. Measures of health that precede the outcomes are available in the NCDS.

Childhood health was monitored through a medical examination at ages 7, 11 and 16. This involved a detailed clinical assessment by the school's medical officer, using a structured questionnaire which asked for details about coordination, growth and development, as well as illnesses and disabilities. Additional information was reported by parents, including absences from school for ill-health, hospital admissions and contacts with general practitioners.

Finally, measures of *behaviour* are derived from several sources. Parental interviews contained some details, such as the leisure activities of their child at age 11, as did the teacher's interview, in providing a measure of behaviour in the school. For age 16, however, the data were reported in most instances by individuals in the study.

After scrutinizing the data available, variables were selected to represent the five broad areas influencing health: 'inheritance' at birth, socio-economic circumstances, education and attitudes, childhood health, and behaviour. More details of the variables selected are given in Chapters 4 and 6 to 10 where they are examined in relation to social class differences in adulthood health. It needs to be recognized, however, that even though the data have many strengths, particularly comprehensiveness, the study was not designed with the present focus specifically in mind. Some information that would have been desirable is lacking; in other instances variables may be relevant to more than one of the broad areas of explanation. Wherever such difficulties occur they will be acknowledged.

2.4 Conclusions

The breadth of data available in the NCDS permits an investigation of each of the areas identified in the conceptual framework proposed for the study of social differences in health (Chapter 1). The large sample allows analyses which integrate several explanations. Furthermore, given the longitudinal nature of the data, it will be possible to take account of the timing of events and circumstances, as they contribute towards social differences in health in early adulthood.

3

Social differences in health in early adulthood

3.1 Introduction

The aim of this chapter is to provide an overview from which we can establish the extent of health differences among young adults and which enables us to select a few measures for more extensive analyses. First though, it is necessary to define what is meant by health and also to identify indicators of social circumstances.

3.1.1 Defining health and ill-health

While recognizing health as a wide concept encompassing much more than an absence of ill-health, the Black Report (DHSS, 1980) gave precedence to mortality rates in its investigation of inequalities in health. The limitations of this approach were appreciated, as they were for other indicators of ill-health such as morbidity prevalence and incidence rates, sickness absence rates and restricted activity rates. Seven years after the Black Report a BMA discussion paper on deprivation and ill-health (BMA, 1987) identified a trend away from the medical model of health (based on the absence of recognizable disease) towards a more positive model based on the optimum development of a person's capabilities, a perceived sense of well-being, and a full role within society.

Measures of mortality and morbidity continue to be the most widely used indicators of 'healthiness' but recently a range of suggestions have arisen as to how the extra dimensions of health might be measured. Whitehead (1988) summarized these developments, emphasizing that 'these new measures are intended to supplement rather than replace traditional indicators'. Despite some scepticism within the medical profession concerning self-reported data, indicators of health are being developed which rely upon a lay person's own reported experience in an attempt to gauge health as a 'positive concept emphasizing social and personal resources as well as physical capabilities' (WHO, 1984).

In representing health in young adulthood a variety of measures will be used: self-reported health and perceived well-being, plus more traditional indices such as illness and disability, and height and weight. These will be referred to as 'health' indices even though particular measures might more accurately describe ill-health, and this practice will be followed in subsequent chapters. However, mortality is omitted due to the small number of deaths in the early twenties (Jones and Sedgwick, 1991).

3.1.2 Indicators of social circumstances

Socio-economic inequality is apparent among young people but is diffi-cult to quantify. Children are regularly categorized in terms of their father's or mother's characteristics. In early adulthood measures depend on the timing of the 'transition to adulthood' for the individual in question. Measures based, for example, on income and occupation will reflect when the person started working and will consequently depend on when he or she left full-time education. Young adults who attended university will have entered the labour force later than those who did not. Similarly, housing circumstances of many young people may reflect parental circumstances rather than their own because they remained at home during early adulthood, while others set up their own house-holds. Despite problems of measurement it is clear nevertheless that while many young adults experienced poverty associated with home-lessness, unemployment and single parenthood, others led sheltered, cushioned and generally affluent lives.

The main indicator of social position that will be used in the present study is the Registrar General's social classification (OPCS, 1980), based broadly on occupation and 'status' of the job. The scale consists of six classes but here we use four in order to provide adequate numbers for the analyses described in subsequent chapters (Table 3.1).

It was possible to place the majority of young adults (96%) into one of these four classes using either current (72%) or last (28%) occupation.

Table 3.1 Number of NCDS subjects in four social class groups at age 23

Social class		Men	Women
I and II	Professional and managerial	1278	1283
IIIN	Other non-manual	1010	3042
IIIM	Skilled manual	2413	560
IV and V	Semi- and unskilled manual	1224	1199
All classes		5925	6084

Well-known problems of occupational class as a measure of social circumstances (DHSS, 1980; Whitehead, 1988; Blaxter, 1986; Goldblatt, 1988) were to some extent mitigated in these data because of the detailed work histories provided and the stage of the life cycle reached by the NCDS sample. Most subjects out of the labour force at the time of the interview could be included on the basis of a recent occupation, and this was especially important in deriving a class for women. Even so, this approach does not overcome objections which, for example, concern the nature of the occupational classification itself. In view of this, alternative measures of socio-economic status are considered later in the chapter.

3.2 Class differences in health

Health measures used in this section – disability, illness, height and weight, self-rated health and emotional well-being – were obtained from the questionnaire administered at age 23 (Appendix A). Examination of these measures is fairly comprehensive at this stage, although details of significance tests are not presented.

The first comparison made here is of the social class distribution in *limiting longstanding illness*. At age 23 subjects in the NCDS were asked whether they had any longstanding illness, disability or infirmity which limited their activities in any way compared to other people of their age. Four per cent of women and 5% of men reported a wide range of problems in response to this question; handicapping conditions such as poor eyesight and other disorders of the eye, deafness, epilepsy or migraine were the most common. The class distribution of reported limiting longstanding illness is given in Figure 3.1 and while it appears that the prevalence is generally higher in manual classes than in non-manual, there is no consistent trend with social class. Others have found similar patterns. For example, West (1988) used comparable data from the GHS to show that class gradients were weak for 20–24 year olds, although they became more pronounced after this age.

NCDS respondents also declared *conditions for which they received regular medical supervision*. Five per cent of men and 9% of women reported such conditions and, of these, skin, genito-urinary and digestive complaints were the most prominent. Prevalence* of all supervised conditions was consistently higher for semi- and unskilled workers (56 per 1000 for men and 106 per 1000 for women) compared with professional groups (48 per 1000 for men and 96 per 1000 for women) but no strong gradients emerged by social class (Figure 3.1). Similarly, for *hospital*

---

* Defined as the proportion of the sample having a condition at age 23.

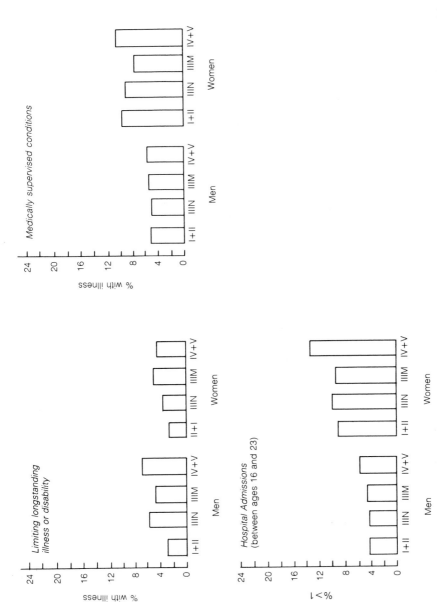

Fig. 3.1 Class* differences in limiting longstanding illness and disability, regularly supervised medical conditions and hospital admissions in young adults in the NCDS.

* The numbers in each social class are shown in Table 3.1.

admissions between the ages of 16 and 23, the greatest proportion of men and women reporting more than one admission occurred among classes IV and V, but differences between other social class groups were small (Figure 3.1).

The measures considered so far combine a wide variety of complaints, possibly obscuring class differences for specific conditions. This can be overcome to some extent by examining the major categories of disease – grouped according to the 9th revision of the *International Classification of Diseases* (ICD) (WHO, 1977) – identified from reported limiting illnesses, medically supervised conditions and hospital admissions (Table 3.2). However, it is important to recognize that the major ICD categories are also broad and heterogeneous categories which cannot be described in any detail.

With admissions for injuries and 'routine' births excluded, hospital admissions remained the largest group and therefore provide the major contribution to the table. After excluding all who reported positively to questions about limiting longstanding illness, supervised conditions, hospital admissions or any other questions about their health, there were 1475 men and 393 women who had reported no problems. Since, in addition, few of these men and women rated their health as poor or fair (Appendix B, Table B.1) they have been labelled here as 'healthy' for the purpose of comparison with study members who did report any ill-health, even though it is appreciated that this is a particularly stringent definition.

Using prevalence ratios,* Table 3.2 shows variations in major ICD categories and in the 'healthy' group. Categories are not mutually exclusive, except for the 'healthy' group. The excess of the latter among male skilled manual workers may, in part, be the result of selection into these particular occupations on the basis of physical fitness (the 'healthy worker effect', Fox and Collier, 1976). Even though the greatest deficit of 'healthy' subjects occurred in classes IV and V, there is no regular class gradient. This is apparent for many of the ICD categories for men, although gradients emerged for disorders of the nervous and sensory organs and for mental conditions, and reverses for disorders of the circulatory system. (An interesting question is whether these contrasting trends could arise in part as a result of 'labelling' by class, in that upper classes might be diagnosed as having organic diseases, while lower classes have nervous or mental problems.)

In contrast, NCDS women exhibit class differences in several categories (Table 3.2). Not surprisingly, therefore, differences are also apparent in the 'healthy' group: the ratio of healthy women in the professional and managerial group was almost double that in the semi- and unskilled

---

* Calculated as the number of observed cases divided by the number expected in each category (base=100).

Table 3.2 Prevalence ratios* for major ICD categories †, according to social class

ICD category

Social class	Infectious	Neoplasms	Endocrine, nutritional, metabolic and immunity	Blood and blood-forming organs	Mental disorders	Nervous and sense organs	Circulatory system	Respiratory	Digestive	Genito-urinary	Complications of pregnancy and birth	Skin and subcutaneous tissue	Musculoskeletal and connective tissue	Congenital anomalies	Poisoning	Operations and investigations	Symptoms	Inadequate	'Healthy'‡
Men	(91)	(19)	(45)	(11)	(98)	(214)	(48)	(208)	(337)	(50)	—	(182)	(174)	(34)	(55)	(300)	(123)	(30)	(1475)
I and II (1280)	94	136	113	46	66	89	132	132	97	103	—	95	81	37	118	125	69	66	92
IIIN (1001)	80	0	72	237	71	98	141	88	79	119	—	101	96	119	81	102	109	42	95
IIIM (2407)	107	116	114	49	97	99	82	90	109	71	—	98	109	89	87	85	91	106	111
IV and V (1240)	110	113	82	144	165	115	68	95	102	138	—	109	107	172	124	103	143	173	70
Women	(68)	(41)	(59)	(46)	(174)	(144)	(105)	(267)	(393)	(389)	(543)	(171)	(155)	(47)	(111)	(506)	(165)	(27)	(393)
I and II (1283)	156	112	100	69	62	91	70	116	101	102	77	120	118	79	78	116	105	99	134
IIIN (2960)	90	103	105	85	70	98	98	106	98	101	96	90	105	93	92	99	84	94	98
IIIM (565)	135	150	76	53	127	79	117	71	116	76	105	104	79	77	138	74	80	90	99
IV and V (1275)	52	100	100	186	194	123	128	83	95	107	130	101	80	148	123	97	141	119	71

$$\text{*Prevalence ratio} = \frac{\text{No. of observed cases per 1000 per social class}}{\text{No. of expected cases per 1000 (from social class composition of entire cohort)}} \times 100$$

Figures in brackets are actual numbers.
†Conditions were identified from reports of limiting longstanding illness, medically supervised conditions or hospital admissions.
‡'Healthy' is defined as having no positive responses to any of the health questions in Appendix A.

manual group (134 compared with 71). Trends for several ICD categories are consistent with this and show declining health with decreasing social class, but this does not apply to all categories. As mentioned above, each major ICD category covers a wide range of problems and the composition of the particular categories will vary with the age group studied. There are also small numbers in some categories. Hence, some trends, such as for respiratory conditions (which is mainly asthma in early adulthood), are inconsistent with those seen at older ages. Furthermore, social class differences in ICD categories for limiting illness and conditions needing medical supervision or hospital admission are influenced by class variation in seeking medical assistance and, subsequently, by treatment practices. There are several suggestions of why this should occur, including class differences in illness behaviour, lay culture and environmental demands (Blane *et al.*, 1990). Consequently, data in Table 3.2 may not be the most appropriate representation of class differences in health among young adults.

An alternative is to use information about particular symptoms. Data were available for *respiratory symptoms, asthma and wheezy bronchitis and for allergies*, which are presented according to social class in Figure 3.2. Respiratory symptoms, ascertained using the Medical Research Council's (1960) approved questions (winter cough or phlegm), were sharply discriminated by social class. Such differences are likely to reduce after allowing for smoking habits (Colley *et al.*, 1973) but they do not disappear entirely (Kiernan *et al.*, 1976).

Whereas asthma and/or wheezy bronchitis were barely differentiated by class (Figure 3.2), and while the figure includes all those declaring an attack of asthma or wheezy bronchitis since their sixteenth birthday, the pattern is similar when confining the comparison to those receiving treatment.

In contrast, there is a negative class gradient for the allergies, eczema and hayfever, although in women the gradient is less consistent, the main contrast being between non-manual and manual groups (Figure 3.2). These data represent reported occurrence in the twelve months preceding the study, during which time hayfever was more common than eczema (Appendix B, Table B.2) thereby contributing most to the class trends. A negative class gradient is also seen in consultations with GPs for hayfever (RCGP, OPCS, DHSS, 1982). In the NCDS, such sharp class contrasts were not evident, however, when comparing reported prevalence of 'migraine or recurrent sick headaches' or 'fits, convulsions, long faints or loss of consciousness'. Indeed, levels of these complaints were similar for each class. Again these findings are consistent with those evident from GP consultations for such problems (RCGP, OPCS, DHSS, 1982).

Indicators of *reproductive health* of women available for the cohort are

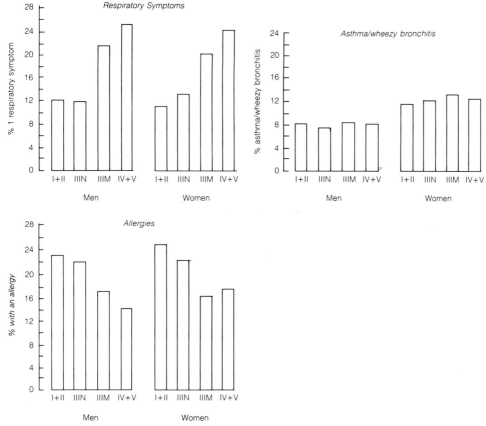

Fig. 3.2 Class* differences in respiratory symptoms,† asthma,‡ and allergies§ among young adults in the NCDS.

* The numbers in each social class are shown in Table 3.1.
† Medical Research Council (1960) approved questions on winter cough or phlegm (Appendix A).
‡ Respondents were asked separately about asthma and wheezy bronchitis (Appendix A).
§ Reported occurrence of eczema and hayfever (Appendix A).
Note: The three conditions identified here are not mutually exclusive.

varied. They include: number of miscarriages, complications during pregnancy and birthweight of offspring. No consistent class trends were evident in the miscarriage rate once allowance was made for class-related rates of pregnancy by age 23; but since lower class women had had more pregnancies it is likely that their health was more affected by this compared with women in higher classes (Tables 3.2 and 3.3).

Reproductive health could also be indicated by the birthweights of women's offspring, although this may be determined largely by the nutritional state of the woman's mother at the time of the woman's

Table 3.3 Social class and miscarriage* in NCDS women by age 23

| | ≥ 2 miscarriages reported among: | | | |
| | Women who have been pregnant | | All women | |
Social class	(Base)	%	(Base)	%
I and II	(239)	2.1	(1283)	0.39
IIIN	(1026)	3.0	(3042)	1.02
IIIM	(260)	2.7	(560)	1.25
IV and V	(798)	2.4	(1199)	1.58

*Miscarriage was reported separately from abortion. No definition was provided, but it is assumed that respondents reported spontaneous and therapeutic abortions as miscarriages and abortions respectively.

birth, rather than the woman's own nutritional state when she has her own children (Baird, 1974, 1985). Low birthweight in the offspring of the 1958 cohort was to some extent determined, therefore, by social circumstances and inheritance in 1958 but, as invariably found (e.g. OPCS, 1984b, 1985), was also associated with current social class. Joffe (1989) compared low birthweights (that is, 2500 g or less) to women in the cohort classified according to the social classes of their fathers and husbands. Only 3.4% of births to women born into classes I and II had low weights, compared with 8.7% in class III and 10.3% in classes IV and V. Similar gradients were apparent by husbands' class: 3.4% in I and II, 8.9% in III and 11.0% in IV and V.

Subsequent *height and weight* by age 23 were also examined and found to vary with social class as determined from current or recent occupation (Figure 3.3). Average height at age 23 was 2.4 cm greater in young men in classes I and II compared with those in classes IV and V. The corresponding difference for young women was 2.8 cm. Further confirmation of class gradients in height are evident from Figure 3.3 which presents class differences in short stature (defined as the shortest 10% – that is, below 1.676 m in men and 1.524 in women).

In contrast with height, however, weight (expressed as means) was lower in non-manual than in manual classes. Consequently, the proportion of young adults identified as overweight or obese (according to definitions recommended by the Royal College of Physicians, 1983) was greatest among manual classes (Figure 3.3). This is consistent with earlier reports of class differences (Stark *et al.*, 1981; Knight, 1984).

Indicators of physical health described above for the NCDS sample can be complemented with measures of psychological or emotional health. Two main indicators were available. The first is based on self-reported psychological or emotional problems between ages 16 and 23, for which specialist help was obtained. The second measure, 'malaise', was derived from self-completion responses to a symptom checklist

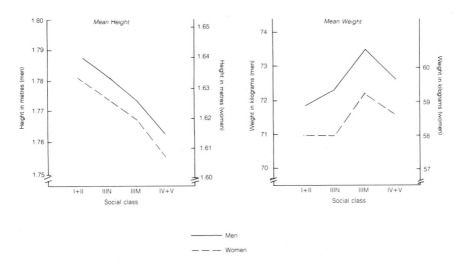

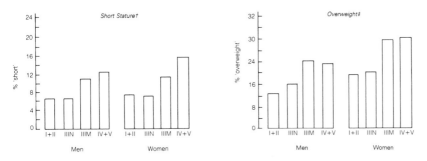

Fig. 3.3 Adult stature, weight and overweight by social class* at age 23.
* The numbers in each social class are shown in Table 3.1.
† Below the bottom decile of the height distribution (1.676 metres for men and 1.524 for women).
‡ According to the Royal College of Physicians' definition (1983): BMI ⩾ 25 (men), BMI ⩾ 23.8 (women).

(Rutter *et al.*, 1970) and is discussed in more detail later in this chapter (page 50). While class differences in emotional health were apparent using either measure, steeper gradients emerged consistently using 'malaise' for both sexes (Figure 3.4). Explanations for such discrepancies will be discussed later (page 52); meanwhile it is worth noting that other researchers have demonstrated that class gradients vary according to the instrument adopted. For example, in a sample of women in Edinburgh, Surtees *et al.* (1983) found a positive relationship between

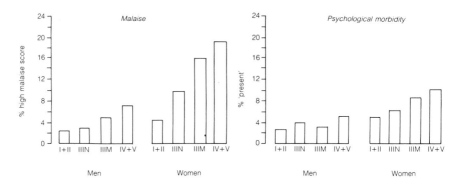

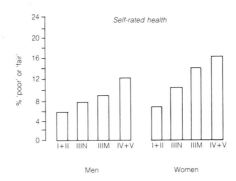

Fig. 3.4 Malaise, psychological morbidity and self-rated health by social class* at age 23.
* The numbers in each social class are shown in Table 3.1.

social class and psychiatric morbidity which varied slightly with the three separate definitions used. Brown and Harris (1978) also reported poorer mental health in lower social class women in Camberwell, London, but conflicting results were produced by Bebbington *et al.* (1981). Reviewing a wide range of such findings, Dohrenwend and Dohrenwend (1974) concluded 'that the most consistent result was an inverse relationship between overall rates of psychopathology and social class'.

Finally, when the sample *rated* their *health* on a four-point scale ranging from excellent to poor, young men and women in lower social classes each perceived their own health to be poorer more frequently than their higher social class contemporaries (Figure 3.4). Findings emerging from the GHS for 20–24 year olds provide corroboration for the class trends that we observe in the NCDS (West, 1988).

At this point it is important to summarize the main findings concerning class inequalities at age 23 and comment upon sex differences. As in other studies, such as the GP morbidity survey (RCGP, OPCS, DHSS, 1982) or for mortality (OPCS, 1978), we have found that class trends vary widely with the measure of health. Differences were not always pronounced, whether using indices based upon service use or symptoms and conditions reported by the respondents. This, as some researchers have suggested, may be because social differences are not as strong for young adults as they are for older ages (Blaxter, 1987; West, 1988). However, some notable trends have emerged and only rarely do these indicate poorer health in higher social classes: this is more generally a feature of lower classes.

Sex differences in reported morbidity have also become apparent, with women reporting more problems than men over a broad range of conditions and symptoms, although some exceptions – limiting long-standing illness, hayfever and some respiratory symptoms – have emerged (Appendix B, Table B.2). This finding is well documented, along with the greater average life expectancy of women in developed countries and the likely explanations. Since several reviews of such differences already exist (Nathanson, 1975, 1977; Silman, 1987; MacIntyre, 1986; Verbrugge and Wingard, 1987) the arguments need not be repeated. It is of interest to note, however, that despite sex differences in reported health problems, trends were fairly consistent for both sexes in relation to class gradients. Figures 3.1 to 3.4 show, for example, that where gradients were particularly weak or strong this applied to men and women. Others have compared class differences and found trends in limiting illness to be similar for both sexes (Arber, 1989).

It might be questioned whether a comparison of social gradients in health between men and women is valid using the existing classification of occupations. While classification of women by their own occupation, as used here, may satisfy some criticisms, other difficulties remain. In particular, women tend to be concentrated in a smaller number of occupations than men, clustering in the lower non-manual and unskilled classes (Roberts and Barker, 1986; Arber *et al.*, 1986), whereas predominantly male occupations cluster in the skilled manual class. Furthermore, men and women tend to do different jobs within a particular class with the result that the same occupational class may have a different meaning for men and women and thus be differently associated with health (Arber, 1989). In view of these problems more meaningful contrasts of social gradients await the development and widespread use of indices of social position which are comparable for men and women (Moser *et al.*, 1988). Meanwhile, alternative socio-economic measures are presented here for some health indices. Those that will be examined and included in further analyses of social inequalities are now discussed.

3.3 Selection of health measures for further analyses

In pursuing this enquiry it was necessary to select a few measures for this relatively healthy stage of the lifespan; four were chosen. As noted at the outset (Chapter 1), the main aim of the study is to examine the relative merits of different explanations for the social class differences that are observed in society. Therefore, measures chosen for further analysis were selected in part because they demonstrated the familiar trend of poorer health in lower social classes. It should not be assumed, however, that the explanatory variables included in the conceptual framework (Figure 1.4) are only relevant to health measures showing a class trend. On the contrary, they may well be as pertinent in explaining a lack of inequality.

A further consideration was that the measures should be appropriate for the stage of life of interest in our particular enquiry. Blaxter (1989) suggested that measures of ill-health may have differing relevance for health inequalities, particularly at different stages in the lifespan. As many illnesses are relatively uncommon in early adulthood, the numbers available for specific conditions may not allow a detailed analysis. Furthermore, in such cases, the conditions are likely to be of limited relevance for the larger part of class differences. Finally, some 'health' measures used in the previous section were not considered for further analysis because they were likely to say more about variations in rates of service use or provision than about differences in morbidity.

Evidence from other studies is important in demonstrating the relevance of particular health problems at different ages. *The Health and Lifestyle Survey* (see page 15 for a brief description of this survey) is especially useful in this respect. Using ratios which relate the occurrence of particular health problems to the overall study population mean (for the survey) Figure 3.5 illustrates how disease and disability increase with age as fitness declines (Blaxter, 1990). In contrast, psychological well-being does not appear to deteriorate with age. Younger ages had the highest ratios for poor psychosocial well-being compared with other ages, and in men the ratios declined steadily with age (i.e. psychosocial well-being improved). Similar findings have been reported for the USA (Weissman, 1987). Furthermore, for all other 'dimensions of health' examined by Blaxter (1990) young adults had a more favourable experience than older adults.

In view of these and the additional considerations outlined below, indices of health that were chosen for further study in the NCDS sample were as follows: self-rated health, 'malaise', psychological morbidity for which medical treatment was obtained, and height. Each of these measures showed a statistically significant increasing linear trend* of 'poor' health with decreasing social class in both men and women. It is important to stress, however, that these are not the only measures of interest, nor will they necessarily be the most appropriate choices at older ages when, for example, disability and functional impairment become more common.

Additional justifications for our selection, and also potential problems, need to be considered separately for each measure.

3.3.1 Self-rated health

Perceived health status is an unusual measure in that it attempts to measure 'health' rather than ill-health. A second, related, advantage is that while 'healthiness' may never be represented by a single indicator, self-assessed health combines a variety of physical and emotional components of well-being that incorporate 'healthiness'. For these (and other) reasons, Blaxter (1985) included self-assessed health as one of several dimensions that need to be covered in any investigation of healthiness.

However, the generality of the rating also creates confusion about what exactly it is measuring. Consequently: 'Such a subjective measure may be dismissed as meaningless, since one does not know what standards people are using, or how their assessments may be affected by an unwillingness to label their own health as poor' (Blaxter, 1990).

Information is accumulating, however, which should clarify some of the difficulties associated with the subjective rating of health. A major contribution has emerged from Blaxter's use of data in *The Health and Lifestyle Survey* (Blaxter, 1990). By comparing subjective assessments – not just with reported levels of illness and disease but also with physiological measures such as blood pressure and tests of lung function, psychosocial measures and demographic factors – she was able to examine what is measured when respondents are asked to rate their own health. Self-assessments, though always with a bias towards 'good' health, were found to be generally accurate, although there were more likely to be people who assessed their health 'anomalously' among younger and older age groups. The strongest influence on self-assessed health was the 'disease' dimension (defined in Figure 3.5) and the weakest was the 'fitness' (physiological) dimension. This applied across all ages. However, 'fitness' was a common concept in self-assessment of health, especially at younger ages, and psychosocial well-being

---

* Using the chi-squared test for trend.

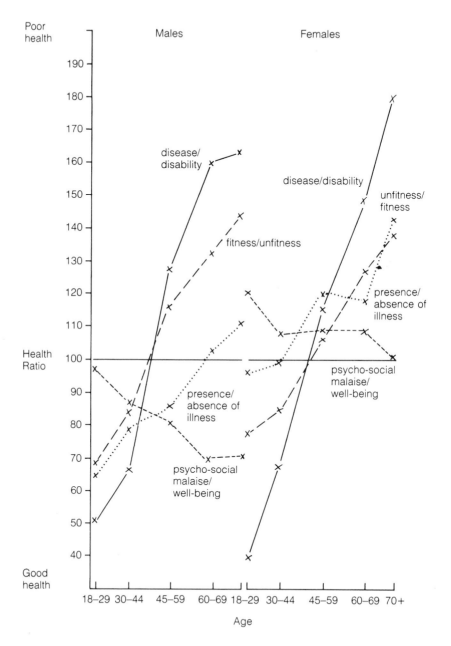

formed a generally popular concept of health. People in manual classes were more likely to take a pessimistic view of their health than others. More specifically, they were more likely to define it as poor when in fact it appeared to be good (on all available evidence) and to agree that it was poor when other measurements suggested that to be the case (Blaxter, 1990).

As in analyses of *The Health and Lifestyle Survey*, 'fair' and 'poor' ratings of health were grouped together for most later analyses of NCDS: 8.4% of young men and 10.7% of young women rated their health in this way. When compared with health problems reported to be limiting longstanding illnesses, medically supervised conditions or those resulting in hospital admission (classified into major ICD categories) the proportions rating their health as fair or poor were represented disproportionately in most categories (Appendix B, Table B.1). In contrast, as was noted earlier, respondents with no reported health problems perceived their health to be generally better than the sample overall.

Comparisons between self-rated health and major ICD categories is only of limited value, however. Self-assessment is likely to be influenced not only by perception but also by coexistence, severity and transience of morbidity. ICD groupings compared separately fail to take such considerations into account. Evidence for associations between subjective rating of health and other health measures selected for further study will be discussed below.

Fig. 3.5 Health ratios* for four dimensions of health showing differences by age and gender (total population mean = 100) in *The Health and Lifestyle Survey* Blaxter (1990).

* Standardized ratios represent the relationship of the group (e.g. age group) to the mean for the total population sample in *The Health and Lifestyle Survey*. A lower value represents less ill-health than the mean; a higher value, greater ill-health.

Health measures:
'Fitness/unfitness' is based on physiological measurements.
'Disease/disability' is based on reported medically defined conditions and degree of disability which accompany them.
'Illness' and 'psychosocial malaise/well-being' are based on reports of symptoms.
For details of physiological measurements, reported conditions, symptoms, etc., see Appendices in Blaxter (1990).

3.3.2 'Malaise'

Psychosocial well-being is an important component of health status and, in recognition of this, most comprehensive health surveys attempt to measure it. A variety of validated instruments are used for this purpose, such as the General Health Questionnaire, the Malaise Inventory and the Present State Examination.

The measure used to define the psychosocial well-being of young adults in the NCDS was the Malaise Inventory, which had been developed from the Cornell Medical Index by Rutter *et al.* (1970). It is important to recognize that the inventory is intended as a screening instrument to identify a tendency towards depression and is not used alone to diagnose depression. Recent evaluations of the Malaise Inventory demonstrate moderate correlations with other measures of stress (a scale of symptoms and the taking of medication related to mental health). It is also thought to provide a reliable representation of the symptoms associated with emotional disturbance, although emotional disturbance was not the dominant dimension of the scale (Hirst, 1983; Hirst and Bradshaw, 1983).

The checklist includes symptoms of anxiety, irritability, depressed mood and psychosomatic illness (Appendix B, Table B.3). In general, women in the NCDS sample gave positive responses to these symptoms more frequently than men, but both sexes identified, most frequently, worrying, annoyance or irritation with other people and being easily upset and, least frequently, physical symptoms apart from backache.

While some researchers have assigned weights to items particularly associated with depression (Osborn *et al.*, 1984), more conventionally a symptom score is derived from the total number of affirmative responses and a cut-off of more than 7 is used to identify a high-risk group (Richman, 1978; Rutter *et al.*, 1976). Using this criteria 4.2% of men in the NCDS and 11.0% of women were identified as having a high malaise score. The higher prevalence among women is consistent across several different measures of psychological health (Goldberg and Huxley, 1980; Rodgers and Mann, 1986) and there is much discussion about what this signifies (Weissman and Klerman, 1977).

Earlier in this chapter, it was evident that the proportion of men and women with a high malaise score declined from social classes IV and V to classes I and II (Figure 3.4). Class gradients were also evident when the average symptom scores were compared.

Young men and women with a high malaise score reported higher rates of limiting longstanding illness, medically supervised conditions or hospital admissions in general than those with a low score, although this varied with the type of condition reported (Appendix B, Table B.4) and they were also more likely to assess their own health as 'fair' or 'poor' overall (Table 3.4). These associations may have arisen through an overlap between the two measures. As mentioned above, psycho-social well-being is thought to be a popular general concept that is used when people assess their own health. The Malaise Inventory also includes some physical symptoms (Appendix B, Table B.3). However, others have found an association between physical and psychological health even after physical symptoms were excluded from the psychiatric measures used (Cox *et al.*, 1987). NCDS findings are consistent with an interdependence of physical and mental health. While in some instances it will be more appropriate to use the full title, Malaise Inventory, in general the term 'malaise' will be used in the remainder of this book.

Table 3.4 Self-rated health and malaise at age 23

	Men				Women			
	High malaise score		Low malaise score		High malaise score		Low malaise score	
Self-rated health	*n*	(%)	*n*	(%)	*n*	(%)	*n*	(%)
Excellent	54	(21)	2941	(49)	98	(14)	2495	(45)
Good	99	(38)	2623	(44)	331	(48)	2653	(48)
Fair	85	(33)	385	(6)	216	(31)	388	(7)
Poor	21	(8)	24	(0.4)	43	(6)	18	(0.3)

3.3.3 Psychological morbidity

While the Malaise Inventory elicited responses for psychological and emotional *symptoms* at age 23, information on psychological and emotional problems experienced since age 16, for which specialist help had been sought, was ascertained separately. Excluding mental handi-cap, 3.6% of men and 7.1% of women were identified from a specific question and also from reports of limiting longstanding mental ill-health or hospital admission or medical supervision for a mental disorder. Conditions included anorexia nervosa, drug and alcohol dependence and personality disorders, but the majority reported depression, anxiety or having deliberately taken an overdose (Appendix B, Table B.5).

In view of the extent to which psychological morbidity was attributed to depression and anxiety, simultaneous detection by the Malaise Inven-tory might be expected to occur. Table 3.5 shows that while the percent-age of those reporting psychological morbidity was higher among high malaise scorers than low scorers, there remained a substantial pro-portion not identified by the Malaise Inventory, especially among young men.

Table 3.5 Malaise and psychological morbidity at age 23

| | Men | | | | Women | | | |
| | High malaise score | | Low malaise score | | High malaise score | | Low malaise score | |
Psychological morbidity*	*n*	(%)	*n*	(%)	*n*	(%)	*n*	(%)
None	194	(75)	5817	(97)	501	(73)	5305	(96)
One or more	65	(25)	159	(3)	188	(27)	251	(4)

*Between ages 16 and 23.

However, differences between the two measures were considerable in respect of: the range of symptoms included; the reference period during which problems were experienced; and, given specialist involvement in one instance and not necessarily in the other, possibly in severity also. The latter remains conjecture, given other pertinent explanations of why some individuals present for treatment, which include differences in willingness to seek medical help and variations in service provision (Cartwright and O'Brien, 1976; Forster, 1976; Whitehead, 1988). Systematic class differences in such explanations may also be relevant in understanding why class differences in psychological and emotional ill-health, as measured by the Malaise Inventory, are steeper than those for psychological morbidity receiving specialist attention, especially for women.

As for people with a high malaise score, the group reporting psychological or emotional problems had poorer perceptions of their health than others of the same age (Table 3.6).

3.3.4 Height

So far, the selected indicators of health have been orientated towards psychosocial health. To some extent, each of these measures will be

Table 3.6 Self-rated health and psychological morbidity at age 23

| | Men | | | | Women | | | |
| | Psychological* morbidity | | No psychological morbidity | | Psychological* morbidity | | No psychological morbidity | |
Self-rated health	*n*	(%)	*n*	(%)	*n*	(%)	*n*	(%)
Excellent	57	(25)	2941	(49)	94	(21)	2503	(43)
Good	97	(43)	2623	(44)	200	(45)	2795	(48)
Fair	58	(26)	420	(7)	122	(28)	490	(8)
Poor	14	(6)	36	(0.6)	27	(6)	35	(0.6)

*Between ages 16 and 23.

influenced by the coexistence of other health problems either in the present (Appendix B, Tables B.1 and B.4) or the past (Power and Peckham, 1990) but they are interpreted here as indicating health largely as perceived at, or recent to, age 23.

Adult height was selected because, in contrast, it provides a more objective physical measurement which is a product of heredity and earlier environment. According to Tanner (1986), height represents the accumulated effects of 'successive shocks, nutritional deprivations, infections and emotional and metabolic disturbances' earlier in life and the measure has, therefore, been used traditionally as representing health status in childhood (Tanner, 1978; Preece 1986; Acheson, 1987; Price *et al.*, 1988). Hence, it is thought to be a simple summary of earlier nutrition, growth, physical and emotional health. It has also been proposed that height provides a useful health indicator for adults (Carr-Hill, 1988; MacIntyre, 1988) since in addition to its relationship with *earlier* health, height is associated with several *later* health-related experiences. Evidence for the latter is well established and includes associations between height and reproductive success in women (Butler and Bonham, 1963; Baird, 1974; Emanuel, 1986) and mortality from coronary heart disease (Marmot *et al.*, 1984; Waaler, 1984), tuberculosis and obstructive lung disease (Waaler, 1984); short stature being associated with the greatest risks.

Even though reasons for the link between height and mortality are not entirely clear, several plausible mechanisms can be formulated. MacIntyre (1988) has presented these diagrammatically, such that short stature results from social deprivation and/or genetic and constitutional factors, and it is these characteristics which influence mortality possibly but not necessarily through short stature.

During childhood, minor temporary illnesses may have a small effect on growth but they probably have no long-term implications. Repeated or chronic illness are considered to be more important as they might affect adult height. Several conditions have been identified as affecting height, but even so only a minority of short children have an identifiable disease (Tanner, 1978).

By basing analyses in this and subsequent chapters on adulthood short stature, we are likely to include a disproportionate number of study members who had a serious condition during childhood. However, since 'short' stature is defined here, arbitrarily, as heights below the lower decile, the majority of those identified by this criteria will probably have had no such problems in childhood. Table 3.7 suggests that this is the case, at least in terms of selected health measures in adulthood, even though young adults categorized as short are more likely than their taller contemporaries to have poorer health according to these measures.

Table 3.7 'Short' stature, self-rated health and psychological morbidity at age 23

Height	'Poor or fair' self-rated health		High malaise score		Psychological* morbidity	
	n	(%)	*n*	(%)	*n*	(%)
Men						
Short	90	(13.5)	47	(7.1)	31	(4.6)
Others	431	(7.8)	209	(3.8)	191	(3.4)
Women						
Short	103	(17.2)	95	(15.7)	50	(8.2)
Others	579	(10.3)	570	(10.1)	388	(6.9)

*Between ages 16 and 23.

As mentioned previously, however, short stature in particular is associated with subsequent risks, at least in terms of mortality. This was one reason for treating the variable height as a dichotomy. Additional advantages, such as standardization of methods for the four health measures, will be presented in Chapter 5.

Before concluding this discussion, it is important to establish whether differences in height in the NCDS sample could be explained by reporting bias. No direct physical measurements were available for age 23; heights were self-reported by the subjects. Self-reporting has been shown to be reliable and valid even for less-educated groups and to be most accurate in young adults compared with older ages, but, even so, bias in reporting varied as a function of level of education (Stewart, 1982; Palta *et al.*, 1982).

It is unlikely that bias could account for the class difference entirely, since differences in height are shown in studies based on measurements. A recent national study estimated average height for 20- to 24-year-old men as 178.0 cm in classes I and II compared with 174.9 cm in classes IV and V (Knight, 1984). For NCDS the figures were 178.6 and 175.0 cm respectively. Similarly, average heights of 162.7 (classes I and II) and 161.5 cm (IV and V) were reported for women using measured data, and 163.4 versus 160.5 cm from the self-reports of NCDS subjects. Some discrepancies might be expected between the two studies because of the sample sizes used at different ages. (The study with measured data at 20–24 years was based on social class samples ranging from 108 to 210, while the range for NCDS was 1281 to 1186.)

Further support for a class difference in NCDS subjects is evident from data obtained at age 16 when heights were measured. Not surprisingly, average heights at age 16 were less than at age 23, but class differences were apparent at the earlier age as well as at 23: 172.0 cm for men in classes I and II compared with 168.9 cm in IV and V, with 162.0 and 159.5 cm respectively among women. It seems unlikely, therefore, that reporting bias could account for class differences in adult height of the NCDS sample.

3.4 Differences in health using alternative measures of socio-economic position

The criticisms of using the conventional occupational class categoriz-ation in studies of health trends were referred to earlier in this chapter (page 36). In response to these criticisms a variety of alternative indi-cators such as housing tenure, car ownership, income and education have been put forward and subsequently related to morbidity and mor-tality (Arber, 1989; Moser *et al.*, 1988; Wilkinson, 1986). Here we con-sider alternative measures available in the NCDS.

3.4.1 Housing tenure

This has been suggested as a useful measure of social position (Moser *et al.*, 1988; Arber, 1989; Fox and Goldblatt, 1982). It is a useful indicator probably because it represents control of resources and wealth – 'material security: credit worthiness in the eyes of building societies, stable employment and ownership of assets' (Hart, 1986). It also has the advantage of being applicable equally to men and women whether or not they are employed.

Figure 3.6 shows marked and consistent differences between owner-occupiers and local authority tenants in the NCDS, using the four selected health measures at age 23; owner-occupiers having generally better health. The differences by tenure are similar to the social class differences shown earlier (Figures 3.3 and 3.4), with the greatest being for malaise and self-rated health, and for women rather than men.

Housing tenure proved to be a useful additional measure of social circumstances in the NCDS (Fogelman *et al.*, 1989). While it may be desirable to repeat the analyses presented later using housing tenure, this measure was not given precedence over occupational class because a substantial proportion of 23 year olds still lived in their parental home or in transient rented accommodation. Furthermore, bias is introduced into comparisons based on tenure because women and young people of working-class origins are more likely to leave home by age 23 (Kier-nan, 1986).

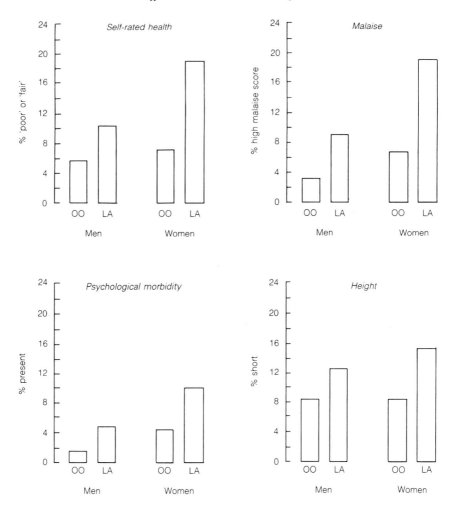

Fig. 3.6 Four health measures by housing tenure.

Housing tenure:
OO = Owner occupied.
LA = Local authority.

3.4.2 Income

As with tenure, income has been suggested as an indicator of social position which can be used to investigate differences in health (Arber, 1989; Cox *et al.*, 1987). It has also been regarded as contributing towards these social differences (Carr-Hill, 1985; Wilkinson, 1986). Difficulties are sometimes experienced in obtaining reliable data, and sources of income other than a main job are not always included.

Nevertheless, there was an attempt to collect such details from NCDS subjects at age 23, and after adjustments were made to allow for family composition (Appendix C, section C.1) the health experiences of four income groups were compared. Figure 3.7 shows poorer health in the lowest income groups on all four selected health measures. For both sexes the highest income group appeared to have better health, although for men there was little differentiation between the two highest income categories. In general, however, the differences in health observed between social groups when occupation is used as the basis of the classification are also apparent when social groups are defined by income. Therefore, income might be used in further investigations into health differences.

3.4.3 Education

Educational attainment has a major advantage as a social index primarily because it is equally available for men and women. It has been used as an alternative to social class in analyses of mortality (Fox and Goldblatt, 1982; Kitagawa and Hauser, 1973) and is especially useful for international comparisons as it overcomes the difficulties of contrasting occupational structures (Valkonen, 1989). Morbidity is also differentiated by educational level (Arber, 1989). Not surprisingly, therefore, classification of NCDS respondents by their highest qualification showed social gradients, and although the gradients were not always consistent, Figure 3.8 shows poorer health at lower levels of education and better health at higher levels.

Using GHS data, Arber (1989) found that limiting longstanding illness was related to education in both men and women, with the least illness among those with degree level education. *The Health and Lifestyle Survey* has also shown gradients in self-perceived health with education and income as well as social class (Blaxter, 1987). Even so, level of education achieved may be limited as a social index. First, most formal educational qualifications are acquired by early adulthood and it is therefore not possible to use those achievements to indicate changes in status thereafter. Second, qualifications are vulnerable to changes in meaning over time, especially between generations, as opportunities and examinations alter. Third, the distribution of qualifications is highly skewed, with the majority of the population having no qualifications.

Table 3.8 demonstrates that this third argument is less applicable to the cohort of young men and women in the NCDS since educational qualifications were well distributed. Even so, education was not accepted as a substitute for own class at 23 because one of the aims of

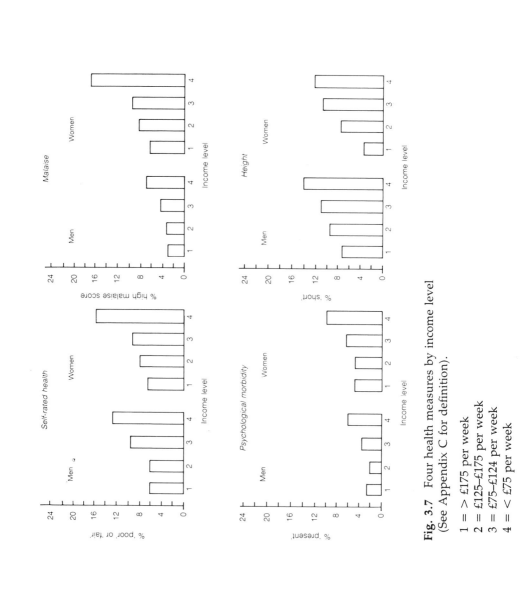

Fig. 3.7 Four health measures by income level (See Appendix C for definition).

1 = > £175 per week
2 = £125–£175 per week
3 = £75–£124 per week
4 = < £75 per week

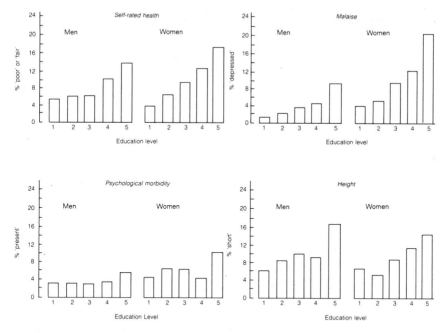

Fig. 3.8 Four health measures by education level.

Education level:

1 = Above 'A' level
2 = 'A' level or equivalent
3 = 'O' level or equivalent
4 = Below 'O' level
5 = None

the investigation is to examine whether education is a contributory factor in the development of social differences in health. Given this, educational achievement both in childhood and on entry to the labour force needs to be considered as explanatory and not as the social stratifier of young adults. Further elaboration of this argument is presented in Chapter 8.

3.5 Conclusions

This chapter demonstrates the extent of social differences in health among young adults, using a variety of indices. Overall, there was a tendency for higher prevalence of reported disease, symptoms of illness and obesity, poorer perceived health and shorter average stature to be found in lower social classes. Although this trend was not uniform,

Table 3.8 Distribution of qualifications attained by age 23 in NCDS subjects

Qualification level	Men (n=6267) (%)	Women (n=6270) (%)
Above 'A' level	19.0	18.0
'A' level or equivalent	21.9	11.1
'O' level or equivalent	28.0	36.7
Below 'O' level	5.4	4.4
None	25.7	29.8

only rarely – as with reported allergies – did the highest classes appear to have poorer health. It has been suggested that differences in health between social groups may not always be as pronounced in early adulthood as in older age groups (Blaxter, 1987; West, 1988). However, distinct trends are evident for particular measures even at 23 years, notably for psychosocial health and height and weight.

From the range of measures presented in this chapter four were chosen for further analyses. Three of these are orientated towards psychosocial well-being. Such measures may well be related to mortality (Kaplan and Camacho, 1983; Kaplan *et al.*, 1987) but for such a young age group correlations are likely to be tenuous, and the choices were made largely because this dimension constitutes one of the main health problems of this age group.

In contrast to the subjective measures of emotional health, height has been selected as a physical marker of past health and as a predictor of future mortality. As with the other measures, it will be referred to as a measure of 'health'. While this may not be the most precise term, it is preferable to unwieldy descriptions that might otherwise result. It is most important to recognize that the four measures do not represent all health in early adulthood, even though each is relevant.

Differences in health were evident for various social indices, namely, housing tenure, income and education. There was little advantage, however, in using an alternative to social class at age 23, given, for example, the problematic nature of housing tenure at this stage in the lifespan and the anticipated role of education in the analyses. It was also possible to overcome some of the criticisms of using current social class since the detailed data for occupation enabled classification of the majority of both men and women. Even so, the argument might still be made that occupation at age 23 (or earlier for those currently not in paid employment) does not provide a good measure of the class that will be achieved later in life. This would apply to other indices representing current circumstances (housing, for example) because early adulthood is a period of transition. Despite its imprecisions, therefore, social class at age 23 (based on current or most recent occupation) was chosen as a useful general guide to social position for this investigation of differences in health in early adulthood.

4

Social mobility and class differences in health

4.1 Introduction

Having shown that social differences in health exist in early adulthood and having identified the indices of health and social position to be used, the aim of this chapter* is to examine the contribution of one potential explanation for health differences, namely, selective social mobility. This explanation has received much attention recently, not just in relation to health but also in connection with the broader issue of the role of genetics in determining social position (Himsworth, 1984, 1986; Goldthorpe, 1985).

According to the selection argument, health differences between social classes are produced as a result of health itself causing social movement: the healthy moving up the social scale and the unhealthy moving down. Empirical support for the concept of health-related mobility accumulated in the 1950s from research on height of women, reproductive outcomes and interclass mobility at marriage (Illsley, 1955). The selection explanation was revived in the early 1980s with a reformulation in mathematical terms (Stern, 1983) and further empirical evidence from the Aberdeen studies (Illsley, 1986). That some selective effects occur is not questioned, but only whether the effect is of sufficient magnitude to account for all or a large part of social class differences in health. Wilkinson (1986), for example, argued that the contribution of selective social mobility is small and needs to be considered alongside other factors such as the accuracy with which differentials in mortality can be assessed.

Much of the evidence for a minimal effect of social mobility is based on older age groups. In the OPCS Longitudinal Study, for example, it

* This chapter is based on a Gower publication: Fogelman, K., Fox, A. J. and Power, C. (1989) Class and tenure mobility, in *Health Inequalities in European Countries;* and on Power, C., Manor, O., Fox, A. J. and Fogelman, K. (1988) *Health Selection,* Social Statistics Research Unit, City University.

was possible to relate deaths between 1976 and 1981 to social class at the 1971 census. Since the mortality gradient by class 5 to 10 years before death was similar to that by social class at death, Fox *et al.* (1985) concluded that for men over fifty years of age health-related mobility between classes did not contribute to mortality differentials. Independent evidence is available from the Whitehall Study (Marmot *et al.*, 1984), which showed that the gradient of coronary heart disease (CHD) mortality persisted among men without, as well as with, any known disease at entry to the study. A similar result was reported for all-cause mortality. Hence, recruitment of sicker men into lower grades in the Civil Service did not explain the mortality gradient.

However, even if selection does not provide an important explanation for class differences at older ages, its effect at younger ages is less clear. It is in early adulthood that the potential for social mobility to explain class differences in health is possibly at its greatest, since social mobility occurring during the transition from class based on parents' occupation to that based on own occupation is undoubtedly health-related. Some support for this is available from the 1946 cohort study in which serious illness in childhood was shown to influence subsequent social mobility (Wadsworth, 1986) but the extent to which this contributes to overall class differences may prove to be small (Wilkinson, 1986).

In the present examination of whether social mobility can explain all or a large part of health differences among NCDS subjects, the same measures of health identified in the previous chapter will be used (i.e. self-rated health, malaise, psychological morbidity and height). At this stage childhood health will not be included among possible explanations for health differences at age 23. As described in Chapter 1, this will be considered separately in a later chapter.

4.2 Measures

Social class data from which mobility was established is as follows:

- *Social class at birth and at 16:* based on father's occupation in 1958 and 1974 (coded according to the Registrar General's classification in 1950 and 1970). Individuals with no male head of household are excluded from these analyses.
- *Social class at 23:* based on the subject's current or most recent occupation (coded according to the Registrar General's 1980 classification).

Class differences in health were tested by calculating the odds of experiencing poor health in classes IV and V relative to classes I and II (details of the odds ratio are presented in Appendix E). If this ratio was greater than 1 (at the 5% level) then differences were regarded as significant.

4.3 Social class at birth and health at age 23

One way in which to investigate whether social mobility accounts for differences in health is to examine differences by class at birth rather than achieved class. While achieved social class (in this case class at age 23) includes the effect of social mobility, social class at birth does not.

Differences in health were examined using this measure (Figure 4.1) and, in general, gradients replicate those shown in the previous chapter for the respondents own class at 23 (Figures 3.3 and 3.4). Similarly, differences in health were examined using housing tenure during childhood as well as in early adulthood and health gradients were evident using either measure of social position (Fogelman *et al.*, 1989). However, the differences appear to be slightly stronger in relation to current social class than to class at birth, suggesting that social mobility may have exaggerated class differences. It is necessary, therefore, to consider social mobility in more detail.

4.4 Social mobility from birth to early adulthood

Before studying relationships between upward and downward mobility and health one must consider the pattern and extent of mobility experienced by the cohort. It is, after all, a combination of high levels of mobility and marked differences in health according to mobility that will exert an influence on health patterns.

Socio-economic mobility is well documented in the UK in the classic studies of Glass and colleagues (Glass, 1954) and the Oxford Mobility Project (Goldthorpe, 1980; Halsey *et al.*, 1980). These studies document the evolving patterns of movement within and between generations of men (Heath, 1981) although patterns for women are less well documented.

Table 4.1 summarizes the mobility experiences of the NCDS cohort. For males and females separately it gives the numbers in each social class at birth, at 16 and at 23; the first two of these are based on social class of father, the last on own social class. The patterns expected from the earlier literature are relatively clear from this table. If, for example, the numbers in different social classes at birth and at 16 are compared, it becomes apparent that fathers were upwardly mobile as their children grew up. At birth 647 (17.5%) of the boys' fathers and 671 (17.7%) of the girls' fathers were in social classes I and II; by age 16 these had risen to 947 (25.5%) and 973 (25.7%) respectively. This upward movement was associated with movement across the manual/non-manual divide and was not confined to movement within the manual and non-

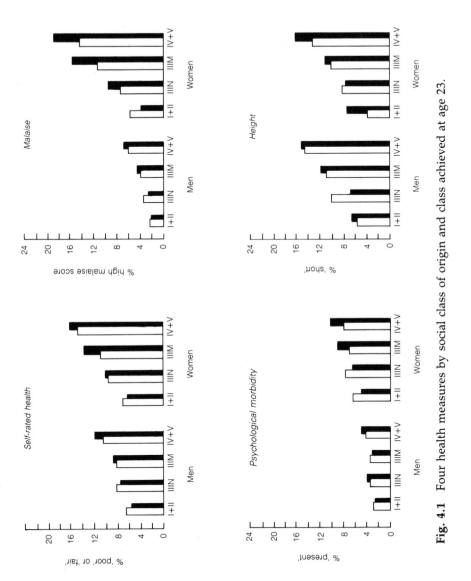

Fig. 4.1 Four health measures by social class of origin and class achieved at age 23.

Table 4.1 Social class at 23 by father's social class at the birth of NCDS member and at age 16, by sex (numbers with complete data)*

Father's class at: birth	16	Men's own class at 23					Women's own class at 23				
		I & II	IIIN	IIIM	IV & V	Total	I & II	IIIN	IIIM	IV & V	Total
I and II	I and II	225	111	95	53	484	209	232	20	36	497
	IIIN	38	25	19	7	89	22	45	7	7	81
	IIIM	20	7	23	8	58	19	35	5	10	69
	IV and V	1	3	9	3	16	5	13	2	4	24
	Total	284	146	146	71	647	255	325	34	57	671
IIIN	I and II	52	45	29	12	138	40	76	6	11	133
	IIIN	41	36	49	15	141	28	79	8	12	127
	IIIM	11	13	35	13	72	23	47	5	20	95
	IV and V	2	4	19	9	34	4	11	2	3	20
	Total	106	98	132	49	385	95	213	21	46	375
IIIM	I and II	88	60	101§	32	281	86	156§	19	26	287
	IIIN	28	27	70	20	145	47	74	14	24	159
	IIIM	**194**	181	**589**	**227**	1191	**210**	**630**	111	**263**	1214
	IV and V	43	25	147§	70	285	32	133§	40	71	276
	Total	353	293	907	349	1902	375	993	184	384	1936
IV and V	I and II	11	8	16	9	44	11	23	7	15	56
	IIIN	7	11	20	14	52	8	32	5	5	50
	IIIM	42	44	177	89	352	47	174	47	85	353
	IV and V	26	83	146	115	253	34	143	41	125	343
	Total	86	101	359	227	773	100	372	100	230	802
Total	I and II	376	224	241	106	947	346	487	52	88	973
	IIIN	114	99	158	56	427	105	230	34	48	417
	IIIM	267	245	824	337	1673	299	886	168	378	1731
	IV and V	72	70	321	197	660	75	300	85	203	663
	Total	829	638	1544	696	3707	825	1903	339	717	3784

*Social class at each of birth, 16 and 23 and height recorded at 23.
Italicized figures are for those also used in Table 4.3.
Bold figures are for those also used in Table 4.4.
Bold and underlined figures are for those also used in Tables 4.3, 4.4 and 4.5.

manual classes. Such trends are consistent with those seen for men of working ages in the OPCS Longitudinal Study (Goldblatt, 1988).

At the same time the table shows the change in employment patterns between the generations and the differences in employment patterns between young men and young women. More sons were in classes I and II at age 23 and fewer were in manual occupations than fathers at the time their sons were born. Just over half the daughters were in social class III non-manual (IIIN) at age 23, whereas the highest concentration of sons (over 40%) was in social class III manual (IIIM).

The feature of the table that is of particular interest from the point of view of social mobility and health is the extent of social class stabilities from birth to 16 and even to 23. Of the 647 sons of men in social classes I and II at the time of the child's birth, 336 (51.9%) were in social classes I and II at 16 and were in non-manual occupations at 23. The comparable figure for 671 daughters was 441 (65.7%). Nearly one-third (589) of the 1902 sons of fathers in social class IIIM at birth were in social class IIIM at 16 and 23. Nearly one-third of the daughters of men in this class remained, from their birth, in the class until 16 and were subsequently found in class III (although most of these women were in IIIN rather than IIIM as a result of different employment opportunities available to women compared with men). Only for class IIIN at birth is there a very marked dispersion of the group during the first 23 years of life.

The patterns described above have implications for the study of mobility and health. Most importantly, while the total amount of mobility was considerable, there were small numbers in those groups representing the least common pathways through life. There were also marked stabilities. Therefore, the relationships between health and mobility will need to be systematic and strong if they are to provide the major explanation of health differences at this age. This issue will be addressed in the next section, by examining the health at 23 of subjects whose social class remained stable and for those who were upwardly and downwardly mobile.

4.5 Social mobility and health

In this section the term 'stable' is used to refer to those whose class was the same at two points in their childhood (birth and age 16), or at one point in their childhood and at 23. Similarly, 'mobility' is used when class differed on these occasions. It must be acknowledged that this overlooks any additional changes that may have taken place between these points, but it seems reasonable to assume that other changes would not be substantial enough to alter the conclusions.

In the description of the stable and the mobile, there are references to the class distribution of the four selected health measures at age 23. These trends were presented in Figure 4.1 but they are shown again in Table 4.2 using a format that is comparable with other tables in this chapter.

Table 4.2 Social class and health at age 23

Health indicator	Men				Women			
	I&II (1278)	IIIN (1010)	IIIM (2413)	IV&V (1224)	I&II (1283)	IIIN (3042)	IIIM (560)	IV&V (1199)
Poor or fair self-rated health (%)	5.5	7.3	8.6	11.8	6.0	9.9	13.6	15.9
High malaise score (%)	2.2	2.6	4.6	6.9	4.2	9.7	15.8	18.9
Psychological morbidity (%)	2.7	4.0	3.1	5.1	4.6	6.3	8.6	10.3
Short stature (%)	6.8	7.1	11.8	14.6	7.2	7.7	10.8	16.0

Trends for each sex and health measure are statistically significant using χ^2 test for trend ($p<0.005$).

4.5.1 'Stable' social class background

Table 4.3 compares the health of those subjects in classes I and II at birth, 16 and 23 with those in classes IV and V. For men, those in class IIIM at each age are also presented. As mentioned above, labour market opportunities for young women differ from those for men in that class III occupations are generally classified as non-manual and so data are

Table 4.3 NCDS subjects with stable social class at birth, 16 and 23,* according to health at age 23

Health indicator	Men†			Women†		
	I&II ($n = 225$)	IIIM ($n = 595$)	IV&V ($n = 115$)	I&II ($n = 209$)	IIIM/N ($n = 631$)	IV&V ($n = 115$)
Poor or fair self-rated health (%)	4.4	9.1	11.3	4.8	8.6	15.2
High malaise score (%)	2.2	3.7	9.6	3.4	9.8	25.0
Psychological morbidity (%)	3.5	2.7	5.2	4.8	5.2	8.8
Short stature (%)	2.7	11.9	13.0	5.3	9.4	19.2

*Identified in Table 4.1.
†The figures shown in parentheses vary slightly according to health indicator, this leads to some discrepancies between numbers here and in Table 4.1.

presented for female subjects whose fathers were in class IIIM during the subjects' childhood but who were themselves in class IIIN. Each of these groups, defined here as stable, is indicated in Table 4.1.

For each of the health indicators the patterns are as expected with significantly stronger differences in malaise, self-rated health and height than in psychological morbidity, and although they appear to be more marked for women than for men, the sex differences were not significant.

This table shows that social class differences in health in the restricted group of subjects whose social circumstances remained stable during their childhood and early adulthood are broadly similar to differences seen in the whole sample when classified by class at birth and at age 23 (Figure 4.1 and Table 4.1) for the whole sample. It may be the case, nevertheless, that there may be different patterns for subjects whose social circumstances had changed and these patterns may contribute to the health differences observed at age 23.

4.5.2 Intergenerational social mobility

Mobility is considered first for those whose own social class at 23 was different to that of their fathers during their childhood. In order to hold constant the effect of father's social class, only those whose fathers were in class IIIM when the subject was born and who were still in the same class when the subject was 16 are included in the analysis. (These groups are indicated in Table 4.1.)

The young men and young women who had moved to a higher social class at 23 reported better health than those who had moved to a lower social class at 23 (Table 4.4). For comparison, figures for those in class IIIM (IIIN for women at 23) throughout their lives are shown again in Table 4.4 as stable, and it can be seen that usually, but not always, they fell between the upwardly and downwardly mobile. The largest differences were, for young men, in malaise and self-rated health and, for young women, in malaise, self-rated health and psychological morbidity.

These data confirm that intergenerational mobility either up or down is associated with differences in health. For men the magnitude of these differences is generally similar to those observed in Table 4.3 between subjects whose class remained stable to age 23. For women the differences observed for height and malaise were significantly wider for the stable than the mobile.

Table 4.4 Intergenerational mobility from social class IIIM* and health at age 23†

| | Mobility between social class in childhood and age 23 | | | | | |
| | Men | | | Women | | |
Health indicator	Upwards ($n = 194$)	Stable ($n = 595$)	Down-wards ($n = 231$)	Upwards ($n = 210$)	Stable ($n = 631$)	Down-wards ($n = 264$)
Poor or fair self-rated health (%)	4.1	9.1	13.4	5.2	8.6	16.3
High malaise score (%)	1.5	3.7	7.4	6.2	9.8	16.7
Psychological morbidity (%)	3.6	2.7	6.5	3.8	5.2	10.6
Short stature (%)	5.2	11.9	12.3	10.0	9.4	14.8

*Indentified in Table 4.1.
†Includes those in class IIIM at birth and age 16.

4.5.3 Social mobility during childhood

As well as intergenerational mobility, the health of those whose parents were mobile during the subject's childhood is also of interest. Again, analyses were limited to those whose fathers were in social class IIIM in 1958. Table 4.5 is further restricted to young men in social class IIIM and young women in social class IIIN at 23. This table indicates whether the father, from the time of the subject's birth, was in a higher, the same or a lower class when the subject was 16. The middle columns for each sex represent those subjects who were in this class at birth, 16 and 23, as in Tables 4.3 and 4.4. Again these groups are identified in Table 4.1.

Table 4.5 Social mobility during childhood only for those in class IIIM* at birth and at 23†, according to health at 23

| | Mobility between birth and age 16 | | | | | |
| | Boys | | | Girls | | |
Health indicator	Upwards ($n = 101$)	Stable ($n = 595$)	Down-wards ($n = 147$)	Upwards ($n = 157$)	Stable ($n = 631$)	Down-wards ($n = 133$)
Poor or fair self-rated health (%)	6.0	9.1	8.8	12.1	8.6	9.7
High malaise score (%)	3.0	3.7	4.1	6.4	9.8	9.8
Psychological morbidity (%)	1.0	2.7	3.4	4.5	5.2	4.5
Short stature (%)	3.0	11.9	13.6	6.4	9.4	7.5

*Class IIIN for women at age 23.
†Identified in Table 4.1.

The numbers of subjects experiencing upward mobility during child-hood is understated in Table 4.5 because the analysis was restricted to those who, at 23, were in the equivalent class to that of their fathers when they were born. As shown in Table 4.1, this is the most likely pattern. Within this restricted group, the differences in health between subjects whose fathers were upwardly or downwardly mobile are rela-tively small (Table 4.5). The only exception is the proportion of young men who were short, which was greater for those whose fathers were downwardly mobile. For each of the other health measures, suggestions of better health for those subjects whose parents were upwardly mobile compared with those whose parents were downwardly mobile, were weak.

4.5.4 Health at 23 controlling for circumstances in childhood

Analyses described in this chapter demonstrate some relationships between social mobility and health in early adulthood, but so far they have been based on selected groups only for illustrative purposes. As evident from Table 4.1, subjects born in social classes other than IIIM – i.e. nearly half the population – have been ignored. These classes also need to be considered if we are to establish the extent to which social mobility explains the social gradient in health at 23. We now attempt to answer this by standardizing the relationship between social class at 23 and health at 23 for earlier social class.

The relationship between social class at 23 and health at 23 was summarized using the Index of Dissimilarity (ID) which measures the percentage of all cases that would need to be redistributed among the classes in order to achieve equal rates for all groups (Preston *et al.*, 1981). The index was then standardized for social class during childhood, and this is shown in Table 4.6 together with the crude or unstandardized percentage. The Index of Dissimilarity is calculated as follows:

$$ID = \Sigma_i \left| \frac{O_i - E_i}{\Sigma O_i + \Sigma E_i} \right|$$

where O_i and E_i are the numbers of cases observed and expected in each category and the summation is over all categories used in the comparison.

A limitation of this index is the lack of any measurement of direction of inequality. The index may, for example, be the same when differ-ences favour the better-off or poorer groups, or even when there is no systematic pattern. This limitation is not critical here since the gradients are generally clear, from better health in classes I and II to poorer health in classes IV and V (Table 4.2).

71

Table 4.6 Index of dissimilarity by sex and health indicator at age 23: crude and standardized* for social class during childhood

Health indicator	Men ($n = 3707$)†	Women ($n = 3784$)†
Poor or fair self-rated health:		
crude	9.8%	12.7%
standardized	7.9%	10.4%
High malaise score:		
crude	16.6%	17.3%
standardized	11.8%	14.6%
Psychological morbidity:		
crude	8.1%	11.8%
standardized	7.5%	10.6%
Short stature:		
crude	12.1%	14.8%
standardized	7.1%	10.8%

*Standardization is based on social class at birth and age 16.
†The numbers vary according to the health index at age 23.

It should also be appreciated that the index weights according to the size of the groups being compared. Classes IIIM and IIIN are the largest groups for men and women and since these are at the centre of the scale this propensity will tend to make the index relatively less sensitive to the values in the extreme groups. This limitation has to be taken into account when interpreting Table 4.6. The measure does have the advantage of using rates for all social classes rather than, as is commonly practised, just comparing the extremes.

The crude ID in Table 4.6 summarizes the class differences shown in Table 4.2 for the health measures used throughout these analyses. The standardized ID is based upon the rates that would be expected from the distribution of social class at birth and at 16. Comparison of the crude and standardized IDs demonstrates the effect of controlling for social class in childhood. Therefore, Table 4.6 provides an indication of the proportion of class differences in health at age 23 that can be 'explained' by earlier class.

Standardization always reduces the ID, but the reduction is rarely substantial. Social gradients in height and, to a lesser extent, malaise are partially explained by the relationship with earlier circumstances, but the gradients of the other two measures are almost independent of any additional effects of social position during childhood.

4.6 Discussion

These findings support hypotheses that subjects who had been upwardly mobile between the ages of 16 and 23 were, on the whole, healthier than those who had been downwardly mobile. This was most marked and consistent for malaise and self-rated health. This conclusion is not likely to be affected by differences in the social origins of the mobile, since the class of origin had been held constant by limiting the analysis to those born to fathers in class IIIM. It remains possible, however, that different patterns could be found for those mobile from other social classes.

Evidence for a relationship between mobility of parents and social class differences in the health of their children when they are young adults was less marked, in general, than the findings associated with intergenerational mobility.

Overall, the evidence presented here does not necessarily mean that mobility explains class differences in health at 23. These differences must first be compared with those observed for subjects whose social class remained relatively stable throughout childhood and early adulthood. This is a large group for whom differences in health are not influenced by mobility. It is striking to note, therefore, that the gradients observed for this group were generally as large as the gradients between the upwardly and downwardly mobile, inter- or intragenerationally.

For social mobility to be an important determinant of health differences at 23, those who were mobile would need to be substantially different in terms of health at 23 from those who were stable, and not just different from the group they were leaving but also different from the group they were joining. At the same time they would need to be numerous enough to influence the weighted averages. Although the upwardly mobile tend to be healthier than the downwardly mobile, the analyses performed so far suggest that the differences between the incomers to the extreme groups and those who had always been in the extreme groups are not sufficient to determine the differences between the extreme groups, irrespective of the numbers who were mobile. This is most clearly shown by analyses which standardized gradients at age 23 for social class during childhood. For most of the four health measures there was a reduction in the gradient, but there remained substantial differences in health at 23 that were not explained by the relationship with earlier social position.

For simplicity, data were presented for cohort members who were allocated to a social class at birth, at 16 and again at 23. This disproportionately excludes some of the most deprived members of the cohort. To some extent this limitation was overcome in work reported in detail elsewhere, by investigating the effects of using an alternative index, housing tenure (Fogelman *et al.*, 1989). Similar conclusions were reached from these analyses, although for both social class and tenure there were some variations between health measures and between the sexes. In particular, there was frequently a contrast between the patterns found in relation to height and the other three measures such that the differences in height between social groups were more readily explained by earlier circumstances. This is not surprising, since early events and genetic influences are likely to be especially important for this health measure. Differences between measures will re-emerge in subsequent chapters.

Further analyses were performed to examine whether our conclusions about social mobility would be affected by the omission of subjects who experienced a period with no male head of household during childhood (Fogelman *et al.*, 1987). This group was excluded from the analyses reported in the present chapter because it was not possible to allocate a social class when no data were available for father's (or father figure's) occupation. This is an important group numerically (10% of the cohort) which has experienced considerable financial and material difficulties and, subsequently, poorer school attainment (Essen and Lambert, 1977; Ferri, 1976; Essen, 1978). Even though the experience of being without a father at some stage during childhood appeared to influence health and depress occupational opportunities, such effects were found to be relatively small in the context of explaining class differences in health in early adulthood.

4.7 Conclusions

The potential for social mobility to explain social class differences in health is possibly at its greatest during early adulthood when the transition from class based on parents' occupation to that based on own occupation occurs. Even so, it is clear from these analyses that while social mobility may be health related, class differences in health cannot be explained entirely through social mobility.

The investigation has not yet included health in childhood and it is important to take account of this and other explanations for class differences in health outlined in Chapter 1. As part of the discussion of each of these explanations, it will be necessary to return to the selection argument, especially in relation to earlier health. Methodological considerations are, however, relevant to all subsequent chapters and these are presented next.

5

Disentangling causal chains

5.1 Introduction

The methods used in Chapter 4 enabled us to consider the relationships between social class measured at two or more points in time and health. More extensive and sophisticated methods are needed to explore the full range of explanations indicated in Figure 1.4.

The choice is determined largely by the main requirements of the analysis. First, the contribution that different factors make to class differences in health should be assessed explicitly and in competition with other factors. As Lundberg (1991) suggests, it is important to distinguish between research that attempts to explain *class differences* in health from other studies that use social factors to explain differences in *health between individuals*. Few studies are, however, explicit in this respect with the notable exception of Valkonen and Martelin (1988) who attempt to explain class differences in suicide in Finland. Also, potential explanations should be considered together in order to assess their relative contribution. Earlier approaches have tended to examine individual explanations in isolation. Again the integrated approach of the Finnish study breaks with this tradition.

A second consideration arises from the study framework (Figure 1.4) and this concerns the representation of different types of explanation. Within the constraints of the data it is important that different explanations are represented as fully as possible.

Third, the approach adopted should reflect the developmental sequence that contributes to class differences in health. In the present context, this suggests that the timing of events and circumstances should be accommodated by the methods of analysis.

5.2 The methodological approach

Two stages of analysis were performed, each corresponding to one of the following objectives:

1. To identify the characteristics which make the most substantial contribution to class differences in health, from *within* each broad explanatory area indicated in Figure 1.4, namely 'inheritance' at birth, socio-economic background, education and attitudes, health and behaviour.
2. To compare *between* broad explanatory areas using the variables identified from the first stage.

5.2.1 Stage 1

It should be clear from the description of NCDS (Chapter 2) that the data available are wide ranging. It will also become apparent in the following chapters that a variety of measures might be relevant to later class differences in health. Information collected at age 23 is included in the analysis if it refers to the period between ages 16 and 23, but measures of current circumstances are excluded on theoretical grounds. This decision may be unnecessarily restrictive, but it reflects a concern that contributory factors had, in general, to precede the measure of health status at age 23. The investigation is therefore limited to measures of earlier circumstances. Despite the exclusion of this set of characteristics there are still many variables to be considered and there is no *a priori* reason for selecting a particular measure in preference to any other.

The problem is overcome by scrutinizing each variable within a particular area of explanation and assessing its contribution to later class differences. The contribution of a variable reflects its simultaneous association with the health measure at age 23 and social class at 23. A series of analyses are performed for each health outcome. In these analyses, social class differences are calculated before any adjustment is made for a potential explanatory variable. The analyses are then repeated, adjusting in turn for each variable in that area of explanation. The differences between the unadjusted and adjusted figures indicate the effect of controlling for that particular variable on the class differences observed.

Class differences, both unadjusted and adjusted for other variables, are estimated by fitting a series of logistic models using SPSS version X (SPSS X, 1986) and BMDP (1985). Details are given in Appendix E. Models with interaction terms have been fitted first, and in most cases the interaction between social class and the explanatory variable was not significant. Results presented in later chapters are based on models that include main effects only. Instances in which interactions did occur are indicated in the relevant tables.

These analyses provide estimates of the odds of poorer health for each social class. The ratio of classes IV and V to classes I and II is presented here as a summary measure of class differences; classes III non-manual (IIIN) and III manual (IIIM) were intermediate in each case. Variables are selected for the second stage of analysis on the basis of the reduction occurring between the unadjusted and adjusted odds ratios; the greatest reductions are taken to indicate the most substantial effects. The variables selected to represent each area of explanation are described at the end of the relevant chapter (Chapters 6 to 10).

In some instances, for example for socio-economic circumstances, the choice of variables is not clear-cut since adjustment for a number of variables results in reductions that are similar in magnitude. In order to overcome this difficulty relevant variables are included in a factor analysis, from which a smaller number of factors are identified. This approach leads to factors that are coherent, but since these factors are derived from several variables (sometimes collected across different ages) they are available for a considerably reduced sample only. This would be problematic in the next stage of the analysis in which additional variables would be introduced and, consequently, such factors were discarded. The implications of this and the eventual selection of one or two variables from the group of prominent variables will be discussed in later chapters.

Throughout stage 1, methods of analysis are standard for each of four health measures selected for further investigation. These methods depend on the categorization of the health measure concerned. Self-rated health and psychological morbidity are categorical variables (see pages 49 and 51) and there is some justification for treating malaise in a similar fashion (see page 50). Height, on the other hand, is primarily a continuous variable, although categories were constructed for analyses presented in the previous chapter. Arguments for a particular focus on short stature were mentioned earlier (Chapter 3) but the question remains as to whether results for adult height would differ if height were treated as a continuous variable. Hence, many of the analyses have been repeated, using analysis of variance for height as a continuous variable, compared with logistic regression for height as a categorical variable. The results from these approaches are similar. Subsequently, all analyses for height use the categories 'short' and 'not short'.

5.2.2 Stage 2

Selection of key variables representing each area of explanation in Figure 1.4 completes the first part of the enquiry. The second stage brings together inheritance, socio-economic circumstances, education, earlier health and behaviour in multivariate analyses. The timing of particular events and circumstances is then taken into account by ordering variables in a temporal sequence.

As for stage 1, unadjusted odds ratios were estimated from logistic models, although in this instance the BMDP (1985) package was used throughout (Appendix E). Unadjusted ratios are recalculated because the samples with complete data for this stage of the analysis differed from those available for stage 1. These unadjusted ratios indicate the magnitude of class differences before any explanatory variables are considered. Confidence intervals are calculated in all stage 2 analyses.

Since inheritance is viewed in general as the start of the temporal sequence, the first step in the multivariate analysis is to consider the influence of the variable representing this area of explanation. Next in time is the variable representing socio-economic circumstances in childhood, and this is included in addition to the inheritance variable. This establishes the effect of socio-economic circumstances above that already accounted for by inheritance. The third variable is then included together with the first and second, and so on until all variables have been included. Thus, at each step the reduction in relative odds indicates the particular contribution that each variable adds to the explanation of class differences. This approach gives an indication of the relative and cumulative effect of individual explanations. Any differences in the odds of poor health that remained in classes IV and V relative to classes I and II at the end of the analyses indicate the extent of class differences that has not been explained.

5.3 Advantages and disadvantages

This approach has several strengths. First, it estimates the contribution of different explanatory variables explicitly and integrates a range of explanations into a single model. Thus, it indicates the order of importance of variables within and between particular explanatory areas identified in the conceptual framework.

By allowing for temporal sequencing of explanations, the method used is consistent with a developmental approach which attempts to construct causal chains. It enables the investigator to assess how particular events and circumstances add to previous events and circumstances that have a known (or estimated) effect. Alternative approaches, such as the ordering of explanations according to the magnitude of their (statistical) effect, lack a theoretical perspective in this context, even though they could be justified in an investigation which relied upon cross-sectional data.

Some features of the study design could, on the other hand, be regarded as weaknesses. Not all of these are particular to the present investigation, as was evident from the discussion of what constitutes an 'explanation' (Chapter 1).

One of the main problems concerns the operational definition of the explanatory areas identified in Figure 1.4. In allocating variables to particular areas it is not always clear whether a variable belongs to one area or another. For example, early family formation characteristics might be considered as individual behaviours or as aspects of socio-economic circumstances. While this problem occurs infrequently, it is important since the location of a variable in one group rather than another might influence its selection for stage 2 of the analysis. Furthermore, each explanatory area would be represented, ideally, by several dimensions relevant to that area. For example, for socio-economic circumstances it would be preferable to include housing tenure *and* financial hardship *and* unemployment and so on, rather than any one of these circumstances alone, since events and circumstances are likely to exert a different effect when occurring in combination. The design of the present study does not allow for this. It is, however, difficult to overcome this problem given current technical limitations.

The method of temporal ordering also has limitations. The sequence of variables does not simply reflect the temporal sequence of events as they occur, but as they were measured in NCDS. If the first stage of analysis leads to the selection of a characteristic or circumstance reflecting later rather than earlier in the child's life, then this will influence the order in which the variable is considered in stage 2. The exclusion of contemporary circumstances at age 23 might also be considered unnecessarily stringent.

In presenting the results, the ratio of classes IV and V to I and II is used as a summary index. The tables would otherwise become too detailed and complex. Classes IIIN and IIIM are intermediate in terms of their health in Figures 3.3 and 3.4, but this does not take account of earlier circumstances. Analyses presented in subsequent chapters are limited, therefore, in attempting to explain differences between extremes of the social class scale rather than the distribution of health across the full scale.

5.4 The samples

The method described above has consequences for sample sizes. So far, limited reference has been made to the completeness and representativeness of the data. Since bias may have occurred as a result of sample attrition, this could affect the validity of the findings.

As shown in Chapter 2 (Table 2.1), there has been a decrease in sample size with successive follow-ups. As this enquiry uses data from each sweep, sample sizes will fluctuate accordingly. All analyses depend on data on health and social class at age 23. The effect of such fluctuations in sample size has been assessed and details are given in Appendix D. As described for earlier ages (Goldstein, 1983) certain disadvantaged groups were under-represented later, but since responders and non-responders were similar in most respects the findings are considered to be generally reassuring. A more detailed comparison of responders and non-responders, which examined the association between social class and health in samples with and without data for earlier health (as measured in Chapter 9), confirmed that sample size variations did not result in significant biases (Power *et al.*, 1990).

Even for the samples requiring several variables collected at different ages, the relationships under consideration (that is, between social class, health at age 23 and earlier attributes) did not appear to be affected by sample attrition. There are some implications in relation to the multivariate analyses, however, and further discussion of these will be presented in Chapter 11.

5.5 Conclusions

Several methodological considerations relevant to the analysis of class differences in health using longitudinal data have been discussed. The approach used in this study permits an initial selection of variables from the wide range that might be considered in relation to class differences in health. This avoids, or at least reduces, the arbitrariness of selection in representing particular explanations. Despite the limitations outlined above, there is also an extent to which the study design integrates several factors in attempting to explain class differences in health. The temporal dimension is particularly valuable in this respect. Finally, an examination of response patterns in the NCDS suggested that there were few serious sample biases in relation to data available for the proposed analyses.

6

'Inheritance' at birth

6.1 Introduction

Of those areas identified in the framework for the study (Figure 1.4), 'inheritance' at birth is the first to occur chronologically, and usually in terms of its impact on the developing child. It is important to emphasize, as explained in Chapter 1, that the term 'inheritance' is not used in the strict genetic sense, but includes all those characteristics and circumstances that exist prior to or at the time of the birth.

There are numerous ways in which inheritance might possibly contribute towards later class differences in health. If genetically determined conditions, such as Down's syndrome or Duchenne muscular dystrophy, were simultaneously associated with social class this could account for class differences in particular health problems. However, purely genetically determined conditions are rare, so even if they were associated with social class they would have little overall effect. It is of more interest, potentially, that individuals can be predisposed to a disease through genetic characteristics, and that these individuals could be differently distributed between social classes. There is, however, little evidence to substantiate this. ABO blood groups are thought to be related to some diseases (Mitchell, 1977; Mourant and Kopec, 1978) and, as some researchers suggest, to social class (Beardmore and Karimi-Booshehri, 1983) but the latter is disputed (Mascie-Taylor and McManus, 1984; Golding *et al.*, 1984; Kelleher *et al.*, 1990). Similarly, there may be preconceptual determinants of adverse pregnancy outcomes, such as low birthweight (Emanuel, 1986) which affect the health of the offspring and which may be related to social class (Alberman *et al.*, 1991).

It has also been argued that differences in health between the social classes are derived from inherited attributes, such as intelligence, which then influence health through health practices and/or social mobility. This is a contentious area of debate as witnessed by, for example, the discourse between Himsworth (1984, 1986, 1989), Goldthorpe (1985) and Humphrey and Elford (1988). In attempting to explain the persistent relative differences in early mortality rates, Himsworth claims that there are class differences in the distribution of people who are

> 'differently endowed with certain polygenetically determined attributes which determine their potential ability to deal with environmental factors whose adverse effects on their offspring could, in the then state of knowledge, be prevented or treated.'

Humphrey and Elford (1988) argue that Himsworth's emphasis on genetics is overstated and this echoes the opinions of Rose *et al.* (1984) in the more general debate about genetics and inequality.

The antenatal environment is also included in our definition of inheritance and characteristics of that environment may affect class differences in health. Smoking is an example of an adverse influence during the antenatal period. It is known that smoking affects birthweight and it is through this relationship that the influence of smoking is now thought to extend into early adulthood, at least in relation to adult stature and level of education achieved (Fogelman and Manor, 1988). Since smoking during pregnancy is class related, it may be one of the factors contributing to later class differences in health.

Birthweight is an important factor to consider in the present context since many studies report that it is associated with adult height (e.g. Kuh and Wadsworth, 1989). Some predictors of birthweight – maternal height, smoking during pregnancy, parity and history of pre-eclampsia during pregnancy – have been shown to be stable over recent generations (Peters *et al.*, 1983). Others, such as unemployment, need further investigation. In one study, based in Glasgow, birthweight was associated with unemployment, size of house, outside lavatory and number of children under age 5 (Cole *et al.*, 1983). However, an analysis of the 1970 birth cohort showed no significant excess of low birthweight associated with unemployment once social class had been taken into account (Golding *et al.*, 1986). Reviewing the evidence, MacFarlane and Cole (1985) argued that it is not whether the father is unemployed at the time of birth that is critical, but whether he is at high risk of unemployment. It is also likely that birthweight is affected by dietary intake during pregnancy. Evidence for this is provided by Doyle *et al.* (1982) who found that mean energy intakes were lower in 76 lower-class women than in 24 upper-class women (1689 and 2050 kcals respectively).

Other material circumstances and parental behaviours during pregnancy, such as attendance at antenatal clinics, may vary with social class but their relationship with subsequent health problems needs further clarification.

Although genetic and environmental influences have been described so far as separate entities, this is an oversimplification since there is interaction between them. Only rarely is it possible to determine the amount of variation attributable to genetic as opposed to environmental influences, despite claims that research techniques have improved recently (Susser and Susser, 1987). A general assessment is elusive since variations in these factors occur in different populations and at different times. In relation to health, there is much debate about the relative influence of genetic and of environmental factors on height and obesity (Rona, 1981; Stunkard *et al.*, 1986). For height, Rona (1981) states:

'The high correlations between parents and their children are, for example, interpreted as the effect of genes on human growth. However, the environment is more similar amongst the two generations in the same family than between families. Therefore, the high parent–child correlation can be seen as the result of the combined effect of environment and genes.'

Furthermore, the increase in height since the middle of the nineteenth century is generally attributed to environmental causes. These arguments are relevant here since adult height is one of four measures selected for investigating class differences in health.

Of the remaining measures, two represent psychological states. As with height, there has been considerable debate over the extent to which inheritance – both genetic and environmental – contributes to psychological conditions. Weissman (1987) reviewed the evidence in relation to depression and she notes the comparatively high risk of problems in the offspring of depressed parents. However, the highly familial nature of some psychological problems is insufficient evidence for a genetic explanation. As Rutter and Madge (1976) argue, disorders in children often differ from those in their parents so that transmission is more readily explained by such factors as marital discord and disturbed family relationships that can accompany psychological problems in the parents.

It is possible, however, that prenatal factors and birth complications have psychological consequences later in life. Rodgers (1990c) summarizes the evidence for this and examines relevant birth factors in the 1946 cohort study. He reported no significant links between birthweight and affective disorder at age 36. Breast feeding was also unimportant, but father's age was associated with later disorder. This relationship was, however, significant only among men.

Consequently, while evidence is not always strong, there are grounds for the inclusion of inheritance in an examination of class differences in the selected health measures. The NCDS contains several measures relevant to inheritance: social class at birth has already been examined in Chapter 4 but is included together with a wider range of variables described below.

6.2 Inheritance measures

Of twelve variables selected, nine were from the original perinatal information, from either mothers' reports or medical records at the time of birth. Father's height was reported by the mother during the parental interview at age 11; and for both parents the age when they completed full-time education was obtained at the 16-year parental interview.

- *Social class at birth:* based on the father's occupation (coded according to the Registrar General's 1950 classification) and grouped into classes I and II; IIIN; IIIM; IV and V; no male head of household.
- *Mother's social class at birth:* based on mother's occupation immediately before pregnancy, coded and grouped as for the father, but excluding the category of no male head of household. It was not possible to classify women who had not worked; as Table 6.1 illustrates, this was a substantial proportion of the sample.
- *Grandfather's social class:* based on the mother's report of her father's occupation at the time she left school, coded and grouped as for mother's class described above.
- *Birthweight:* recorded in ounces.
- *Gestation:* the number of days elapsing between the first day of the last menstrual period and the birth of the baby, grouped as: 273 days or less; 274–281 days; 282–288 days; 289 days or more.
- *Birthweight for gestational age:* sex specific centiles were calculated for each completed week of gestation between 31 and 43 weeks inclusive, and then grouped as: under 10th centile; 10th to 24th centile; 25th to 50th; 51st to 75th; 76th to 90th; over 90th.
- *Smoking in pregnancy:* as reported by the mother for the second half of her pregnancy, and grouped as: none; 1–9 per day; 10–19 per day; 20 or more per day.
- *Mother's age:* at the time of the birth and grouped as: 22 or younger; 23–26; 27–31; 32 or older.
- *Age father finished education:* grouped as: up to 14 years 11 months; 15 years to 17 years 11 months; 18 years or over.
- *Age mother finished education:* grouped as for the father.
- *Father's height:* reported by the mother, to the nearest inch.
- *Mother's height:* self-reported or sometimes measured, to the nearest inch.

6.3 Results

Tables 6.1 to 6.4 present, separately for each health measure, the odds of poor health for those in classes IV and V relative to those in classes I and II. The odds ratios (explained in Appendix E) are shown, first, as unadjusted figures, that is they reflect the data in Figures 3.3 and 3.4, although not entirely since the figures indicate the gradient across all four social classes and the ratios represent the extreme classes only. The unadjusted odds ratios were greatest for malaise: women in classes IV and V having odds of five times those in classes I and II and men about a threefold differential.

Table 6.1 Relative odds of subjects rating their health as 'poor' or 'fair' (classes IV and V versus I and II) adjusting for 'inheritance' at birth

'Inheritance' variables	(n)	Men		(n)	Women	
		Unadjusted	Adjusted		Unadjusted	Adjusted
Social class at birth	(5467)	2.33	2.17	(5664)	2.90	2.54
Mother's social class	(2159)	2.01	1.98	(2196)	2.45	2.33
Grandfather's social class	(4630)	2.40	2.29	(4790)	2.74	2.55
Birthweight	(5398)	2.45	2.42	(5622)	2.92	2.88
Gestation	(5048)	2.38	2.38	(5205)	2.93	2.91
Birthweight for gestation	(4811)	2.42	2.42	(5009)	2.85	2.79
Smoking in pregnancy	(5885)	2.28	2.21	(5772)	2.86	2.81
Mother's age	(5603)	2.30	2.29	(5787)	2.92	2.93
Age father finished education	(4253)	2.46	2.42	(4368)	3.39	3.04
Age mother finished education	(4350)	2.53	2.50	(4486)	3.22	3.01
Father's height	(4824)	2.78	2.71	(4966)	3.33	3.27
Mother's height	(5396)	2.23	2.21	(5575)	2.92	2.89

Table 6.2 Relative odds of high malaise score (classes IV and V versus I and II) adjusting for 'inheritance' at birth

'Inheritance' variables	(n)	Men		(n)	Women	
		Unadjusted	Adjusted		Unadjusted	Adjusted
Social class at birth	(5459)	3.22	2.77	(5657)	5.24	4.52
Mother's social class	(2157)	4.94	4.20	(2194)	4.17	3.83
Grandfather's social class	(4628)	2.92	2.84	(4782)	5.44	5.20
Birthweight	(5390)	2.98	2.97	(5615)	5.42	5.32
Gestation	(5041)	3.38	3.34	(5200)	5.72	5.64
Birthweight for gestation	(4804)	3.13	3.12	(5001)	5.91	5.87*
Smoking in pregnancy	(5527)	3.18	2.92	(5707)	5.33	5.06
Mother's age	(5595)	3.21	3.18	(5779)	5.33	5.34
Age father finished education	(4247)	3.09	2.70	(4360)	5.24	4.73
Age mother finished education	(4344)	3.19	3.03	(4479)	4.99	4.78
Father's height	(4820)	2.94	2.78	(4958)	5.55	5.31
Mother's height	(5389)	2.98	2.89	(5568)	5.24	5.10

*Significant interaction ($p<0.05$).

Table 6.3 Relative odds of psychological morbidity between ages 16 and 23 (classes IV and V versus I and II) adjusting for 'inheritance' at birth

'Inheritance' variables	Men			Women		
	(n)	Unadjusted	Adjusted	(n)	Unadjusted	Adjusted
Social class at birth	(5473)	2.01	1.87	(5668)	2.44	2.47
Mother's social class	(2161)	2.49	2.66	(2198)	2.60	2.60
Grandfather's social class	(4636)	2.02	2.01	(4793)	2.23	2.19
Birthweight	(5403)	2.20	2.21	(5626)	2.39	2.40
Gestation	(5054)	2.28	2.28	(5208)	2.28	2.26
Birthweight for gestation	(4816)	2.23	2.23	(5012)	2.36	2.36
Smoking in pregnancy	(5591)	1.99	1.90	(5776)	2.35	2.26
Mother's age	(5609)	2.03	2.03	(5791)	2.36	2.36
Age father finished education	(4258)	1.86	1.79	(4370)	2.73	2.92
Age mother finished education	(4355)	1.67	1.76	(4489)	2.66	2.82
Father's height	(4828)	2.08	2.00	(4969)	2.53	2.52
Mother's height	(5401)	1.99	1.96	(5579)	2.40	2.39

Table 6.4 Relative odds of 'short' stature (classes IV and V versus I and II) adjusting for 'inheritance' at birth

'Inheritance' variables	Men			Women		
	(n)	Unadjusted	Adjusted	(n)	Unadjusted	Adjusted
Social class at birth	(5439)	2.38	2.16	(5635)	2.50	2.14
Mother's social class	(2147)	2.83	2.67	(2184)	2.14	1.91
Grandfather's social class	(4606)	2.26	2.13	(4763)	2.44	2.39
Birthweight	(5362)	2.33	2.16	(5594)	2.38	2.16
Gestation	(5018)	2.21	2.23	(5179)	2.35	2.33
Birthweight for gestation	(4787)	2.27	2.28	(4984)	2.26	2.09
Smoking in pregnancy	(5500)	2.28	2.23	(5741)	2.36	2.23
Mother's age	(5568)	2.31	2.29	(5756)	2.43	2.35
Age father finished education	(4238)	1.84	1.70	(4352)	2.34	2.20
Age mother finished education	(4330)	1.85	1.71	(4465)	2.39	2.23
Father's height	(4792)	2.29	1.76	(4941)	2.40	1.89
Mother's height	(5362)	2.32	1.99	(5546)	2.37	1.94

It is important to note the variation in the unadjusted odds ratios – a pattern that will be repeated in subsequent chapters. Among the unadjusted figures (Tables 6.1 to 6.4) mother's social class was something of a special case as this was only available for those mothers who were working at the beginning of their pregnancy, and the number with data was less than half that for other variables. Even for the other variables, however, there was considerable variation in the unadjusted odds ratios. The figures for a particular health measure should be the same since they represent the same contrast – between classes IV and V and classes I and II. The fluctuation was due to differences in the numbers in each analysis, resulting from varying proportions with data for a specific explanatory variable. Considering the variation in the sample size, the magnitude of the odds ratio and its standard deviation, some variation in the unadjusted figures is to be expected. Nevertheless, it was necessary to examine the representativeness of the samples. Details, given in Appendix D, suggest that despite sample attrition the relationships under consideration were not generally affected.

Tables 6.1 to 6.4 also present odds ratios adjusted for the inheritance variables. As described in the methods, the difference between the unadjusted and adjusted odds ratios indicates the contribution of the inheritance variables to later class differences in health.

The overall impression from Table 6.1 is that, for men, few variables resulted in any substantial reductions; the decreases associated with adjusting for social class at birth and grandfather's class were the largest. Even allowing for these, the major part of the difference in self-rated health between the social classes at 23 was still unexplained. The women's results were similar, except that parents' education also appeared to make a contribution.

In general, the effects of the inheritance variables were not substantial in relation to malaise (Table 6.2). However, social class at birth consistently reduced the odds ratios for both men and women (from 3.22 to 2.77 and from 5.24 to 4.52 respectively) and, given this, it was not surprising that the age at which the father finished his education also affected the class differentials.

No reductions of this magnitude emerged for psychological morbidity (Table 6.3). The largest reductions were associated with social class at birth for men and smoking in pregnancy for women, but the general implication of this table is that class differences in psychological morbidity were quite independent of these individual inheritance measures.

Relative odds of short stature are shown in Table 6.4, and in this instance reductions occurred in relation to several 'inheritance' variables. Mother's height and father's height had the greatest effects but social class at birth and, to a lesser extent, birthweight, consistently reduced class differentials.

6.4 Discussion

It might be anticipated from the introduction to this chapter that not all of the inheritance variables would be relevant to all four health outcome measures. Even so, it was surprising that apart from adult height, many inheritance variables were found to have no notable impact on class differences. This may be a function of the inheritance measures included in the study. Few physical characteristics of the parents were recorded in the NCDS and no psychological measures were available. Inheritance measures were predominantly environmental, although parents' height and to some extent the child's birthweight, are genetically and environmentally determined.

On the other hand, social class at birth appeared to be important, and there are two main reasons why this should be so. First, social class at birth is a measure that represents several aspects of the social and material circumstances of the family at that time; it seems that this is of more relevance than specific elements represented by other variables. Second, children inherit a position in the social structure and this has wide-ranging implications for economic and occupational status (hence wealth and security), housing, scholastic attainment and, as Rutter and Madge (1977) suggest, crime and delinquency, psychiatric disorder and parenting behaviour. Despite considerable mobilities in society, there is an extent to which such circumstances and attributes are transmitted from one generation to the next. However, it is important to note that while class origins were generally relevant to health outcome measures, substantial class differentials remained after adjustment for this variable.

Inheritance, as broadly defined in this book, was generally more relevant to class differences in adult stature than to the other health outcome measures. This was not surprising since, as mentioned earlier, many studies show high correlations between parents' and children's heights; and between birthweight and subsequent adult height. While it is also known that birthweight and parents' heights are class related, few studies attempt to demonstrate the extent to which such factors account for class differences in height. The analyses included in this chapter achieve this.

Of the variables examined, birthweight, parents' heights and social class had the greatest impact on class differences in adult short stature. These findings are consistent with those observed earlier for class differences in height in childhood (Goldstein, 1971). The present analyses did not cover all the factors identified in the introduction, such as unemployment of the father at the time of birth, but many such factors are thought to affect birthweight, which was included. It is important to note that social class differences remained after taking account of inheritance variables separately, but this may not be the case if inheritance variables are considered together. This will be discussed further in Chapter 11.

It is the purpose here to determine how inheritance at birth should be represented in the next stage of the investigation. Although it does not appear to play a major role for all health outcomes, it should be represented in later analyses so that its relative contribution can be assessed.

6.5 Conclusions

This chapter has summarized the arguments for examining inheritance at birth in relation to later class differences in health. Despite these arguments inheritance, as measured here, was only important for differences in adult height, and perhaps early adulthood malaise. One inheritance variable, social class at birth, was notable (as indicated by the reductions in relative odds) even though the reductions associated with this variable were not always substantial. Social class at birth was therefore selected to represent inheritance in the next stage of analyses for self-rated health, malaise and psychological morbidity, although the last was for men only. Smoking in pregnancy was selected for the women's analyses of psychological morbidity. Social class at birth was also relevant to adult height, but since the greatest contribution towards class differences appeared to be related to parents' heights these were selected for further analyses.

7

Socio-economic circumstances during childhood and adolescence

7.1 Introduction

Socio-economic circumstances were identified by the Black Report (DHSS, 1980) as a major source of social inequalities in health. As indicated in the framework in Chapter 1 (Figure 1.4) this broad area of explanations encompasses conditions in the home, at work and at each of their respective localities, which might possibly influence health either directly or indirectly. However, the present enquiry concerns origins of class differences in health at a particular age, namely early adulthood, so the focus of analysis shifts towards the home and its environment rather than the workplace.

Little is known about how socio-economic conditions during childhood affect class differences in health but it is plausible that they are influential. Support for this hinges upon the suggested relationship between poor early conditions and subsequent mortality (Forsdahl, 1977) and other health outcome measures. In young adults, for example, the effects of air pollution and overcrowding on chest illness in childhood re-emerge in relation to respiratory symptoms at age 25 (Kiernan et al., 1976). It has also been suggested that influences such as family size affect height throughout childhood and into adulthood (Tibbenham et al., 1983). However, such longitudinal evidence is still rare and many other potential influences are identified from cross-sectional studies, although establishing causality from these studies is notoriously problematic.

Methodological problems were encountered in, for example, studies examining the effects of quality of housing upon health (Martin, 1987; Strachan, 1988). Even so 'the relationship between housing conditions and health has been accepted in public policy since the 19th century' (BMA, 1987) and this relationship is thought to result from a wide range of influences. Poor-quality housing might affect either physical or mental health through dampness and mould, type of structure and location, amenities and domestic comfort, and also lack of privacy and crowding. In addition, there is wide acceptance that characteristics of the neighbourhood, which are closely associated with quality of housing, influence health through pollution and other general environmental hazards such as unsafe roads and poor availability of local resources and amenities.

There are other material circumstances, such as level of income and stability of employment, that have an indirect influence on health as they determine the general availability of resources – housing, fuel, food and transport. At low levels of income, for example, it has been suggested that the diets of children and teenagers may be especially susceptible to deficiencies (Cole-Hamilton and Lang, 1986). Access to cars can also facilitate the use of local resources, including health care.

In addition to material circumstances, it has been suggested that social characteristics such as social networks, social support, family and household structures and domestic responsibilities have implications for health. Some evidence exists for mortality (Berkman and Breslow, 1983; Orth-Gomer and Johnson, 1987) and also for morbidity (Brown and Harris, 1978). Madge and Marmot (1987) reviewed the expanding literature on social support and concluded that, while more stringent investigations are needed, there is probably some association between a person's pattern of social contact and his or her health.

Many influences considered so far might affect class differences in health among young adults. Some of these are, however, more pertinent than others to the four health measures examined here. Notably, for psychological health there has been sustained interest in the influence of early childhood environment, particularly in relation to family disruption resulting from parental death, divorce or separation. In Britain, longitudinal data from the 1946 cohort study provides some substance to claims that separation during childhood has adverse effects on subsequent mental state in adulthood (Rodgers, 1990b). However, the effect of such factors was not strong and may be associated with circumstances surrounding family disruption rather than the break itself. While it is not anticipated that a large effect will be observed, it is nevertheless relevant to examine the role of family disruption on class differences in psychological health.

Evidence linking psychological health of young adults to their recent socio-economic circumstances is possibly stronger than that for earlier influences. For example, the adverse consequences of insecure employment or unemployment are well recognized (Smith, 1987). Using prospective data, Banks and Jackson (1982) showed the deleterious effect of unemployment on psychological health in young men. Similar results have been obtained for women (Surtees *et al.*, 1983) although it is more problematic to investigate unemployment in women: married women not in paid employment are generally classified as housewives rather than as unemployed. Research for women has concentrated on the protective effect of paid employment outside the home on mental health. Positive effects have been found, although not in all groups of women (Warr and Parry, 1982a). Paid employment and unemployment are strongly class related and should, therefore, be investigated in the present study.

So also, should characteristics of family structure in early adulthood. Marital status is associated with morbidity, such that those who live with a spouse have more favourable mental health than the single, widowed, divorced or separated. Relationships may differ for men and women, with marriage possibly incurring greater negative effects for women (Gove, 1972; Gove and Tudor, 1973) and positive effects for men. Family responsibilities, including the number and ages of children, are also relevant especially for the mental health of women (Brown and Harris, 1978). Hence, family formation patterns should be considered in the present enquiry, especially since, as with unemployment, they are strongly class related at this stage of the lifespan.

It is more problematic to identify socio-economic influences on self-rated health because research for this health measure is limited. However, given associations between self-rated health and psychological health (Chapter 3) it might be anticipated that many potential influences mentioned above for psychological health, particularly those relating to recent socio-economic circumstances – economic and marital status, family responsibilities – might also be relevant to people's assessment of their own health.

Adult height, on the other hand, would be expected to relate to earlier socio-economic conditions. Several influences have been suggested as particularly relevant: family size was mentioned above while parents' unemployment and region of residence have also been identified (Rona *et al.*, 1978), all of which need to be considered in an analysis of class differences in adult stature, together with other proxy measures for living conditions in early life.

The timing of particular socio-economic events and circumstances may be relevant to the four health measures considered here. For example, Wadsworth (1979) illustrated how the timing of a family disruption can affect the risk of delinquency and psychiatric illness in young adults, at least in men. Early family breaks – that is, before age 5 – were associated with higher risks than those for later breaks. Nevertheless, it is anticipated that, for all four health measures except height, recent circumstances will be more influential than earlier circumstances.

Measures from NCDS selected to represent socio-economic circumstances are now described. Since data are available throughout childhood the timing of circumstances can be considered.

7.2 Socio-economic measures

Variables selected from the NCDS parental interviews include:

- *Social class (at ages 7, 11 and 16):* father's occupation, coded to the Registrar General's classification and grouped as: I and II; III non-manual; III manual; IV and V; no male head of household.
- *Family situation (at ages 7, 11 and 16):* the study child's situation, grouped as: with both natural parents; all others.
- *Housing tenure (at ages 7, 11 and 16):* family's housing tenure, grouped as: owner-occupiers; local authority tenants; all others.
- *Crowding (at ages 7, 11 and 16):* ratio of people in the household to rooms in the home, grouped as: less than one; one to one and a half; greater than one and a half.
- *Household amenities (at ages 7, 11 and 16):* access to hot water supply, fixed bath and indoor lavatory, grouped as: sole use of all three facilities; sharing or lacking any.
- *Father's unemployment (at ages 7, 11 and 16):* whether or not the father was reported as unemployed in 1965, 1969 and 1974.
- *Free school meals (at ages 11 and 16):* whether or not any child in the household was currently in receipt of free school meals.
- *Family size (at age 11):* number of children under the age of 21 in the household, grouped as: one or two; three or four; five or more.
- *Family income (at age 16):* income from all sources, as reported by the mother, grouped into approximate thirds (Micklewright, 1986).
- *Region (at age 16):* place of residence, grouped as: North England; Midlands; South England; Wales; Scotland.
- *Neighbourhood (at age 16):* family's place of residence classified into 37 categories of Census enumeration districts (ACORN) and further grouped into: better-off neighbourhoods; deprived neighbourhoods; others (Webber, 1977; Ghodsian and Fogelman, 1988).

Variables collected from cohort members themselves:

- *Unemployment (by age 23):* the proportion of economically active time between leaving school and the 23-year interview spent unemployed, grouped as: none; up to 7%; greater than 7% (Payne, 1983).
- *Marital status (at age 23):* grouped as married and never married.
- *Living alone (at age 23):* grouped as married or cohabiting and living alone.
- *Age married (by age 23):* month and year of marriage, grouped as: teenage; age 20–23; never married.
- *Number of children (by age 23):* total number of children in the family, including adopted, foster and stepchildren.

- *Age at first child (by age 23):* grouped as: teenage; age 20–21; age 22–23; no children.

This list of variables represents most of the relevant socio-economic circumstances described in the introduction to this chapter, although in some instances (such as income) the data are less comprehensive than in others. More serious limitations occur in respect of data describing the neighbourhood (in terms of physical hazards, pollution, local facilities). Details about work and its environment were not included in the analyses because data in the NCDS generally describe contemporaneous working conditions rather than those preceding health status at age 23.

7.3 Results

Tables 7.1 to 7.4 illustrate, separately for each health measure, the odds ratios of poor health before and after adjusting for the social and economic variables described above.

As mentioned in the previous chapter in relation to 'inheritance' at birth variables, there were variations in the number of respondents with complete information for each variable and this resulted in fluctuations in the unadjusted odds ratios. Since this enquiry is dependent upon classification of health and social class during early adulthood, the maximum sample available is that shown for age 23 (page 29) and the requirement of other variables for the analyses reduces sample sizes even further. An investigation of sample variation, while limited to a selection of variables, did not suggest that the fluctuations were such as to undermine the analyses described in this chapter.

Comparing the adjusted and unadjusted relative odds in Table 7.1 it is apparent that class differentials in poor self-rating of health were reduced after allowing for several of the socio-economic variables. Of those measures representing circumstances in childhood, adjustments for social class, housing tenure, crowding and family size resulted in the greatest reductions in relative odds. In the case of crowding (at age 11), for example, relative odds were reduced from 2.57 to 2.33 in men and 3.20 to 2.88 in women. For the period between ages 16 and 23, the reductions were even greater: adjusting for unemployment and age at first child for men and women respectively reduced the relative odds from 2.33 to 1.90 and 2.97 to 2.26. However, odds ratios remained largely unaffected by adjusting for region of residence at age 16 and family situation, household amenities and father's unemployment at different ages. Class differentials in poor self-rated health were also similar before and after adjusting for family income at age 16 but were reduced after adjusting for another index of (lack of) wealth, namely receipt of free school meals by the study child or another member of his or her family.

Table 7.2 shows similar trends for malaise in that some reduction in odds ratios occurred after adjusting for earlier social class, housing tenure, crowding, family size and free school meals. Differentials remained largely unaffected by family situation, household amenities and father's unemployment. The respondent's own experience of

Table 7.1 Relative odds of subjects rating their health as 'poor' or 'fair' (classes IV and V versus I and II) adjusting for socio-economic background

Socio-economic variables	(n)	Men Unadjusted	Adjusted	(n)	Women Unadjusted	Adjusted
At age 7:						
Social class	(4973)	2.05	1.95	(5190)	3.08	2.67
Family situation	(5166)	2.14	2.09	(5361)	3.08	3.07
Tenure	(5135)	2.12	1.98	(5333)	3.13	2.76
Crowding	(4961)	2.08	1.91	(5152)	3.23	2.87
Amenities	(5121)	2.13	2.12	(5309)	3.15	3.05
Father's unemployment	(4459)	2.33	2.27	(4637)	3.37	3.30
At age 11:						
Social class	(4952)	2.55	2.35	(5129)	3.25	2.78
Family situation	(5040)	2.57	2.51	(5202)	3.20	3.15
Tenure	(5021)	2.58	2.37	(5191)	3.20	2.61
Crowding	(5017)	2.57	2.33	(5189)	3.20	2.88
Amenities	(4966)	2.57	2.45	(5136)	3.15	3.15
Father's unemployment	(4904)	2.59	2.47	(5061)	3.24	3.12
Free school meals	(4964)	2.55	2.41	(5140)	3.21	2.90
Family size	(5018)	2.56	2.38	(5189)	3.20	2.87
At age 16:						
Social class	(4347)	2.55	2.37	(4440)	3.10	2.80
Family situation	(4447)	2.57	2.50	(4574)	3.18	3.10
Tenure	(4436)	2.57	2.53	(4563)	3.18	2.61
Crowding	(4397)	2.61	2.47	(4518)	3.16	2.86
Amenities	(4370)	2.51	2.48	(4490)	3.11	3.12
Father's unemployment	(4119)	2.52	2.51	(4175)	3.25	3.20
Free school meals	(4383)	2.53	2.37	(4515)	3.18	2.90
Family income	(3997)	2.76	2.76	(4110)	3.49	3.27
Region	(4447)	2.57	2.54	(4575)	3.19	3.22
Neighbourhood	(4942)	2.21	2.07	(5068)	2.63	2.41
By age 23:						
Unemployment	(5891)	2.33	1.90	(6049)	2.98	2.66
Marital status	(5919)	2.31	2.34	(6079)	2.97	2.90
Living alone	(5919)	2.31	2.33*	(6079)	2.97	3.03*
Age married	(5919)	2.31	2.31	(6078)	2.97	2.69*
Number of children	(5919)	2.31	2.21	(6079)	2.95	2.36*
Age at first child	(5858)	2.33	2.25	(6079)	2.97	2.26*

*Significant interactions (*p*<0.05).

unemployment was, however, associated with a reduction in class differentials: relative odds in men were 3.32 before and 2.52 after adjusting for this variable, and the corresponding figures for women were 5.20 and 4.65. While adjustment for age of marriage and children also resulted in reductions in relative odds in both sexes, these were more marked among women than men.

In examining class differentials in psychological morbidity, however, fewer socio-economic variables reduced the differentials and there was

Table 7.2 Relative odds of high malaise score (classes IV and V versus I and II) adjusting for socio-economic background

		Men			Women	
Socio-economic variables	(*n*)	Unadjusted	Adjusted	(*n*)	Unadjusted	Adjusted
At age 7:						
Social class	(4967)	2.65	2.28	(5183)	5.23	4.40
Family situation	(5160)	2.79	2.78	(5355)	5.23	5.19
Tenure	(5129)	2.82	2.34	(5327)	5.28	4.55
Crowding	(4957)	2.85	2.31	(5148)	5.35	4.78
Amenities	(5115)	2.78	2.61	(5304)	5.50	5.40
Father's unemployment	(4456)	2.63	2.45	(4631)	5.84	5.72
At age 11:						
Social class	(4947)	3.24	2.66	(5122)	5.60	4.70
Family situation	(5035)	3.21	3.10	(5194)	5.58	5.53
Tenure	(5016)	3.22	2.61	(5183)	5.57	4.56
Crowding	(5012)	3.16	2.79	(5181)	5.70	4.86
Amenities	(4961)	3.26	3.08	(5128)	5.67	5.62
Father's unemployment	(4899)	3.07	2.92	(5054)	5.62	5.40
Free school meals	(4959)	3.20	2.81	(5133)	5.60	5.10
Family size	(5013)	3.21	2.85	(5181)	5.57	5.04
At age 16:						
Social class	(4340)	3.40	2.85	(4431)	5.01	4.14
Family situation	(4441)	3.28	3.19	(4565)	5.02	4.85
Tenure	(4430)	3.29	2.85	(4554)	5.17	4.04
Crowding	(4342)	3.33	2.92	(4512)	5.10	4.65
Amenities	(4364)	3.31	3.03*	(4482)	5.03	5.03
Father's unemployment	(4113)	3.00	3.03	(4184)	5.25	5.16
Free school meals	(4377)	3.27	2.96	(4507)	5.26	4.84*
Family income	(4003)	3.11	2.92	(4102)	5.17	4.88
Region	(4441)	3.28	3.26	(4566)	5.03	5.09
Neighbourhood	(4935)	3.64	3.48	(5059)	5.28	4.88
By age 23:						
Unemployment	(5883)	3.32	2.52	(6039)	5.20	4.65
Marital status	(5911)	3.31	3.30*	(6070)	5.29	5.36
Living alone	(5911)	3.31	3.31*	(6070)	5.29	5.55
Age married	(5911)	3.31	3.16	(6069)	5.29	4.98
Number of children	(5911)	3.31	3.04	(6069)	5.30	4.28
Age at first child	(5850)	3.33	3.05	(6059)	5.30	4.13

*Significant interactions ($p<0.05$).

less consistency between the sexes (Table 7.3). Of the variables representing childhood and adolescence, social class at age 16 appeared to be most important for men, compared with family situation and housing tenure at age 16 for women. In respect of later circumstances, however, trends resembled those for poor self-rated health and malaise in that adjusting for unemployment reduced the odds ratios, and the effects of age at first child and number of children were observed for women only.

Table 7.3 Relative odds of psychological morbidity (classes IV and V versus I and II) adjusting for socio-economic background

Socio-economic variables	Men (n)	Unadjusted	Adjusted	Women (n)	Unadjusted	Adjusted
At age 7:						
Social class	(4978)	1.76	1.83	(5193)	2.61	2.61
Family situation	(5171)	1.93	1.83	(5365)	2.47	2.43
Tenure	(5140)	1.86	1.91	(5337)	2.48	2.40
Crowding	(4965)	1.89	1.74	(5156)	2.36	2.32
Amenities	(5126)	1.87	1.80	(5313)	2.46	2.53
Father's unemployment	(4463)	1.95	1.87	(4640)	2.73	2.74
At age 11:						
Social class	(4957)	1.98	1.90	(5132)	2.51	2.46
Family situation	(5045)	2.02	1.93*	(5205)	2.51	2.45
Tenure	(5026)	1.93	1.97	(5194)	2.51	2.43
Crowding	(5022)	1.98	1.87	(5192)	2.51	2.47
Amenities	(4971)	2.11	1.94	(5139)	2.50	2.55
Father's unemployment	(4909)	1.90	1.92	(5064)	2.48	2.44
Free school meals	(4968)	2.00	1.93	(5143)	2.51	2.39
Family size	(5023)	2.02	1.92	(5192)	2.51	2.35
At age 16:						
Social class	(4351)	1.75	1.58	(4443)	2.63	2.58
Family situation	(4452)	1.74	1.63	(4577)	2.70	2.49
Tenure	(4441)	1.74	1.90	(4566)	2.70	2.57
Crowding	(4402)	1.72	1.65	(4521)	2.65	2.62
Amenities	(4375)	1.75	1.69	(4493)	2.61	2.65
Father's unemployment	(4124)	1.75	1.77	(4186)	2.69	2.64
Free school meals	(4388)	1.73	1.69	(4518)	2.72	2.72
Family income	(4008)	1.80	1.79	(4113)	2.86	2.79
Region	(4452)	1.74	1.75	(4578)	2.70	2.80
Neighbourhood	(4948)	2.08	2.22	(5071)	2.33	2.32
By age 23:						
Unemployment	(5896)	1.96	1.49	(6052)	2.38	2.03
Marital status	(5923)	1.95	2.03	(6083)	2.37	2.64
Living alone	(5923)	1.95	2.05	(6083)	2.37	2.65*
Age married	(5923)	1.95	1.95	(6082)	2.37	2.31
Number of children	(5925)	1.95	1.95*	(6083)	2.37	2.08
Age at first child	(5864)	1.96	1.98	(6073)	2.38	1.96*

*Significant interactions ($p<0.05$).

Class comparisons of 'short' stature have been adjusted for socio-economic circumstances during childhood and adolescence only (Table 7.4). Later circumstances, reported for the period between ages 16 and 23, were not included since they were unlikely to influence the attainment of adult height. Height is largely determined by age 18 in women and 20 in men, even though a minority grow after these ages (Sinclair, 1985). The table shows that, in general, the greatest reductions in relative odds occurred after adjusting for social class, housing tenure, crowding and family size, and this was consistent for both sexes.

Table 7.4 Relative odds of 'short' stature (classes IV and V versus I and II) adjusting for socio-economic background

Socio-economic variables	(n)	Men		(n)	Women	
		Unadjusted	Adjusted		Unadjusted	Adjusted
At age 7:						
Social class	(4943)	2.16	1.75	(5165)	2.46	1.85
Family situation	(5135)	2.37	2.34	(5334)	2.50	2.46
Tenure	(5104)	2.35	2.04	(5307)	2.46	1.98
Crowding	(4933)	2.43	2.13*	(5126)	2.43	2.19
Amenities	(5091)	2.33	2.25	(5282)	2.49	2.38
Father's unemployment	(4429)	2.32	2.20	(4614)	2.56	2.49
At age 11:						
Social class	(4920)	2.32	1.89	(5103)	2.47	2.24*
Family situation	(5007)	2.28	2.23	(5176)	2.48	2.43
Tenure	(4988)	2.25	2.05	(5165)	2.48	2.01
Crowding	(4984)	2.23	1.95	(5164)	2.47	2.19
Amenities	(4933)	2.23	2.21	(5110)	2.47	2.42
Father's unemployment	(4872)	2.29	2.13*	(5035)	2.52	2.42
Free school meals	(4931)	2.28	2.00	(5116)	2.47	2.36
Family size	(4985)	2.26	2.04	(5164)	2.48	2.31
At age 16:						
Social class	(4320)	1.90	1.64	(4420)	2.28	1.80
Family situation	(4419)	1.84	1.81	(4552)	2.29	2.24
Tenure	(4408)	1.85	1.63	(4541)	2.30	1.90
Crowding	(4369)	1.87	1.67	(4498)	2.31	2.08
Amenities	(4344)	1.88	1.84	(4469)	2.31	2.30
Father's unemployment	(4095)	1.93	1.90	(4171)	2.23	2.19
Free school meals	(4356)	1.90	1.74	(4495)	2.28	2.14
Family income	(3976)	1.97	1.97	(4090)	2.29	2.19
Region	(4419)	1.84	1.79	(4553)	2.29	2.18
Neighbourhood	(4910)	2.45	2.30	(5040)	2.60	2.28

*Significant interactions (*p*<0.05).

7.4 Discussion

It was possible to examine a range of socio-economic circumstances in attempting to explain class differences in health in early adulthood.

Surprisingly, several variables identifying adverse social and economic situations, such as lacking basic household amenities, father's unemployment or not living with natural parents (family situation) contributed minimally, if at all, to later class differences in health. For father's unemployment the findings may be partially explained by the small size of the group affected (1.8% at age 7, 2.6% at 11 and 1.1% at 16) but this would not apply to other variables. The family situation variable was used to indicate a family disruption which, as mentioned earlier, might be expected to contribute towards class differences in malaise and psychological morbidity. That this contribution was not particularly noteworthy could reflect insufficient differentiation in the categories used (living with both natural parents and all others). The consistency of findings with those of Rodgers (1990b) suggests, however, that family disruption may not be a particularly important factor.

Several indices of circumstances during childhood and adolescence were more important – namely, social class, housing tenure, crowding, family size and receipt of free school meals – although results for psychological morbidity were less consistent than for the other health measures. Given the stage of life of individuals in the study, these socio-economic variables necessarily characterize earlier home environment rather than the workplace, but some recent experiences – unemployment and family formation – were also considered.

In general these more recent socio-economic circumstances were of greater salience than earlier circumstances, except for adult height. For self-rated health, malaise and psychological morbidity, unemployment between leaving school and age 23 was associated with a reduction in class differentials for both sexes, although this was especially pronounced among men. As noted by others (Bartley, 1988) and as will be shown in Chapter 11, unemployment contributes to health differences because, proportionately, unemployment is experienced by more people in lower social classes than in higher social classes and, in consequence, the lower social classes are more exposed to the ill-effects associated with unemployment. Payne *et al.* (1984) examined whether social class mediated between unemployment and psychological ill-health among married men aged 25–39 and they found that both working-class and middle-class samples were similarly affected by unemployment. For women the relationship between unemployment and ill-health is more contentious, but findings from the present study suggest that there is a contribution towards class differences even though this may not be as great as that evident for men.

In contrast, recent family formation factors were seen to be especially relevant to women while barely impingeing on class differences for men. Such findings will be discussed more fully in Chapter 11, but at present it is noteworthy that social class differences in family formation have become apparent, particularly among women, by age 23, but less so among men. Also, women are more commonly the child carers in our society and this appears to engender psychological ill-effects (Tennant, 1985).

For adult height, the contribution of socio-economic circumstances was apparent at the earliest age, 7, for which data were available and continued to be evident thereafter. Not all socio-economic circumstances had a notable impact on class differences, even though some of these, such as unemployment of parent, have previously been related to height (Rona *et al.*, 1978). General indicators of socio-economic circumstances – social class, housing tenure and crowding – had a greater effect than other variables, probably because they summarize several dimensions of living conditions. Also, the social class of the parents is associated with the parents' height, which was shown in the previous chapter to be of considerable importance in relation to height differences between classes in their offspring. Many variables are inter-correlated not just within this chapter, but also between chapters.

However, not all socio-economic variables identified above for height or for the other health measures could be included in the next stage of analysis. There were grounds for representing more recent circumstances in the next stage, since these appeared to be especially important for the three health measures in which they were examined. Consequently, unemployment was selected for all three measures for men and self-rated health and psychological morbidity for women. Family formation also needed to be represented in the women's analyses but it was not clear which variable should be selected. Similar difficulties were experienced in selecting a variable to represent socio-economic circumstances in childhood and adolescence, since several variables had reduced class differentials in poor health.

As explained in Chapter 5, relevant variables were included in a factor analysis in an attempt to overcome this problem, and factors were derived which summarized (i) childhood and adolescent circumstances and (ii) family formation in early adulthood. However, sample sizes were so substantially reduced (page 77) that the factors had to be abandoned and, although several variables had affected the class contrasts in these two areas, the one that achieved the most substantial reduction in the odds ratio was selected.

Variables selected for the next stage of analysis are given in Table 7.5. Housing tenure at age 11 was chosen for self-rated health and malaise and social class at age 7 was chosen for height. Earlier circumstances were not represented in the next stage of analysis for psychological morbidity (reductions in the odds ratios had been negligible) although recent circumstances were selected for this and other health measures.

Table 7.5 Variables selected to represent socio-economic circumstances in further analyses of class differences in health in early adulthood

Health measure at age 23	Selected variables	
	Men	Women
Self-rated health	• Housing tenure at age 11 • Unemployment	• Housing tenure at age 11 • Unemployment • Age at first child
Malaise	• Housing tenure at age 11 • Unemployment	• Housing tenure at age 11 • Age at first child
Psychological morbidity	• Unemployment	• Age at first child • Unemployment
Short stature	• Social class at age 7	• Social class at age 7

Before concluding this chapter, it is important to recognize that while a range of circumstances were considered, these did not include pollution, hazards and facilities in the neighbourhood and at work, as well as recent income and wealth. Further details of social networks and support would also be desirable. In addition, there is an extent to which some of the variables designated as socio-economic could also be regarded as (cultural) behavioural. For example, family formation characteristics qualify for inclusion as social factors as they have both social and economic causes and consequences (Kiernan, 1986; Smith and Mumford, 1980) but arguments might also be presented to include childbearing (especially teenage pregnancy) as a health-related behaviour (over which the individual exerts choice). Moreover, as mentioned in Chapter 1, there are different interpretations of what constitutes an 'explanation' of class differences in health; some have argued that the distinction between socio-economic and (cultural) behavioural is artificial (Blaxter, 1983; Blane, 1985).

7.5 Conclusions

From the range of socio-economic circumstances considered in this chapter there were many that appeared to contribute towards class differences in health. Analyses of self-rated health, malaise and psychological morbidity suggested that more recent circumstances were particularly important and this ensured that they would be included in the next stage of analysis. The selection of variables representing earlier circumstances was more problematic since several of those considered would have been appropriate. Some differences emerged for men and women, especially in terms of the recent characteristics that were associated with class differences in their health. Finally, there were also differences between health measures: while reductions in odds ratios suggested that earlier circumstances were particularly relevant to height, recent circumstances were generally more relevant to the other health measures.

Education, attitudes and beliefs

8.1 Introduction

In the framework presented in Chapter 1, education, attitudes and beliefs were designated as constituting a broad area of explanation for class differences in health. This is in recognition of the role played by education in determining positions in the social hierarchy and of that played by knowledge, attitudes and beliefs in affecting the propensity to follow sensible health practices, such as a balanced diet and physical activity, which thereby influence health.

Both roles were discussed in the Black Report, although in relation to cultural/behavioural explanations rather than as a separate area. The report recognized that education is the major basis for selection into occupations and thus plays a substantial part in determining entry into social groups. Leaning heavily on Bernstein's (1971) theories of language development and social differentiation, they argued

'. . . that the educational system tends to be substantially developed and maintained in conformity with the class system or with that pattern of differential material advantages or disadvantages, and social opportunities or obstacles, which govern both the place taken in the system by the individual child and the chances of that child having a successful career within the system. On this reasoning, level of education becomes difficult to treat as intrinsically independent of class.'

This prompted some researchers to suggest that educational level is a more useful indicator of socio-economic status than occupational class (e.g. Kitagawa and Hauser, 1973). The advantages of this approach were outlined in Chapter 3. However, it is important to stress that while educational qualifications are heavily influenced by class of origin they are also a major sorting mechanism through which social mobility acts and influences class of destination (Halsey *et al.*, 1980; Goldthorpe,

1980). Use of education as the indicator of socio-economic position would preclude any investigation into the contribution of this mechanism to social differences in health.

As well as providing a passport to other advantages, education can, as expressed by the BMA Board of Science and Education (BMA, 1987) '. . . affect health . . . directly, through a person's knowledge of healthy life-styles and disease prevention'. Individuals used to collecting and interpreting information will be in a better position to acquire knowledge than others less skilled in this activity. This is evident in, for example, knowledge about the nutrient content of food (Whichelow, 1988). Communication with health professionals will also be easier for those with better education. It is not surprising, therefore, that knowledge about health-damaging or health-promoting practices is then used more in some groups than in others. For example, uptake of cervical and antenatal screening is greater, and the decline in smoking more pronounced, among well-educated groups.

Knowledge, as health educators appreciate only too well, is but one step in the adoption of a healthy lifestyle. Attitudes and intentions are of great importance (Ajzen and Fishbein, 1980) and these are not always congruent with health knowledge. Hence, many recent studies incorporate these dimensions in their attempts to explain behaviours such as smoking (Marsh and Matheson, 1983) and breast self-examination (Calnan and Rutter, 1986). An absence of a relationship between knowledge and attitudes is not uncommon, as shown for example in relation to AIDS (Morton and McManus, 1986). Even when knowledge is improved, changes in attitudes do not necessarily follow (Bagnall, 1991). Furthermore, Graham's research (1989) into women's smoking suggests that the relationship between knowledge, attitudes and behaviour can even be paradoxical, since knowledge about healthy lifestyles may be only one of several influences shaping attitudes and behaviour.

There is little evidence to suggest that education/knowledge, attitudes and beliefs are relevant for class differences in the specific health measures being examined here. However, as mentioned above, education is a major sorting mechanism for occupations and entry to the labour market during early adulthood is a particularly important time in this respect.

In addition, it could be envisaged that education/knowledge would directly affect psychological health through its influence on the extent to which particular roles are felt to be socially and personally desirable. Among women, for example, Warr and Parry (1982a, b) suggest that there are interrelationships between education, desirability of paid employment, home role attitudes and employment role attitudes, which in turn affect psychological health. Educational achievement might influence aspirations and self-images including self-esteem and perceived efficacy. Such attributes are not generally easy to identify, but they may be a part of a wider constellation of factors contributing to psychological health (Brown *et al.*, 1986) and, in the present context, to the rating young adults give to their own health at age 23.

A considerable amount of information would be needed to determine knowledge, attitudes and beliefs of the young people in NCDS. Only limited data are available on attitudes and beliefs, but educational attainment was tested throughout childhood and adolescence. Educational measures therefore provide the focus of the present chapter, although attitudes and beliefs will require greater emphasis in future studies.

8.2 Educational measures

Eleven variables were selected from those available within NCDS to explore the extent to which education contributes to subsequent social class differences in four health outcomes:

- *Arithmetic at age 7:* scores on a problem arithmetic test devised by the National Foundation for Educational Research (NFER) specifically for the study (Pringle *et al.*, 1966). Scores on this and the four attainment tests given below were grouped into thirds for analyses presented in this chapter.
- *Reading at age 7:* scores on the Southgate reading test (Southgate, 1962), assesses word recognition and reading comprehension and is particularly suitable for identifying backward readers.
- *Mathematics at age 11:* a test constructed by the NFER specifically for the cohort study.
- *Reading at age 11:* a test constructed by the NFER, to be parallel with the Watts–Vernon test of reading comprehension.
- *General ability at 11:* a test containing equal numbers of verbal and non-verbal items (Douglas, 1964).

The following three variables are based on data collected from schools in 1978 on each cohort member's public examination results. A single overall measure of school-based examination attainment has been created. However, because of the different examination structures in Scotland and England and Wales, this was not possible for measures of achievement in the two single subjects, and results for these variables are for England and Wales only.

- *Mathematics qualifications:* grouped as: none; up to CSE grade 2 or GCE 'O' level grade D; CSE grade 1 or 'O' level grade C or better; GCE 'A' level.
- *English qualifications:* grouped as for Mathematics.

- *Overall qualifications:* grouped as, none or CSEs to grade 2 only; up to four GCE 'O' levels (or SCE 'O' grades in Scotland) at grade C or better, or CSEs grade 1; more than four 'O' levels (or 'O' grades) but not more than one 'A' level (or 'H' grade in Scotland); two or more 'A' levels (or 'H' grades).

The remaining measures are all derived from information obtained in the 23-year interview.

- *Highest qualification obtained by 23:* grouped as, two 'A' levels or equivalent or higher (includes degrees, HNC/HND and other advanced level qualifications); 'O' levels and equivalent up to one 'A' level and equivalent (includes ONC/OND, TEC/BEC, City and Guilds, etc.); qualifications below 'O' level and none.
- *Education and training:* summarizes post-school experience as, no post-school education or formal training; some formal work-related training (of at least 14 days' or 100 hours' duration); some post-school education aiming for a qualification (may be combined with training).
- *Age of finishing full-time education:* grouped as, at minimum school-leaving age; up to 18 years 3 months; above 18 years 3 months.

The effect of 23-year variables (i.e. the final three listed above) on class differences in 'short' stature was not examined since, as mentioned in Chapter 7, events taking place after adult height was achieved by almost all could not be regarded as contributory.

8.3 Results

As in the two previous chapters, unadjusted and adjusted odds of poor health in social classes IV and V relative to classes I and II are presented as ratios for the four health measures separately (Tables 8.1 to 8.4). The most striking finding is that reductions in class differentials are generally greater than those observed in previous chapters, although this applies less for psychological morbidity.

Comparison of the effect of adjusting for educational measures at different ages is complicated, as it was for inheritance and socio-economic variables, by variations in the samples. The tables suggest a trend, however, in that earlier educational attainment had a smaller effect than later attainment or qualifications: reductions in relative odds associated with 7-year reading and arithmetic attainment were generally smaller than those for the 11-year test scores; and the latter were smaller than for the end-of-school qualification variables. For example, the odds ratio of poor or fair self-rating of health among women reduced from 3.26 to 2.49 after adjusting for reading ability at age 7, 3.24 to 2.31 for tests at age 11 and 2.89 to 1.76 for English qualifications at age 16.

Table 8.1 Relative odds of subjects rating their health as 'poor' or 'fair' (classes IV and V versus I and II) adjusting for educational achievement

Educational variables	Men			Women		
	(n)	Unadjusted	Adjusted	(n)	Unadjusted	Adjusted
At age 7:						
Arithmetic	(5216)	2.32	2.06	(5423)	3.22	2.66
Reading	(5236)	2.41	1.86	(5428)	3.26	2.49
At age 11:						
Mathematics	(5109)	2.33	1.74	(5258)	3.24	2.15
Reading	(5110)	2.33	1.76	(5260)	3.24	2.31
General ability	(5109)	2.33	1.74	(5262)	3.24	2.17
At end of schooling:						
Mathematics qualifications†	(3742)	2.43	1.91	(3846)	2.89	2.01
English qualifications†	(3742)	2.40	1.70	(3846)	2.89	1.76
Overall qualifications	(5131)	2.57	1.92	(5309)	2.78	1.68
By age 23:						
Highest qualification	(5919)	2.31	1.49	(6080)	2.97	1.41
Education and training	(5915)	2.31	1.27	(6079)	2.97	2.18
Age finished education	(5419)	2.31	1.76	(6080)	2.97	1.99*

†England and Wales only.
*Significant interactions ($p < 0.05$).

Table 8.2 Relative odds of high malaise score (classes IV and V versus I and II) adjusting for educational achievement

Educational variables	Men			Women		
	(n)	Unadjusted	Adjusted	(n)	Unadjusted	Adjusted
At age 7:						
Arithmetic	(5211)	2.89	2.58	(5416)	5.02	4.22
Reading	(5231)	2.99	2.23	(5421)	5.07	4.03
At age 11:						
Mathematics	(5105)	3.28	1.99	(5251)	5.72	3.47
Reading	(5106)	3.28	2.30	(5253)	5.72	3.84
General ability	(5105)	3.28	1.91	(5255)	5.60	3.71
At end of schooling:						
Mathematics qualifications†	(3734)	3.97	2.51	(3837)	5.84	4.01
English qualifications†	(3739)	4.18	2.58	(3837)	5.82	3.75
Overall qualifications	(5125)	4.10	2.69	(5301)	5.54	3.26
By age 23:						
Highest qualification	(5911)	3.31	1.50	(6070)	5.29	2.66
Education and training	(5907)	3.31	2.17	(6069)	5.29	3.82
Age finished education	(5911)	3.31	2.28	(6070)	5.29	3.82

†England and Wales only.

Table 8.3 Relative odds of psychological morbidity between ages 16 and 23 (classes IV and V versus I and II) adjusting for educational achievement

		Men			Women	
Educational variables	(*n*)	Unadjusted	Adjusted	(*n*)	Unadjusted	Adjusted
At age 7:						
Arithmetic	(5221)	2.03	2.03	(5427)	2.29	2.10
Reading	(5241)	2.09	1.89	(5432)	2.31	2.16
At age 11:						
Mathematics	(5114)	1.65	1.27	(5261)	2.53	2.13
Reading	(5115)	1.65	1.48	(5263)	2.53	2.48*
General ability	(5114)	1.65	1.31	(5265)	2.54	2.23
At end of schooling:						
Mathematics qualifications†	(3746)	2.10	2.00	(3848)	2.35	2.12
English qualifications†	(3746)	2.09	1.79	(3848)	2.46	2.10
Overall qualifications	(5135)	2.04	1.63	(5313)	2.42	2.08
By age 23:						
Highest qualification	(5425)	1.95	1.61	(6084)	2.37	1.94
Education and training	(5920)	1.95	1.87	(6083)	2.37	2.26*
Age finished education	(5911)	1.95	1.57	(6084)	2.37	2.05

†England and Wales only.
*Significant interactions ($p<0.05$).

Table 8.4 Relative odds of 'short' stature (classes IV and V versus I and II) adjusting for educational achievement

		Men			Women	
Educational variables	(*n*)	Unadjusted	Adjusted	(*n*)	Unadjusted	Adjusted
At age 7:						
Arithmetic	(5188)	2.40	2.04	(5393)	2.55	2.36
Reading	(5207)	2.43	1.97	(5397)	2.49	2.05
At age 11:						
Mathematics	(5080)	2.33	1.71	(5229)	2.63	2.13
Reading	(5081)	2.33	1.77	(5231)	2.63	1.99
General ability	(5080)	2.33	1.79	(5233)	2.68	2.13
At end of schooling:						
Mathematics qualifications†	(3717)	2.05	1.63	(3830)	2.56	2.02
English qualifications†	(3717)	2.04	1.61	(3830)	2.55	1.92
Overall qualifications	(5100)	2.12	1.29	(5282)	2.47	1.74
By age 23:						
Highest qualification	(5883)	2.33	1.54	(6045)	2.46	1.54
Education and training	(5879)	2.33	1.71	(6044)	2.49	1.90*
Age finished education	(5911)	2.33	1.82	(6045)	2.46	1.84

†England and Wales only.
*Significant interactions ($p<0.05$).

At age 7, adjusting for reading test scores produced greater effects than arithmetic test scores (women's psychological morbidity was an exception), but at age 11 there was no consistent pattern of differences between the three tests. For end-of-school measures, qualifications in English were again associated with greater reductions in class differentials than Mathematics qualifications. Reductions occurring after adjustment for overall qualifications at the end of school were substantial, especially for self-rated health and malaise where they ranged between 25% and 41%. These effects tended to be larger than those observed for age of finishing full-time education.

However, the largest reductions were found for the measures obtained at 23, particularly the level of the highest qualification obtained by that age. For both sexes, class differentials in malaise were halved by taking this measure into account, and the same applies to women's self-rated health. Reductions associated with post-school education and training were not always as substantial as those for highest qualification achieved by age 23. Tables 8.1 and 8.2 suggest that involvement in education or training since leaving school is more important for class differentials among men than among women.

8.4 Discussion

Overall, these results indicate that educational achievement makes an important contribution to class differentials in health, although, of the four health measures examined, psychological morbidity appears to be more independent of education than the others. In general, reductions were greater than those seen in earlier chapters and several variables – which are themselves highly correlated – demonstrate this. As anticipated in Chapter 1 (Figure 1.5), the effect of earlier education appeared to have diminished over time and more recent educational achievements made the most notable contribution to the class differences in health at age 23. This is not surprising in view of the opening remarks in this chapter. Although earlier attainment will be strongly predictive of ultimate school achievement, the qualifications attained at the end of schooling will contribute most directly to early employment. Post-school education and training are also important, especially for men, since more men than women undertake training, and this is only partially offset by the tendency for more women to continue their education (Fogelman, 1985).

That part of the effect of education and training is indirect – as it is not independent of social class – is suggested by the results for short stature. The direct effect on height of educational attainment later in childhood can hardly be substantial. Nevertheless, that such variables bring about a sizeable reduction in class differentials for short stature indicates that this is likely to reflect the influence of earlier social background and inheritance factors on educational attainment and physical growth. This is indicated by the high correlation between qualifications and social class.

On the other hand, greater reductions in class differentials were found in relation to self-rated health and malaise, so there is still a possibility that education plays a more direct role, at least in these areas. As suggested earlier in the chapter, this could be achieved through the influence of education/knowledge on aspirations and attitudes about home and work roles in particular and self-image in general. In consequence, self-rated health and malaise could be affected. A better understanding of the mechanisms involved depends, however, on further investigations focusing more directly on attitudes and beliefs. At older ages and for other health measures, knowledge could have a more general effect on lifestyles and disease prevention.

In relation to the present study, the purpose here is to select a variable for the next stage of analysis. If this were to be made on statistical grounds alone, then the highest qualification obtained by the age of 23 would be chosen, as this explains the greatest proportion of the class differences in almost every case. However, this is inappropriate in the present enquiry since it is the one variable that is most structurally intertwined with occupational class. The purpose of the final analysis will be to determine the extent to which the class differences remain after allowing for other variables that may influence health and class and are not simply other ways of characterizing social position. Furthermore, qualifications at 23 will to some extent reflect job-related opportunities, as well as the converse. Almost half the cohort had undertaken some work-related training, and about one-third had obtained their highest qualification in this way (Fogelman, 1985).

For these reasons level of qualifications at the end of schooling was selected for the next stage of analysis. This has three advantages: it is clear that it reflects school experience; it pre-dates entry into the labour market and thus will not be influenced by employment experiences; it represents most directly those qualifications that will have influenced the level of entry into the labour market and is therefore an appropriate measure to test the educational contribution to subsequent class differences in health.

8.5 Conclusions

The contribution of education to class differences in health among young adults was examined and found to have an important effect.

Conclusions

This may be because education influences the level of occupation achieved and thereby social class; and/or because of relationships with self-rating of health and malaise, through associated attitudes and beliefs. Given the close relationship between qualifications obtained by age 23 and social class, an earlier measure of achievement, at the end of schooling, was chosen for the next stage of analysis.

9

Health in childhood and adolescence

9.1 Introduction

In summarizing the conceptual framework used in the study, Figure 1.4 may be interpreted as depicting health as an outcome measure only. This occurs because it is difficult to convey the dynamic nature of the interrelationships in such a summary. However, there are two main reasons why the earlier health experience of young adults should be considered in relation to subsequent class differences in health.*

First, health is known to influence social mobility in such a way that the healthy tend to move up the social scale while the unhealthy move down (Illsley, 1955, 1986; Wadsworth, 1986). Mobility, which is selective on the basis of health, has the potential to contribute towards the unequal distribution of ill-health across social groups. This was discussed previously in Chapter 4 and although we confirmed that social mobility was related to health at age 23, these analyses did not look at the effects of ill-health prior to social mobility. It is therefore necessary to examine the contribution of earlier health – that is, in childhood and adolescence – partly because of the potential influence of health selection.

A second reason is that early health might influence class differences in later health through the persistence or consequence of early class differences in health problems. In this case the origins of class differences observed at age 23 might be found in patterns of health, and their causes, experienced earlier. However, the relevance of childhood health for adult health is not well understood. Neither are there clearly established social class differences in childhood ill-health, since many measures of morbidity rely upon use of health services that may be class-biased (Blaxter, 1976, 1981). It is probable, however, that overlying

* Some of the material in this chapter has been published previously in Power *et al.* (1990).

the divergent class trends for specific childhood illnesses (Butler and Golding, 1986; Davie *et al.*, 1972; Fogelman, 1983) is a pattern of poorer health in lower social classes. Evidence for this emerges from a comparison of all serious illness (involving hospital admission of a minimum of 28 consecutive days or school absence of three consecutive weeks or more in total) by social background in the 1946 cohort (Wadsworth, 1986). In this study the chances of boys having a serious illness increased significantly with falling social class, although no similar association was found for girls. Furthermore, social class differences in boys' health persisted from childhood and adolescence through to early adulthood. In addition, there are well-documented class gradients in childhood height (Douglas and Simpson, 1964; Goldstein, 1971; Rona *et al.*, 1978), which is a widely recognized index of nutritional and health status (MacIntyre, 1988; Preece, 1986; Price *et al.*, 1988; Acheson, 1987).

To explain class differences in four selected measures of health among young adults, health problems at different stages in childhood and adolescence need to be considered. Some findings have already been reported (Power *et al.*, 1990) but an account is provided here which justifies the choice of health measures for the next stage of analysis. A wide variety of indices of early health problems are available in the NCDS and those selected for inclusion in the analyses are described below.

9.2 Measures of ill-health

During childhood and adolescence, medical examinations were carried out by the schools health service specifically for the NCDS and, in a home interview, parents were also asked to report the child's past and present health problems. Data up to age 7 were subsequently categorized into morbidity groups constructed to resemble those used by Starfield *et al.* (1984). Details are given elsewhere (Power and Peckham, 1988) but a brief description of the groups used here is as follows:

- *Ear and throat illness:* including repeated infections, problems with tonsils or adenoids, running ears or otitis.
- *Other acute illness:* including urinary infections, fits or convulsions not identified as epilepsy, tuberculosis, glandular fever, pneumonia, abdominal operations (common childhood infectious diseases were not included).
- *Asthma, bronchitis and wheezing.*
- *Allergies, namely eczema and/or hayfever.*
- *Chronic conditions:* predominantly physical or mental handicap, but

also sensory (speech, vision, hearing) defects and other chronic (cardiovascular, urogenital, epilepsy) problems.

- *Psychosocial problems:* maladjustment, enuresis and/or soiling.
- *Psychosomatic complaints:* both headaches and digestive problems.

Hence, a wide range of data was utilized in classifying ill-health by age 7, but similar measures are not available for older ages. In view of this, cruder indicators were selected to represent ill-health at ages 11 and 16. Height and stage of puberty were included as nutritional and health status indicators (Tanner, 1978) while school absence resulting from ill-health was selected as a measure of the total burden of health problems. In addition, it was desirable to include a proxy for severe problems, as these might be expected to have long-term effects and data concerning ascertained handicap were available from the study. The details of 11- and 16-year measures are:

- *Absence from school in the preceding year for reason of ill-health or emotional disturbance:* as reported by parents. The number of days absence was subsequently categorized into those with more than one week in total and those with less.
- *Height:* as measured at ages 7, 11 and 16.
- *Stage of puberty:* derived from doctors' rating of axillary hair development and categorized into two groups, mature and immature at age 16.
- *Ascertained handicap:* reported by doctors in a special examination carried out for the study. The doctors consulted school health records and identified children with any condition severe enough for the local education authority to provide special education. The majority of children included in this category were, in the terminology of the time, educationally subnormal (Walker, 1982).

Information on ill-health beyond age 16 was not considered since later health problems were ascertained at age 23 – that is, simultaneously with the four health outcomes to be explained. However, an exception was made for women since a recent pregnancy or any complications from a pregnancy might substantially influence class differences in how women rate their health and overall well-being and there are marked class differences in the experience of pregnancy by age 23. Furthermore, in the case of self-rated health and malaise, data for pregnancy do precede the health measures. Therefore, the final indicator included in this section was:

- *Recent pregnancy:* that is, a pregnancy in the year preceding interview at age 23 – and any reported complications of a pregnancy before age 23.

9.3 Results

Class differentials in health at age 23, adjusted for previous health, are presented in Tables 9.1 to 9.4. In general, the tables suggest that the effect of such characteristics up to age 7 was negligible since class differentials were similar before and after adjusting for the early indices. There are some notable exceptions to this: not surprisingly, class differences in 'short' stature reduced considerably, after accounting for height at age 7 (Table 9.4). The reduction was of a similar magnitude in men (from 2.49 to 1.43) and women (from 2.35 to 1.26). To a lesser extent, adjusting for height during childhood also affected later class differences in malaise (Table 9.2).

Considering next the contribution of health later in childhood, adjusting for height at age 11 reduced the relative odds of short stature in adulthood, as had been the case for height at age 7, but no other health variables appeared to substantially affect class differentials in shortness (Table 9.4).

Table 9.1 Relative odds of subjects rating their health as 'poor' or 'fair' (classes IV and V versus I and II) adjusting for earlier health

		Men			Women	
Indicator of health	(n)	Unadjusted	Adjusted	(n)	Unadjusted	Adjusted
Age 0 to 7:						
Ear and throat illness	(4696)	2.12	2.12	(4776)	3.29	3.30*
Other acute illness	(4819)	2.21	2.22	(5037)	3.12	3.10
Asthma/bronchitis	(5135)	2.10	2.13*	(5326)	3.10	3.06
Allergies	(4982)	2.07	2.10	(5151)	3.15	3.16
Chronic condition	(4995)	2.19	2.13	(5174)	3.11	3.08
Psychosocial	(4970)	2.07	2.08	(5144)	3.16	3.08*
Psychosomatic	(5117)	2.11	2.11	(5315)	3.11	3.06
Height	(4868)	2.27	2.14*	(5011)	3.23	3.05
Age 11:						
School absence due to ill-health	(5010)	2.55	2.49	(5183)	3.16	3.08
Height	(4658)	2.50	2.37	(4821)	3.09	2.97
At age 16:						
School absence due to ill-health	(4404)	2.48	2.23	(4528)	3.18	2.87
Ascertained handicap	(4429)	2.53	2.33	(4538)	2.80	2.86
Height	(4243)	2.23	2.18*	(4345)	3.35	3.29
Puberty	(4245)	2.19	2.16*	(4317)	3.36	3.36
At age 23:						
Pregnancy				(6080)	2.97	3.01*
Complications of pregnancy				(6080)	2.97	2.85

*Significant interactions ($p<0.05$).

Table 9.2 Relative odds of high malaise score (classes IV and V versus I and II) adjusting for earlier health

Indicator of health	Men			Women		
	(*n*)	Unadjusted	Adjusted	(*n*)	Unadjusted	Adjusted
Age 0 to 7:						
Ear and throat illness	(4691)	2.86	2.86*	(4772)	5.65	5.65
Other acute illness	(4813)	2.68	2.68	(5032)	5.16	5.13
Asthma/bronchitis	(5129)	2.81	2.82	(5320)	5.30	5.26
Allergies	(4976)	2.78	2.80*	(5145)	5.42	5.41
Chronic condition	(4990)	3.02	2.97	(5168)	5.39	5.34
Psychosocial	(4996)	2.91	2.83	(5138)	5.44	5.23
Psychosomatic	(5112)	2.92	2.92	(5309)	5.31	5.23*
Height	(4863)	2.78	2.48	(5011)	5.38	5.12
Age 11:						
School absence due to ill-health	(5007)	3.21	3.11	(5175)	5.55	5.47
Height	(4655)	2.97	2.74	(4816)	5.61	5.33
At age 16:						
School absence due to ill-health	(4398)	3.26	2.85	(4519)	5.03	4.62
Ascertained handicap	(4423)	3.54	3.16	(4528)	4.06	4.36
Height	(4238)	3.58	3.36	(4338)	5.56	5.35
Puberty ˅	(4239)	3.20	3.13	(4310)	5.85	5.87*
At age 23:						
Pregnancy				(6070)	5.29	5.41
Complications of pregnancy				(6070)	5.29	5.11

*Significant interactions (*p*<0.05).

For self-rated health, malaise and, to a lesser extent, psychological morbidity, the most consistent reductions in relative odds were achieved after adjustment for school absence for ill-health at age 16 (Tables 9.1 to 9.3). In men, for example, the relative odds of poor or fair rating of health were 2.48 before adjusting for school absence and 2.23 after adjustment: the corresponding figures in women were 3.18 and 2.87 respectively (Table 9.1). Adjustment for ascertained handicap at age 16 also resulted in a reduction in relative odds for both self-rated health and malaise among men, but not in women.

Finally, the relative odds in self-assessed health, malaise and psychological morbidity in women remained largely unaffected after adjustment for a recent pregnancy or complications during pregnancy.

Table 9.3 Relative odds of psychological morbidity between ages 16 and 23 (classes IV and V versus I and II) adjusting for earlier health

		Men			Women	
Indicator of health	(n)	Unadjusted	Adjusted	(n)	Unadjusted	Adjusted
Age 0 to 7:						
Ear and throat illness	(4700)	1.82	1.80	(4780)	2.26	2.26
Other acute illness	(4824)	1.89	1.89	(5041)	2.41	2.40
Asthma/bronchitis	(5140)	1.86	1.86	(5330)	2.51	2.50
Allergies	(4986)	2.00	2.04	(5155)	2.42	2.41*
Chronic condition	(4999)	2.15	2.11	(5178)	2.39	2.38
Psychosocial	(4974)	2.19	2.08	(5148)	2.44	2.39
Psychosomatic	(5122)	1.92	1.92	(5319)	2.52	2.47
Height	(4872)	2.04	1.94	(5021)	2.43	2.49
Age 11:						
School absence due to ill-health	(5015)	1.98	1.93	(5186)	2.50	2.46
Height	(4663)	2.08	1.98	(4824)	2.56	2.57
At age 16:						
School absence due to ill-health	(4409)	1.63	1.59	(4531)	2.65	2.45
Ascertained handicap	(4434)	1.76	1.56	(4541)	2.13	2.67*
Height	(4248)	1.93	1.94	(4348)	2.92	2.98
Puberty	(4250)	1.85	1.86*	(4320)	2.88	2.88*
At age 23:						
Pregnancy				(6084)	2.37	2.46
Complications of pregnancy				(6084)	2.37	2.28

*Significant interactions ($p<0.05$).

9.4 Discussion

In contrast to other potential influences discussed in previous chapters – such as those associated with qualifications at the end of school and recent unemployment – the reductions in relative odds reported here for measures of earlier health appear to be less substantial. Previous health, especially early in childhood, was largely irrelevant to class differences in self-rated health, malaise and psychological morbidity among young adults.

Height measured as early as age 7, on the other hand, made a substantial contribution towards adulthood class differences in short stature. While this is not surprising, since class differences in height are known to exist in childhood (Goldstein, 1971), inclusion of an earlier measure can indicate the extent to which explanations for adulthood short stature are located before age 7 and, conversely, the extent to which they are not.

117

Table 9.4 Relative odds of 'short' stature (classes IV and V versus I and II) adjusting for earlier health

Indicator of health	Men			Women		
	(*n*)	Unadjusted	Adjusted	(*n*)	Unadjusted	Adjusted
Age 0 to 7:						
Ear and throat illness	(4667)	2.57	2.57	(4753)	2.51	2.51
Other acute illness	(4790)	2.49	2.50	(5010)	2.37	2.37
Asthma/bronchitis	(5105)	2.35	2.36	(5299)	2.52	2.51
Allergies	(4952)	2.37	2.37	(5126)	2.44	2.43
Chronic condition	(4965)	2.46	2.43	(5147)	2.50	2.48
Psychosocial	(4941)	2.41	2.40	(5119)	2.43	2.36*
Psychosomatic	(5089)	2.39	2.39	(5288)	2.48	2.49
Height	(4839)	2.49	1.43	(4994)	2.35	1.26
Age 11:						
School absence due to ill-health	(4977)	2.22	2.23	(5157)	2.52	2.53
Height	(4627)	2.31	1.59	(4796)	2.49	1.49
At age 16:†						
School absence due to ill-health	(4376)	1.80	1.79	(4507)	2.34	2.32
Ascertained handicap	(4401)	1.84	1.68	(4516)	2.39	2.25
Puberty	(4215)	2.05	1.99	(4296)	2.48	2.45

†At age 16 height was not used as an indicator of development, since women in particular and many men would have achieved their adult height by this age.
*Significant interactions ($p < 0.05$).

For the other early adulthood health measures, there are several explanations why health in early life may not provide an important contribution towards class differences. First, the most common conditions experienced in childhood and adolescence, e.g. acute ear and throat infections, are generally relatively minor and self-limiting and as such they do not exert a long-term effect upon class differences in health. Second, groups affected by potentially lasting and serious conditions might experience downward social mobility (Wadsworth, 1986) but this would need to be substantial in order to exert a strong influence on the levels of morbidity within each class.

However, it is important to note that more recent health, specifically school absence through ill-health at age 16, had a greater impact on later class differences than earlier health. This had been anticipated (Figure 1.5) but remains a tentative conclusion in view of the wider range of indicators used to characterize health in childhood compared with adolescence. Not only were fewer indices used to characterize the latter but they were also cruder. School absence, for example – which, according to the parents of the study members, resulted from ill-health – could nevertheless include unjustified absenteeism. This is likely to have been a greater problem at age 16 than at age 11 (Fogelman *et al.*,

1980). A further limitation of this indicator is that it gives no idea of severity of ill-health since it could represent a high level of minor illness. School absence has been used as a measure of ill-health by others (Charlton and Blair, 1989) but variations in reasons for children being 'off school sick' should not be underestimated (Prout, 1988).

Ascertained handicap was also used to indicate health problems at age 16. The difficulties associated with this measure differ from those described above for school absence but are important in the present context. As Table 9.5 shows, the number of young people ascertained as having a handicap is small and they are disproportionately less likely to have held a job by age 23. Few of these subjects could be allocated to a social class and so the impact of this variable on class differences in health was likely to be minimal. Furthermore, even when an adjustment for ascertained handicap resulted in reductions in relative odds that were greater than those for other measures of childhood health, this could not be used in the next stage of analysis because the small numbers would be problematic for the multiclassification involved. The contribution of this variable can only be assessed, therefore, from the simple analyses presented in this chapter.

Table 9.5 Social class distribution at age 23 of those with ascertained handicap at age 16

	Men		Women	
Social class at age 23	% with ascertained handicap at 16 ($n = 187$)	% without ascertained handicap at 16 ($n = 5821$)	% with ascertained handicap at 16 ($n = 108$)	% without ascertained handicap at 16 ($n = 5584$)
I and II	2.7	16.5	0.9	17.6
IIIN	3.2	13.2	7.4	40.3
IIIM	17.6	30.8	6.5	7.3
IV and V	26.6	14.4	30.6	15.7
Unknown	50.3	25.2	54.6	19.1

Measures of earlier health included psychosocial and psychosomatic conditions at age 7. These are especially relevant to selected health outcomes at age 23, since in part they indicate emotional well-being early in childhood. As mentioned in the introductory remarks to this chapter, persistence of emotional disorders and/or related consequences is a mechanism by which earlier health could contribute to subsequent health differences. Some evidence exists for associations between childhood and adult psychological disorders although associations are not always strong and depend upon the type of disorder (Rutter, 1972; Robins, 1979, 1986; Rutter and Garmezy, 1983; Rodgers, 1990a). It is of interest, therefore, that measures for age 7 made no notable impact on class differences in malaise and psychological morbidity at age 23. Measures of emotional well-being later in childhood (ages 11 and 16) have not yet been considered. This is rectified to some extent in the following chapter, which assesses the contribution of individual behaviour towards class differences in health in young adults. Among the behaviours examined is a rating of behaviour at school, as perceived by the teacher, which was obtained for several stages during childhood. These measures might also be interpreted as indicators of psychiatric disorder, although in the absence of further details they do not enable a psychiatric diagnosis to be made (Rutter *et al.*, 1970). Even so, findings in relation to the behaviour ratings are relevant to an assessment of the importance of earlier health to later class differences in young adults, and will be discussed again in subsequent chapters.

9.5 Conclusions

Earlier health should be included in an examination of class differences in health because of selective social mobility, and also in order to detect whether later differences have their origins in childhood health. Height was found to be an example of the latter and heights at ages 7 and 11 were chosen, therefore, for the multivariate stage of analysis of adult short stature. Apart from this, health early in childhood was not found to be an important influence on subsequent class differences, although health in adolescence appeared to be more important. School absence at age 16 was chosen for the multivariate analyses of self-rated health, malaise and psychological morbidity (women only). In the case of psychological morbidity in men, earlier health was shown to be largely ineffective in reducing class differentials and so no measure was selected for the later analyses.

10

Individual behaviour

10.1 Introduction

Arguments for cultural/behavioural explanations for social inequalities in health were presented in the Black Report (DHSS, 1980) and updated in *The Health Divide* (Whitehead, 1988). While both reports provide comprehensive summaries, it is necessary to reiterate the arguments briefly in introducing this chapter so that relevant explanatory factors can be considered in relation to social differences in health among young adults.

Behavioural factors encompass a range of lifestyles and practices, some of which are regarded as important determinants of poor health. According to the Black Report, this group of factors includes excessive consumption of harmful substances, refined foods, tobacco and alcohol, lack of exercise, underutilization of preventive care, vaccination, ante-natal surveillance or contraception. Some would argue that individuals invite harm to themselves and their children through their personal choice or dispositions towards particular behaviours while others attribute the shaping and reinforcement of lifestyles to social structures.

Whichever view is taken of the extent to which lifestyles are voluntary, variation in harmful or protective behaviours between social groups is likely to contribute towards class differences in health. Poorer health in lower social classes might arise, therefore, from more dangerous practices and low levels of health-promoting activities in these groups. A notable illustration of this is evident from a comparison of smoking habits and smoking-related diseases by social class (Whitehead, 1988; Blaxter, 1987; Pugh *et al.*, 1991). Controlling for the effect of smoking habits and other behaviours and/or their related risk factors diminishes social differences in mortality, but there remains some social class gradient that is unexplained (Marmot *et al.*, 1984; Berkman and Breslow, 1983; Kaplan, 1985; Pocock *et al.*, 1987). Preliminary evidence from *The Health and Lifestyle Survey* suggests that conclusions would be similar for morbidity, as indicated from physiological measures such as lung function and blood pressure (Blaxter, 1987).

Many behavioural patterns become established during adolescence and early adulthood and exert their effects on health later in life. Immediate or short-term effects are not always known but some behaviours are relevant, potentially, to the selected health measures of interest here.

More stringent investigations are needed to establish the extent of risks associated with particular behaviours, but the evidence available suggests, for example, that leisure activities and physical exercise in particular can promote mental health (Taylor *et al.*, 1985; Sports Council, 1984). Level of fitness could also affect how young adults assess their own health (Blaxter, 1990).

Alcohol consumption is another potentially relevant behaviour. Early adulthood is a stage of life of particularly high levels of consumption, and although serious health hazards that affect older age groups (Royal College of Physicians, 1987) have yet to be incurred, there are nevertheless consequences of drinking heavily at younger ages (Plant *et al.*, 1985). These could have negative effects on mental health and contribute to a young adult's rating of his or her own health. Smoking has also been related to many health problems, although the direction of the relationship is unclear for mental health.

Overeating might also have a detrimental effect on physical and mental health in early adulthood, if it results in overweight or obesity. Psychological effects of being overweight are not thought to be evident at older ages (Crisp and McGuiness, 1975) but adolescence and early adulthood are periods of particular weight consciousness (Bruch, 1974; Stewart and Brook, 1983) and psychological problems could ensue.

Social contact was discussed in relation to psychological health in Chapter 7. Some of the variables examined – for example, early marriage – could be regarded as measures of both socio-economic circumstances and individual behaviour. Similarly, there is an overlap between childhood health, as discussed in the previous chapter, and behaviour since there is an obvious behavioural component of some childhood health measures, notably psychosocial health and psychosomatic conditions. Investigation of patterns of behaviour was, however, far from complete in these earlier chapters and further analyses of individual behaviour are warranted. For the purpose of the present investigation, childhood behaviour might be relevant, first, because it represents an early indication of psychological health which *continues* into adulthood; second, because it signifies personal dispositions which are risk factors for subsequent psychological problems; and, third, because it influences the sorting process by which individuals are allocated to social classes. Evidence now exists in support of a link between early behaviour, especially in teenage years, and subsequent adult psychiatric disorder (Rodgers, 1990a).

This chapter examines whether the social class distribution of selected measures of health in early adulthood is influenced by preceding behaviours and what the magnitude of such an effect might be. Evidence linking potential influences identified above and adult height is more limited than for the other three health measures. Diet during childhood may be more relevant to adult height, but data contained in NCDS do no allow examination of this. Consequently, it is anticipated that individual behaviour as represented here will not contribute to class differences in this health measure.

10.2 Measures of behaviour

The measures used in the analyses were as follows:

- *Leisure pursuits:* Individuals rated the frequency with which they were engaged in leisure activities at ages 11 and 16 that were conducted outside school hours. Three pastimes were selected to represent active and sedentary pursuits, namely, playing sports, reading and watching TV. Each was graded according to frequency of participation ('often', 'sometimes' or 'never or hardly ever').
- *Consumption habits:* At age 16 individuals in the study provided detailed information on how often and how much alcohol and tobacco they consumed; individuals were characterized according to whether they smoked and whether they had consumed an alcoholic drink in the week preceding the survey. Ideally dietary habits would also be included in the analyses but this information was not available in the study. Doctors rating of overweight at age 16 (grouped as obese, normal and thin) was therefore included as a proxy measure, albeit crude, of overconsumption.
- *Behaviour at school:* This was assessed by teachers using the Bristol Social Adjustment Scale (Stott, 1969) at age 11 and the Rutter Behaviour Scale (Rutter, 1967) at age 16. As in earlier work on the cohort the ratings were divided into: 'deviant' behaviour, the top 13% of ratings; 'normal', the 50% with the lowest scores; with intermediate scores forming the third category (Ghodsian *et al.*, 1980). Fuller details of the scales and their categorization are given in Appendix C, section C.2.

Information available for leisure activities and consumption of alcohol and tobacco at age 23 was omitted from the analyses because their simultaneous data collection with the health indices called into question their role in the causal process. In other relevant areas, such as preventive care, antenatal surveillance and contraception, the data were not available from the NCDS and so it was not possible to represent these health-related behaviours in the analyses.

10.3 Results

Class differences in the four selected indices of health in early adulthood were adjusted for the leisure activities, consumption and school behaviours described above (Tables 10.1 to 10.4).

Table 10.1 compares odds of rating health as 'poor' or 'fair' in classes IV and V relative to classes I and II both before and after adjusting for behavioural characteristics. For men and women, unadjusted and adjusted relative odds were similar for all variables considered, except for behaviour at school rated at ages 11 and 16 and smoking at age 16. The reduction associated with teachers' rating of behaviour at age 16 was from 2.34 to 1.65 in men and from 3.39 to 2.57 in women, and that for adolescent smoking was from 2.27 to 1.99 and 3.05 to 2.82 in men and women respectively.

This pattern was fairly consistent for each of the indices of psycho-social and emotional ill-health, in that adjustment for behaviour at school and smoking habits reduced the relative odds, while adjustment for other behaviours was largely ineffective in this respect. Generally, the reductions associated with school behaviour rated at age 16 were

Table 10.1 Relative odds of subjects rating their health as 'poor' or 'fair' (classes IV and V versus I and II) adjusting for health behaviour

Health behaviour variables	Men			Women		
	(n)	Unadjusted	Adjusted	(n)	Unadjusted	Adjusted
At age 11:						
Leisure time spent:						
playing sports	(4926)	2.33	2.33	(5101)	3.07	3.06*
reading	(4926)	2.34	2.34	(5101)	3.07	2.90
watching TV	(4926)	2.33	2.32	(5101)	3.18	3.18
Behaviour at school	(5117)	2.40	1.99	(5250)	3.25	2.59
At age 16:						
Leisure time spent:						
playing sports	(3934)	2.12	2.12	(3801)	2.96	2.97
reading	(4060)	2.25	2.25	(4336)	3.14	3.14*
watching TV	(4330)	2.35	2.33*	(4542)	3.20	3.15
Smoking	(4463)	2.27	1.99	(4659)	3.05	2.82
Drinking	(4486)	2.27	2.27*	(4663)	3.08	3.06
Overweight	(4267)	2.18	2.14	(4371)	3.35	3.33
Behaviour at school	(4632)	2.34	1.65	(4811)	3.39	2.57

*Significant interactions ($p<0.05$).

Table 10.2 Relative odds of high malaise score (classes IV and V versus I and II) adjusting for health behaviour

Health behaviour variables	Men			Women		
	(n)	Unadjusted	Adjusted	(n)	Unadjusted	Adjusted
At age 11:						
Leisure time spent:						
playing sports	(4923)	3.31	3.31	(5096)	5.38	5.39
reading	(4923)	3.33	3.31	(5097)	5.60	5.31
watching TV	(4923)	3.31	3.31	(5098)	5.74	5.72
Behaviour at school	(5111)	3.11	2.48	(5243)	5.61	4.47
At age 16:						
Leisure time spent:						
playing sports	(3932)	3.55	3.54	(3798)	5.74	5.75
reading	(4059)	3.83	4.15	(4332)	4.85	4.89*
watching TV	(4327)	3.97	3.90	(4537)	5.06	4.94
Smoking	(4460)	3.74	3.13	(4654)	5.13	4.47
Drinking	(4483)	3.80	3.82	(4658)	5.20	5.21
Overweight	(4261)	2.99	3.20*	(4364)	5.78	5.74
Behaviour at school	(4627)	4.37	2.66	(4802)	5.74	4.03

*Significant interactions ($p<0.05$).

Table 10.3 Relative odds of psychological morbidity (classes IV and V versus I and II) adjusting for health behaviour

Health behaviour variables	Men			Women		
	(n)	Unadjusted	Adjusted	(n)	Unadjusted	Adjusted
At age 11:						
Leisure time spent:						
playing sports	(4929)	1.62	1.62*	(5104)	2.37	2.37
reading	(4929)	1.59	1.63	(5104)	2.41	2.40
watching TV	(4929)	1.72	1.71*	(5106)	2.48	2.49
Behaviour at school	(5123)	1.63	1.39	(5253)	2.48	2.10
At age 16:						
Leisure time spent:						
playing sports	(3938)	2.31	2.30	(3803)	2.53	2.65
reading	(4064)	2.28	2.31	(4339)	2.65	2.65
watching TV	(4334)	2.20	2.19*	(4545)	2.83	2.83
Smoking	(4467)	2.21	1.93	(4662)	2.49	2.21
Drinking	(4490)	2.21	2.24	(4666)	2.47	2.49
Overweight	(4272)	1.87	1.88*	(4374)	2.81	2.80
Behaviour at school	(4636)	2.28	1.53	(4814)	2.50	1.77

*Significant interactions ($p<0.05$).

Table 10.4 Relative odds of 'short' stature (classes IV and V versus I and II) adjusting for health behaviour

Health behaviour variables	Men			Women		
	(n)	Unadjusted	Adjusted	(n)	Unadjusted	Adjusted
At age 11:						
Leisure time spent:						
playing sports	(4897)	2.20	2.20	(5074)	2.63	2.63
reading	(4897)	2.14	2.15	(5075)	2.62	2.44
watching TV	(4896)	2.26	2.24	(5077)	2.53	2.55
Behaviour at school	(5086)	2.36	2.22	(5222)	2.65	2.60
At age 16:						
Leisure time spent:						
playing sports	(3916)	2.29	2.29	(3789)	2.60	2.60
reading	(4037)	2.11	2.12	(4319)	2.38	2.29
watching TV	(4306)	2.14	2.15	(4524)	2.42	2.42
Smoking	(4438)	2.16	2.19	(4639)	2.44	2.41*
Drinking	(4461)	2.16	2.12	(4643)	2.43	2.39
Overweight	(4237)	2.00	2.02	(4350)	2.50	2.48
Behaviour at school	(4602)	2.26	2.05	(4709)	2.39	2.16

*Significant interactions ($p < 0.05$).

greater than for age 11. For malaise, for example, adjusting for behaviour rating at age 11 reduced class differentials from 3.11 to 2.48 in men but after adjusting for the rating at age 16 the comparable figures were 4.37 and 2.66 (Table 10.2). Adjusting for smoking at age 16 produced smaller, but nevertheless substantial, reductions in some instances: from 3.74 to 3.13 in the relative odds of malaise in men.

Neither behaviour rating nor smoking at age 16 appeared to exert a comparable effect upon class differences in short stature (Table 10.4) but leisure time reading at age 11 did result in a reduction of relative odds among women, as it had also for relative odds of malaise in women (Table 10.2).

10.4 Discussion

A clear pattern has emerged from this analysis of behaviour in that, with two notable exceptions, these factors were found to be generally unimportant in accounting for class differences in four selected measures of health in early adulthood. On the other hand, allowing for behaviour rated by teachers and smoking behaviour in adolescence consistently reduced class differentials in self-rated health, malaise and psychological morbidity for men and women, but, as anticipated, adult height remained largely unaffected.

The contribution of the teachers' rating of adolescent behaviour was particularly notable, but in view of the complexity of the rating it is not altogether clear how this should be interpreted. However, as outlined in the introduction (page 122), several mechanisms can be postulated.

10.4.1 Continuity in psychological disorders

The first is that the teachers' assessment of behaviour provides a good approximation of adolescent emotional well-being and that malaise and psychological morbidity at age 23 show problems continuing into adulthood. The Bristol Social Adjustments Guide (BSAG) was originally designed for 'detecting and diagnosing maladjustment, unsettledness or other emotional handicap in children of school age' (Stott, 1969) and the purpose of the Rutter scale was to provide a screening instrument for psychiatric disorder (Rutter *et al.*, 1970). Rutter and his colleagues caution against diagnosis of psychiatric disorder on the basis of the scales alone, but it seems plausible that they provide an approximation of adolescent emotional health. If there is continuity of psychological problems, as indicated by behaviour assessed at age 16 and malaise and psychological morbidity at age 23, then factors contributing to class differences in the former are particularly relevant in the present investigation.

10.4.2 Early behaviour predisposes to subsequent psychological problems

Second, 'deviant' behaviour identified from the teachers' assessments may detect particular personal characteristics and/or patterns of social interaction which predispose towards later emotional health problems. For example, the rating provides an indication of the individuals in relation to their social world. Social contacts and social networks are thought to influence health (Berkman and Breslow, 1983) and evidence for the importance of this is accumulating (Madge and Marmot, 1987). Several items on the Rutter scale refer to the study children's standing with their peers ('not much liked by other children', 'tends to be on own') so that social isolation or popularity can be inferred, although it may or may not be under the control of the individual. Other characteristics included in the scale, such as being afraid or unresponsive (Appendix C, section C.2), could also be precursors to later psychological problems.

10.4.3 Behaviour-related social mobility

Third, behaviour at 16 may influence allocation of individuals to social classes and through either mechanism described above – continuity of psychological problems and predisposing behaviours – thereby affect the social distribution of psychological health at age 23. Therefore, further analyses of social class, social mobility and behaviour rating were conducted to examine these relationships within NCDS.

Table 10.5 illustrates that, in general, those with a 'normal' behaviour rating at age 16 were more likely to move up the social scale than those with a 'deviant' rating. For example, of 276 men and 331 women in classes IV and V at age 16 and rated as having 'normal' behaviour, 42 (15.2%) and 51 (15.4%) moved to classes I and II at age 23, compared with 2 out of 124 men (1.6%) and 5 out of 87 women (5.7%) rated as 'deviant'. Conversely, 'deviant' rating at age 16 was associated with greater downward social mobility by age 23 than a 'normal' rating. This is apparent among 68 'deviant' men and 38 'deviant' women in classes I and II at age 16, of whom 14 (20.6%) and 10 (26.3%) moved to classes IV and V at age 23; of 564 'normal' men and 663 'normal' women in classes I and II at age 16, only 51 (9.0%) and 46 (6.9%) moved to classes IV and V by age 23. However, Table 10.5 also suggests that social class differences in behaviour existed before social mobility had taken place; that is, differences in behaviour were apparent by age 16 as indicated by father's class. Comparing 'deviant' rating in classes IV and V with that in classes I and II, there were 124 boys out of 634 (19.6%) and 68 out of 903 (7.5%) using social class at age 16; this changed to 166 out of 682 (24.3%) and 28 out of 779 (3.6%) using class at 23. Similarly for girls, there were 87 out of 647 (13.4%) and 38 out of 939 (4.0%) using class at 16; this changed to 130 out of 689 (18.9%) and 28 out of 777 (3.6%) using class at age 23.

In summary, behaviour problems developed disproportionately in lower classes compared with higher classes, *and* behaviour was also associated with social mobility, thereby influencing the subsequent class distribution of related psychological health. Support is available, therefore, for an effect of class on behaviour/psychological problems and conversely, for an effect of behaviour/psychological problems on social class.

The interpretations presented above are not mutually exclusive and it would be impossible to disentangle their respective effects. Before moving on to discuss behaviours other than those rated by teachers it is of interest to establish whether subsequent health measures (at age 23) were associated with particular behaviour problems at age 16. Items in the Rutter score (Appendix C, section C.2) are generally grouped in such a way as to differentiate children whose problems are primarily 'emotional' from others with 'conduct' problems, although this is not always accepted if the rating is used without any other means of assessment (Ghodsian, 1977). In applying the subclassification to the deviant group in the NCDS, there was no preponderance of one category over the other, but 'emotional' disorder was predominant among adolescent

Table 10.5 Social class at age 23 by father's social class when NCDS members were aged 16 by behaviour rating and sex. (Numbers with complete data)

Behaviour rating at age 16	Father's class of NCDS member at age 16	Men's own class at 23					Women's own class at 23				
		I&II	IIIN	IIIM	IV&V	Total	I&II	IIIN	IIIM	IV&V	Total
Normal	I and II	268	139	106	51	564	256	330	31	46	663
	IIIN	83	56	72	19	230	70	123	14	23	230
	IIIM	168	129	336	105	738	192	488	83	133	896
	IV and V	42	50	125	59	276	51	181	34	65	331
	Total	561	374	639	234	1808	569	1122	162	267	2120
Intermediate	I and II	83	62	86	40	271	65	122	20	31	238
	IIIN	22	31	62	28	143	27	71	13	16	127
	IIIM	63	68	313	137	581	73	269	52	155	549
	IV and V	22	12	123	77	234	15	93	31	90	229
	Total	190	173	584	282	1229	180	555	116	292	1143
Deviant	I and II	10	16	28	14	68	4	17	7	10	38
	IIIN	2	1	14	15	32	2	7	3	13	25
	IIIM	14	17	111	77	219	17	44	22	64	147
	IV and V	2	2	60	60	124	5	20	19	43	87
	Total	28	36	213	166	443	28	88	51	130	297
Total	I and II	361	217	220	105	903	325	469	58	87	939
	IIIN	107	88	143	62	405	99	201	30	52	383
	IIIM	245	214	760	319	1538	282	801	157	352	1592
	IV and V	66	64	308	196	634	71	294	84	198	647
	Total	779	583	1436	682	3480	777	1765	329	689	3560

girls and 'conduct' disorder among boys (Appendix C, Table C.2). It is pertinent to this discussion, however, that it was not just the 'emotional' group who had raised odds of poor health in early adulthood, since the antisocial or 'conduct' group was also affected (Appendix C, Table C.3).

Furthermore, the association between adolescent behaviour and later health was maintained across each of the self-rated health, malaise and psychological morbidity measures (Appendix C, Table C.3). This suggests that there are some similarities in the adulthood health outcomes examined, at least in respect of their origins. Self-rating of health in young adults would appear, therefore, to be heavily influenced by emotional well-being, even though the overlap between individuals identified by different measures is by no means complete (Chapter 3).

As mentioned in the previous chapter, there is an extent to which the behaviour rating could be included in more than one of the broad areas identified in the study framework (Figure 1.4). Smoking, on the other hand, is regarded conventionally as a health-related behaviour which may affect class differentials in health. The contribution of smoking towards class differences in mortality is well established and analyses reported here suggest that smoking also contributes towards differences in health observed at a younger age, in fact not long after smoking habits have become established. Class differences in smoking in the NCDS sample were already apparent by adolescence and still entrenched at age 23 (Table 10.6). However, class differences in psychological problems could exist prior to differences in smoking and it is not apparent from analyses presented so far whether smoking influences psychological health in early adulthood or vice versa. The following chapter goes some way towards resolving this. Even so, if differences in smoking persist or widen as they have in the mothers of these young people (Pugh *et al.*, 1991) then the influence of smoking upon class differences in health is unlikely to diminish as the cohort ages.

Table 10.6 Social class (at age 23) and smoking habits at ages 16 and 23

	% smoking (*n*)			
	Men		Women	
Social class at age 23	at age 16	at age 23	at age 16	at age 23
I and II	24 (238)	29 (367)	23 (235)	32 (409)
IIIN	29 (220)	32 (322)	32 (738)	36 (1079)
IIIM	42 (766)	44 (1057)	43 (180)	49 (275)
IV and V	48 (427)	52 (631)	48 (422)	55 (658)
All classes	37 (1651)	40 (2377)	34 (1575)	40 (2421)

Unlike smoking and school behaviour, other personal habits that were considered did not appear to contribute towards class differences in health. For some behaviours this could have occurred because they were unrelated to health, as defined by our four measures. Alternatively, or in addition, class differences may not have become firmly established during adolescence, even though they may become evident during the twenties and thereafter (Cox *et al.*, 1987). For example, involvement in sporting activities did not vary greatly before age 23 (Table 10.7) nor were class gradients in being overweight pronounced during adolescence. Nevertheless, these behaviours could contribute to class differences in health at older ages rather than in early adulthood since, for example, the effects of being overweight or lack of exercise may take several years to emerge.

Table 10.7 Social class (at age 23) and participation in sporting activities at ages 11, 16 and 23

	% participating in sporting activities* (*n*)					
	Men at age:			Women at age:		
Social class at age 23	11	16	23	11	16	23
I and II	53 (587)	73 (649)	44 (563)	36 (359)	49 (422)	32 (404)
IIIN	57 (482)	74 (519)	47 (477)	37 (953)	43 (818)	22 (660)
IIIM	57 (1140)	75 (1186)	40 (973)	40 (181)	43 (145)	17 (93)
IV and V	52 (507)	72 (550)	36 (436)	38 (370)	50 (348)	14 (166)
All classes	55 (2716)	74 (2904)	41 (2449)	37 (1899)	46 (1733)	22 (1323)

*Includes those reporting that they 'often' participated in sporting activities in their spare time (at ages 11 and 16) and those who took part in sporting activities once a week or more (at age 23).

It is also possible that the results for behavioural factors considered here may be limited by the measures used. For example, participation in leisure activities outside school is not a measure of the total amount of exercise that individuals undertake, but of their orientation towards sporting or more sedentary activities. Nor are the behavioural measures included in our analyses fully comprehensive: dietary intake during childhood may be relevant to differences in adult height but cannot be examined in this population of young adults.

10.5 Conclusions

The variables covered by this chapter on individual behaviour encompass a range of lifestyles and personal habits that could have a differential effect on the health of social groups. In the context of four measures of health in young adults, NCDS data permitted the inclusion of prominent areas of interest, namely, participation in leisure activities, smoking and drinking habits and being overweight, and an assessment of school behaviour. Since these behaviours were found to be largely irrelevant for class differences in adult short stature, a behaviour measure was not chosen for the multivariate analysis of this health outcome. In contrast, smoking in adolescence and behaviour in school appeared to contribute towards class differences in the other health measures, and so both were selected for inclusion in the later analyses.

11

Integrating and comparing explanations for class differences in health

11.1 Introduction

Each of the groups of explanatory variables that were introduced in the theoretical framework (Chapter 1) have now been examined individually (Chapters 6 to 10). So far, however, the influence of each variable on class differences in four selected health measures has been established from simple comparisons only. This chapter proceeds to the second stage of analysis, outlined in Chapter 5, by bringing together several key explanatory variables in an attempt to explain health differences.

The conclusions to Chapters 6 to 10 identified variables that appeared to make the greatest contribution to health differences (as indicated by the reduction in relative odds achieved after adjustment for separate variables). These are shown in Table 11.1, according to the area of explanation they represent. Despite the large number of variables examined, the table shows considerable similarity in those selected for further analysis. For example, social class at birth, the behaviour score and smoking habits at age 16 were chosen from their respective groups of explanatory variables as they appeared to make the greatest contribution to class differences in health. Whereas, for education and attitudes only one variable was selected – namely, the level of qualifications achieved at the end of schooling – as an appropriate summary measure of the many educational variables that reduced health differences. Similarities between explanatory variables selected for further analyses of self-rated health, malaise and psychological morbidity may in part reflect similarities in the measures themselves, while for adult height, not surprisingly, the variables tended to differ.

Further analyses of health differences required complete data for several variables (identified in Table 11.1) and, accordingly, sample sizes were substantially reduced. It is important to digress at this point to determine the effects of this.

Table 11.1 Variables selected for multivariate analyses of four health measures

Area of explanation	Index of health at age 23							
	Men				Women			
	Self-rated health (n = 2652)	Malaise' (n = 2650)	Psychological morbidity (n = 3632)	Height (n = 2951)	Self-rated health (n = 2827)	Malaise' (n = 2839)	Psychological morbidity (n = 3190)	Height (n = 3073)
'Inheritance' at birth	Social class at birth	Social class at birth	Social class at birth	Parent's height	Social class at birth	Social class at birth	Mother smoking during pregnancy	Parent's height
Socio-economic circumstances	Housing tenure at 11 and unemployment between 16 and 23	Housing tenure at 11 and unemployment between 16 and 23	Unemployment between 16 and 23	Social class at 7	Housing tenure at 11 and age at first child and unemployment between 16 and 23	Housing tenure at 11 and age at first child	Age at first child and unemployment between 16 and 23	Social class at 7
Education/attitudes	End of school qualifications	End of school qualifications	End of school qualifications	End of school qualifications	End of school qualifications	End of school qualifications	End of school qualifications	End of school qualifications
Health in childhood and adolescence	School absence*	School absence*		Height at ages 7 and 11	School absence*	School absence*	School absence*	Height at ages 7 and 11
Behaviour	Smoking and behaviour score at age 16	Smoking and behaviour score at age 16	Smoking and behaviour score at age 16		Smoking and behaviour score at age 16	Smoking and behaviour score at age 16	Smoking and behaviour score at age 16	

*School absence through ill-health between age 15 and 16.

11.2 Response

Two main problems arose, the first of which concerned the representativeness of the samples available for this stage of the analysis. Response comparisons reported in Appendix D show that these samples differed significantly from the original sample in several respects. However, when the relationship of earlier characteristics with social class at age 23 was examined, which is the focus of this investigation, only for one health outcome measure, adult height, did significant biases remain. In general, the results of these analyses were reassuring. However, they were contingent, in part, upon the solution to the second problem associated with a reduced sample.

The second problem concerned the number of variables selected for analysis, which as currently structured, would result in too few observations for multi-classification due to the reduced sample size. In order to avoid this difficulty variables were regrouped (Appendix D, Table D.3) and for the analyses of height, one parental measure (the average of the mother's and father's heights – midparent height) was used rather than two separate variables for the mother and father. So while the final categorization was not as finely differentiated as originally conceived, it enabled the simultaneous inclusion of all variables in the analyses. As mentioned above, regrouping of variables had some advantages in terms of response comparisons (Appendix D).

11.3 Results

Returning to the main focus of this chapter, results of the multivariate analyses will be given, but, before proceeding, the first tables in this section attempt to clarify the underlying relationships operating within the analyses. As explained in Chapter 5, the contribution of each variable towards class differences in health reflects their simultaneous association with both the health outcome measure and social class at age 23. These associations are discussed separately.

11.3.1 Selected explanatory variables and health outcomes

Relationships between explanatory variables and health outcomes, presented in Table 11.2, are summarized by odds ratios which contrast the odds of poor health in one subgroup (for example, smoker at age 16) with the other subgroup for the variable (non-smoker in our example). This table demonstrates how all the variables, apart from social class at birth and housing tenure, were significantly associated with each of three health outcomes – namely, self-rated health, malaise and

Table 11.2 Associations between poor health and selected earlier characteristics,§ expressed as relative odds

Area of explanation/selected variables§	Men†			Women†		
	'Poor' or 'fair' self-rated health	High malaise score	Psychological morbidity	'Poor' or 'fair' self-rated health	High malaise score	Psychological morbidity
'Inheritance' at birth:						
Social class (manual versus non-manual)	1.36	1.36	1.17	1.67*	2.02*	1.10
Socio-economic circumstances:						
Housing tenure at age 11 (renters versus owners)	1.19	1.64*	1.19	1.89*	2.02*	1.05
Unemployment by age 23 (one or more periods versus none)	1.68*	1.74*	3.49*	1.35*	1.43*	1.94*
Age at first child (child by 23 versus no child)	–	–	–	1.85*	2.10*	1.44*
Education/attitudes:						
End of school qualifications (none versus one or more)	1.83*	3.09*	1.32*	2.73*	3.17*	1.62*
Health in childhood/adolescence:						
School absence through ill-health‡ (>1 week versus <1 week)	2.07*	3.00*	1.36	1.85*	1.79*	1.47*
Behaviour:						
Smoking at 16 (smoker versus non-smoker)	1.80*	2.67*	1.60*	1.67*	2.23*	1.78*
Behaviour score at 16 ('deviant' versus 'normal')	3.16*	4.56*	3.97*	3.17*	4.10*	3.28*

§Indicated in Table 11.1 (refer to Appendix D, Table D.3, for details of categories).
†Based on samples shown in Table 11.1.
‡During preceding year.
*95% confidence interval excludes 1.

psychological morbidity. (Adult height is excluded from the table; the explanatory variables selected for this health measure differ substantially from those for the other three.) The highest relative odds, which were greater than threefold, emerged for the behaviour rating ('deviantly' rated 16 year olds versus those rated as 'normal') and this applied to both sexes on each health measure. Relative odds in excess of three were also apparent for qualifications at the end of school and school absence in relation to malaise, although the latter applied to the men only.

11.3.2 Selected explanatory variables and social class at 23

Next, explanatory variables were examined in relation to social class at age 23 and again the contrast is expressed as relative odds (Table 11.3). For example, for class at birth the table indicates the odds of having manual class origins (as opposed to non-manual origins) for those in classes IV and V at age 23 relative to those in classes I and II at 23. Of the explanatory variables examined both school behaviour and qualifications at the end of school were strongly associated with class at age 23 (the relative odds were greater than 10 in each case). School absence, on the other hand, with relative odds of 2.31 in men and 2.48 in women, showed a weaker association. This suggests that school absence will provide a weaker contribution towards class differences in health than the behaviour rating or qualifications at the end of school. Table 11.3 also shows raised relative odds for women according to the variable age at first child, suggesting that this may be an important characteristic in the multivariate models.

11.3.3 Multivariate analyses

Consideration of Tables 11.2 and 11.3 provides some indication of the relative importance of selected explanatory variables, but better evidence is available from multivariate analyses.

Tables 11.4 to 11.7 present the odds of poor health among those in classes IV and V relative to those in classes I and II, adjusting for inheritance at birth, socio-economic background, education, earlier health and behaviour. Results are given for men and women and the four health measures separately. The unadjusted figures are provided at the top of each table and, subsequently, the relative odds are adjusted for variables in the sequence given in the tables. As explained in Chapter 5, the ordering of variables reflects a temporal sequence but references to cases in which the timing is not so clear will be made in the text. It is also important to restate at this point that the reduction in relative odds occurs as the cumulative effect of adjusting for the first

Table 11.3 Associations between social class at 23 and selected earlier characteristics,§ expressed as relative odds (classes IV and V versus I and II)

Area of explanation/selected variables§	Men (*n* = 2652)†	Women (*n* = 2827)†
'Inheritance' at birth:		
Social class (manual versus non-manual)	3.68*	4.54*
Socio-economic circumstances:		
Housing tenure at age 11 (renters versus owners)	3.74*	5.70*
Unemployment by age 23 (one or more periods versus none)	4.05*	2.17*
Age at first child (child by 23 versus no child)	3.58*	11.35*
Education/attitudes:		
End of school qualifications (none versus one or more)	11.25*	12.78*
Health in childhood/adolescence:		
School absence through ill-health‡ (>1 week versus <1 week)	2.31*	2.48*
Behaviour:		
Smoking at 16 (smoker versus non-smoker)	3.72*	3.00*
Behaviour score at 16 ('deviant' versus 'normal')	14.60*	10.97*

§Indicated in Table 11.1 (refer to Appendix D, Table D.3, for details of categories).
†Based on sample selected for self-rated health (Table 11.1).
‡During preceding year.
*95% confidence interval excludes 1.

variable, and then the second in addition to the first, and so on until all variables have been included.

All but two of the analyses in Tables 11.4 to 11.7 show that a significant class difference (indicated by 95% confidence intervals) became non-significant after adjusting for all the variables in the model. The exceptions occurred in the comparison of malaise in young women (Table 11.5) which was notable because the unadjusted relative odds were greatest for this group and in self-rated health among men (Table 11.4), although the class differential remaining at the end of this analysis was of borderline significance only (95% confidence interval = 1.03, 3.01).

Comparing the relative odds before adjustments were made with those achieved after controlling for all the explanatory variables, there were reductions of over 50% for two out of four health measures among men, and three out of four among women. As will emerge from the description of individual health measures given below, some variables were particularly prominent in producing these results.

a) Self-rated health

Table 11.4 shows comparatively small reductions in the relative odds of poor or fair rating of health after adjustment for 'inheritance' at birth as represented by social class. Subsequently, the introduction of housing tenure at age 11 into the analysis was associated with no further reduction beyond that already established among the men, but for women the class differential was almost one-fifth less than the unadjusted odds ratio as a result of allowing for socio-economic circumstances during childhood and 'inheritance' at birth. Even so, substantial class differentials in poor rating of health, of almost threefold in men and over twofold in women, persisted after allowing for the combined influences of these earlier circumstances.

Table 11.4 Relative odds of subjects rating their health as 'poor' or 'fair' (classes IV and V versus I and II) adjusting for 'inheritance' at birth, socio-economic background, educational achievement, earlier health and behaviour; 95% confidence intervals shown in brackets

	Men (*n* = 2652)
Unadjusted	3.04 (1.83, 5.05)
Adjusted for:	
Social class at birth	2.90*
and Housing tenure at 11	2.91*
and Behaviour score at 16	2.25*
and School absence through ill-health†	2.09*
and Smoking at 16	1.96*
and End of school qualifications	1.86*
and Unemployment	1.71*

	Women (*n* = 2827)
Unadjusted	3.28 (2.12, 5.05)
Adjusted for:	
Social class at birth	3.00*
and Housing tenure at 11	2.66*
and Behaviour score at 16	2.16*
and School absence through ill-health†	2.05*
and Smoking at 16	2.00*
and End of school qualifications	1.62*
and Unemployment	1.58
and Age at first child	1.52

†Age 15–16.
*95% confidence interval excludes 1.

The next variable introduced into the analysis was the behaviour score at age 16, which had reduced the class differentials by about a third in the simple analyses (Table 10.1). This effect was diminished by simultaneously allowing for class at birth and housing tenure during childhood, but the contribution was still comparatively substantial, especially for men. Henceforth, variables included in the analyses along with class at birth, housing tenure and adolescent behaviour, made a smaller contribution to the overall reduction in relative odds.

Even so, it is noteworthy that the later variables still exerted some effect. For example, adjusting for male unemployment between ages 16 and 23 reduced the relative odds from 1.86 to 1.71 – not a large reduction but one achieved after adjusting for six earlier variables. For women, a twofold difference in odds remaining after adjustment for social class at birth, housing tenure and school behaviour was not greatly affected by the addition of two further variables into the model (school absence through ill-health and smoking at 16 years) but the odds were then reduced by 11% after allowing for qualifications at the end of schooling.

The sequence in which variables were included into the models had an obvious temporal ordering in most cases. However, the ordering of variables was not as clear when more than one variable was included for a particular age; for example, behaviour rating, school absence through ill-health and smoking all refer to age 16. Arbitrary decisions were taken in such cases (as indicated in Table 11.4). Although they are not presented here, further analyses were performed to assess how these arbitrary orderings affected the results and, in general, the main findings were not substantially altered.

b) Malaise
Trends for malaise (Table 11.5) resemble those described above for self-rated health, with the most substantial reductions occurring after allowing for behaviour score at age 16 and qualifications at the end of school and, among women, for social class at birth and housing tenure at age 11. It was particularly striking, however, that odds of malaise among women in classes IV and V were more than two and a half times those in classes I and II even after controlling for all seven major influences.

c) Psychological morbidity
Table 11.6 shows that class contrasts in psychological morbidity were also affected by behaviour score at 16, and this effect was largely undiminished by prior adjustment for earlier circumstances. The odds ratio reduced by 35% in men and 27% in women further to that achieved by the 'inheritance' variable. However, trends for this health measure differed from self-rated health and malaise in other respects. In particular, socio-economic circumstances between ages 16 and 23, represented

Table 11.5 Relative odds of malaise (classes IV and V versus I and II) adjusting for 'inheritance' at birth, socio-economic background, educational achievement, earlier health and behaviour; 95% confidence intervals shown in brackets

	Men (*n* = 2650)
Unadjusted	3.90 (1.95, 7.82)
Adjusted for:	
Social class at birth	3.48*
and Housing tenure at 11	3.58*
and Behaviour score at 16	2.55*
and School absence through ill-health†	2.28*
and Smoking at 16	2.01
and End of school qualifications	1.58
and Unemployment	1.58

	Women (*n* = 2839)
Unadjusted	5.84 (3.63, 9.40)
Adjusted for:	
Social class at birth	5.24*
and Housing tenure at 11	4.58*
and Behaviour score at 16	3.62*
and School absence through ill-health†	3.50*
and Smoking at 16	3.30*
and End of school qualifications	2.75*
and Age at first child	2.68*

†Age 15–16.
*95% confidence interval excludes 1.

here by unemployment since leaving school, produced a substantial reduction in the relative odds of psychological morbidity in men (that is, of 12%), even though four other variables had already been accounted for. In contrast to self-rated health and malaise, the contribution of qualifications to class differentials among women were no longer apparent in the analyses for psychological morbidity.

d) Adult height
Some common themes have emerged from results for self-rated health, malaise and psychological morbidity, but findings for adult height show a different pattern altogether since class contrasts were affected largely by variables characterizing 'inheritance' and early childhood (Table 11.7). Thus, adjusting for the average of the mother's and father's heights (midparent height) substantially reduced the relative odds of short stature in adulthood, and the height of the individual at age 7 further reduced the relative odds for both men and women.

There are considerable advantages to be gained from the inclusion of an earlier (related) measure of the early adulthood health outcome. For

Table 11.6 Relative odds of psychological morbidity (classes IV and V versus I and II) adjusting for 'inheritance' at birth, socio-economic background, educational achievement, earlier health and behaviour; 95% confidence intervals shown in brackets

	Men ($n = 3632$)
Unadjusted	2.32 (1.34, 4.03)
Adjusted for:	
Social class at birth	2.26*
and Behaviour score at 16	1.51*
and Smoking at 16	1.47
and End of school qualifications	1.56
and Unemployment	1.20

	Women ($n = 3190$)
Unadjusted	2.33 (1.46, 3.72)
Adjusted for:	
Mothers smoking during pregnancy	2.27*
and Behaviour score at 16	1.71*
and School absence through ill-health†	1.66*
and Smoking at 16	1.60
and End of school qualifications	1.59
and Unemployment	1.47
and Age at first child	1.48

*95% confidence interval excludes 1.
†Age 15–16.

Table 11.7 Relative odds of short stature (classes IV and V versus I and II) adjusting for 'inheritance' at birth, earlier health, educational achievement and socio-economic background; 95% confidence intervals shown in brackets

	Men ($n = 2951$)
Unadjusted	2.43 (1.60, 3.68)
Adjusted for:	
Midparent height†	1.71*
and Social class at 7	1.68*
and Height at 7	1.17
and Height at 11	1.15
and End of school qualifications	1.10

	Women ($n = 3073$)
Unadjusted	2.27 (1.55, 3.32)
Adjusted for:	
Midparent height†	1.65*
and Social class at 7	1.38
and Height at 7	0.93
and Height at 11	0.90
and End of school qualifications	0.97

*95% confidence interval excludes 1.
†The average of the mother's and father's heights.

example, in the analyses of adulthood short stature described above, class differentials no longer existed after the introduction of height at age 7 in addition to 'inheritance', suggesting that explanatory events occurring after this age are of negligible importance relative to those occurring before this age. Inclusion of an earlier indicator of the later health measure under consideration can, therefore, indicate the stage of life for a particular health measure that is likely to be especially influential in accounting for class differences.

A related advantage is that, having allowed for influences up to a specific age, it is then possible to clarify the extent to which later events and circumstances add to these earlier contributions. Furthermore, allowing for earlier health improves an appreciation of class differences in health that follow rather than predate particular circumstances. As an illustration, the effect of unemployment on health can be established only after the state of health that preceded unemployment has been taken into account. The same argument applies to an examination of class differences in health. This point will be pursued in the discussion, but here it is necessary to return to the analyses of adulthood short stature and Table 11.7.

The table suggested that further examination of earlier circumstances was warranted. So far, relationships between class differences and the 'inheritance' variables were examined in separate analyses (Chapter 6) except for midparent height, which was included in the multivariate model. However, social class at birth and, to a lesser extent, birthweight had also appeared to contribute to class differences and these variables could be examined in addition to midparent heights in order to achieve a more complete view of the contribution of 'inheritance'.

Additional analyses were therefore conducted and the results are given in Table 11.8. It was difficult to impose a temporal sequence here, although the timing of variables was considered. The table shows that adjustment for the additional inheritance variables does achieve a further reduction (beyond that in Table 11.7) before height at age 7 is introduced, but the resultant relative odds were still significantly different from 1 and only became non-significant when height at age 7 was included.

Finally, although each area of the study framework was represented in the analyses for comparison, this was a formality in cases where the contribution was marginal. Consequently, such variables were excluded from a further set of analyses that examined the simultaneous relationship between health, social class at 23 and the remaining explanatory variables. Table B.6 in Appendix B illustrates the extent of differences between extreme classes after allowing for other variables and contrasts this with differentials relating to the other variables. Substantial differentials remained in some cases – for example, when comparing the

Table 11.8 Relative odds of short stature (classes IV and V versus I and II) adjusting for 'inheritance' at birth, and childhood height

	Men ($n = 3664$)
Unadjusted	2.36 (1.65, 3.37)
Adjusted for:	
Midparent height†	1.63*
and Social class at birth	1.67*
and Birthweight	1.55*
and Height at 7	1.11

	Women ($n = 3818$)
Unadjusted	2.31 (1.66, 3.23)
Adjusted for:	
Midparent height†	1.59*
and Social class at birth	1.47*
and Birthweight	1.38
and Height at 7	0.97

*95% confidence interval excludes 1.
†The average of the mother's and father's heights.

odds of psychological morbidity in men who had been unemployed since leaving school with those who had not. Odds of poor health in the 'deviant' relative to the 'normal' behaviour groups were also significantly raised, even after simultaneous account had been taken of the other variables. Together with the comparisons in Table 11.2, this demonstrates the extent to which self-rated health, malaise and psychological morbidity at age 23 were differentiated not just by social class but by behaviour rating, in particular at age 16.

11.4 Discussion

As stated in the introduction, the purpose of this chapter was to assess the relative and cumulative contribution of potential explanations for class differences in health among young adults. The analyses presented here allow some conclusions in this respect, although it is important to reiterate how methodological considerations necessarily affect the interpretation of the results.

Perhaps the most important of these considerations is that while a temporal sequence has a logical attraction, we cannot presume that because particular circumstances or characteristics *precede* others that relationships are *causal*. It may even be the case that the true or 'causal' relationships have been obscured by allowing for earlier circumstances with which later characteristics are associated. In other words, it is not possible to determine from a study such as this, if at all, whether earlier variables confound later 'causal' relationships. But even if this were the case, the earlier variables might be considered as 'causal' to the extent that they influence the later attributes (beliefs, behaviours and social circumstances) which become closely intertwined. It is no surprise, therefore, that causes of class differences are difficult to unravel.

Also, the contribution of areas identified in the theoretical framework – inheritance at birth, socio-economic circumstances, health, behaviour and education – depend, in part, upon the breadth of characteristics representing a particular area (i.e. the number of variables in the analysis). This is illustrated for adult height, since the contribution of 'inheritance' was assessed from analyses using several variables (Table 11.8) and a single variable (Table 11.7). A further problem is that wide confidence intervals surrounded the relative odds, despite the large samples studied. Hence, it is difficult to decide when class differences in the health outcomes have been 'explained' adequately.

Nonetheless, the analyses described in this chapter are useful in respect of this enquiry. Multivariate analyses allow simultaneous consideration of a variety of potential explanations and enable us to comment upon their relative contribution. It is thus possible, for example, to compare the influence of 'inheritance' with that of later individual behaviour. Moreover, these observations do not appear to be undermined by the sample attrition that had occurred in constituting the groups for analysis. A comparison of different samples suggests that those used in the present chapter represented the relationships under consideration (Appendix D), although for analyses of adult height shown in Table 11.8 the effect of class at birth is underestimated.

In the discussion of class differences in health which follows, the contribution of particular characteristics will be considered in relation to the groups of potential explanations that have provided the framework for this enquiry (Figure 1.4).

'Inheritance' at birth was relatively unimportant in accounting for class differences, especially in men, and also especially for the psychological morbidity measure. Its effect could be underestimated as a result of regrouping the explanatory variable social class at birth from five original categories into just two: non-manual and manual. However, categories for several other variables in the multivariate analyses were also collapsed and it is relative to these other variables that 'inheritance' was being assessed.

Contrasting with this general finding, 'inheritance' appeared to be more influential in the case of height, accounting for a large part of the excess odds of short stature in classes IV and V when compared to classes I and II. This important contribution may be enhanced if more 'inheritance' variables are introduced into the final models. However, it is of interest to note that class differentials in short stature persisted after controlling for 'inheritance' – although not significantly for women – and it remains possible that class differences will not be totally explained by 'inheritance' factors. A similar conclusion is suggested from the work of Kuh and Wadsworth (1989) who showed that class differences in adult height were reduced but not eliminated by a combination of factors, including birthweight, birth order, number of siblings, parents' height and father's education. Further, although the methods differ from those used here, the total contribution of such factors towards class differences is estimated to be of a similar magnitude in both studies.

For adult short stature the present work confirms that differences originate in factors operating early in life. Attempts to further disentangle the relative influences of such factors were made but were not exhaustive. It is important to note in this respect that the nature and timing of the data may not be adequate for this task; for example, information on diet may be relevant to class differences in adult stature and it would also be desirable to monitor circumstances between birth and age 7.

At this point it is pertinent to consider the extent to which social and economic circumstances during childhood affected class differences in the other health measures in addition to those aspects represented in 'inheritance'. For self-rated health and malaise early circumstances were considered separately from recent socio-economic circumstances; while for psychological morbidity the simple analyses in Chapter 7 had already suggested that early circumstances were relatively unimportant. Analyses presented in this chapter suggest that early socio-economic background was important for self-rated health and malaise among women, but unimportant for these health measures among men, once 'inheritance' (social class) at birth was taken into account.

The contribution of *recent* socio-economic background was diminished considerably because of the stage in the analyses at which variables representing this (unemployment and age at first child) were introduced. It is particularly in relation to these influences, therefore, that previous remarks about causality and ordering of variables in the models (page 144) apply. The results do not suggest that recent socio-economic background is unimportant, but that after taking several earlier background factors (i.e. those in Tables 11.4 to 11.6) into account with which they are inter-correlated, the additional effect of, say recent family formation, is minimal.

Even so, not all of the effect of unemployment was removed, particularly for young adult men. This is an interesting finding in view of the characteristics already accounted for in the analyses. It is particularly important that the behaviour score had already been included. As argued in Chapters 9 and 10, this measure can be regarded, to some extent, as an indicator of psychological well-being. Since behaviour was ascertained *before* unemployment, the approach adopted here allows estimation of the contribution of unemployment towards social class differences in health that is unaffected by the prior movement of the psychologically unfit into the lower social classes. In other words, the contribution of unemployment cannot be attributed to health selection. The use of longitudinal data, therefore, has important implications for this attempt to unravel the processes through which class differences develop, and overcomes limitations that are inherent in investigations which rely on cross-sectional data.

All explanations for differences in self-rated health, malaise and psychological morbidity that have been considered, tend to be over-shadowed by the rating of school behaviour, which was judged by the teacher. This measure was notable for a consistent and comparatively substantial reduction in class differentials. Such consistencies are likely to reflect similarities in the health outcome measures (i.e. they were intended as measures of psychological health or were influenced by it) as well as common origins of social differences among young adults.

The complexities of the behaviour rating have been discussed in Chapter 10 and in section C.2 of Appendix C. This enquiry has not resolved (a) whether the rating detects behaviours that will be hazard-ous for later emotional well-being through the isolation and disapproval they may incur or (b) whether emotional problems detected by the teachers continue into early adulthood. However, it is apparent from the results presented in this chapter that 16 year olds identified as 'deviant' from the teachers' ratings had significantly raised odds of poorer health at age 23 and were also more likely to be members of a lower social class during their early working lives.

Among women the contribution of the behaviour rating was affected by the prior inclusion of social class at birth and housing tenure during childhood, but this effect was less pronounced in men. Consequently, it may appear as though the rating provides a more powerful expla-nation for class differences in health for men than for women, and reference to the simple relationships (Tables 10.1 to 10.3) shows that there is some evidence for this, especially for the malaise health out-come. Moreover, the comparisons of the behaviour rating with health outcomes on the one hand and social class at 23 on the other (Tables 11.2 and 11.3) were suggestive of slightly stronger associations for men than women, and this is compatible with an enhanced role for school behaviour in men.

One possible explanation is that the transition from school to early adulthood involves changes in life circumstances that are more con-ducive to symptoms of malaise in women than in men (for example, women get married earlier and will have experienced longer periods at home by age 23, some of them with young children) and this weakens the association between emotional problems at ages 16 and 23. An alternative or perhaps compounding explanation is that disparities between the measures and their methods of symptom assessment (by teachers at age 16 and self-rating at age 23), together with sex differences in symptom reporting, would affect identification of psychological problems. There is support for this since illness is considered to be less stigmatizing for women: 'the female gender role may contribute to the inclination to give attention to and evaluate ambiguous or mild body cues as symptoms of illness' (Hibbard and Pope, 1983). Men may be more reluctant to admit to symptoms or consult with a doctor than women, but so far insufficient data are available to evaluate this (Nathanson, 1975). In the present context, it is intriguing that such influences might affect the relationships observed for behaviour rating and malaise in men and women, but not also for self-rated health (Table 11.2).

While the school behaviour rating bridges two groups of potential explanations for class differences, earlier health and behaviour, there is only weak evidence for an additional contribution from the other variables representing these two groups. In general, therefore, much of the effect of school absence through ill-health and adolescent smoking had become subsumed by variables included in the analyses at an earlier stage, although this was less applicable to men. There is an advantage, however, in considering behaviour before school absence through ill-health which relates to the adequacy of the childhood health measure. The latter is likely to be affected by unjustified absenteeism, but by adjusting for school behaviour prior to the health measure such problems can be minimized.

Even when school absence through ill-health was considered before the behaviour rating, and the contribution of the former was thereby increased, the behaviour rating remained more prominent in terms of reducing class differences in poor health. Earlier health and behaviour therefore emerge as comparatively important areas of explanation for differences in the health measures examined here, but mainly through the behaviour rating at age 16.

The final group of explanatory variables investigated in relation to class differences among young adults comprised education and training. As expected, qualifications at the end of school were strongly associated with subsequent social class and health at age 23 and these relationships underscore the simple analyses in Chapter 8 in which the education variables made a substantial impact on class differences in health. This contribution was appreciably diminished in analyses presented in this chapter. However, reductions were achieved after several other explanations – 'inheritance', early socio-economic background, health and behaviour – had already been taken into account. As for socio-economic variables representing recent experiences of young adults, the analyses shown here suggest that the contribution of education is exclusive of any effect of earlier emotional health (indicated by behaviour rating at age 16) on educational achievement and, thereby, subsequent class differences. Since education, as represented by qualifications at the end of school, made a contribution to class differences in self-rated health and malaise after prior consideration of other factors, there is an argument for a direct role of education (see Chapter 8).

11.5 Conclusions

In general, class differences in health have largely been explained by the characteristics and circumstances examined in this chapter. The main exception was the difference in malaise among women. For all health measures, odds ratios of poor health in classes IV and V compared with classes I and II were reduced by more than a third and in several instances more than halved. The method of analysis used showed the extent to which particular characteristics contributed to class differences after *preceding* characteristics had been taken into account. In this respect, the method indicates the cumulative impact of a sequence of events and circumstances.

The analyses provided justification for all of the broad areas of potential explanation to be considered in relation to class differences, but some explanations were more prominent for specific health outcomes than others. 'Inheritance' was especially important for differences in height, and although it appeared to be much less so for the other health measures, its contribution towards differences among women (self-rated health and malaise) is noteworthy. Socio-economic background, separated into earlier and later circumstances, was especially relevant to psychological morbidity in men and self-rated health and malaise in women, but some of the effect of the socio-economic variables was necessarily reduced by adjustments for other variables.

Earlier indicators of health most closely related to the adult health outcome – namely, height and possibly the behaviour rating – were, as expected, particularly influential in explaining class differences. Nonetheless, it is interesting that adolescent behaviour does not explain entirely class differences in malaise, psychological morbidity or self-rated health. Education and later socio-economic circumstances are also relatively important in explaining class differences in these health outcomes. Despite some variations, the findings suggest some common origins in class differences in self-rated health, malaise and psychological morbidity.

12

Discussion

Social differences in mortality, which have been documented for the British population since the last century, are now found in many countries. There are also several studies which show that, as well as having shorter lives, people in lower social classes experience more morbidity and disability than those in higher classes. In developed nations the attenuation of these differences constitute an important challenge. To ignore this challenge is unjust (Chalmers, 1985) and may also be short-sighted since recent studies suggest that reduced socio-economic inequality is necessary for an improvement in our national average life expectancy (Marmot and Davey-Smith, 1989; Wilkinson, 1989).

If differences are to be minimized more precise knowledge is needed of how social position is related to health and disease. This challenge provides the impetus for the research described in this book. Several strategies might be useful in this respect. A society-wide approach – that is, one looking at macro level explanations – provides one alternative. Another, which is the one chosen for the present study, focuses on the life course of individuals. Both approaches can be justified; each informs the other and, as with most research, it is likely that neither can provide all the answers.

The main aim of the work described here was to:

1. attempt to 'explain' differences in health between social classes in a national sample of young adults;

and in order to do this, two additional aims were identified:

2. to suggest a framework for investigating health differences within a population which (a) brings together several potential explanatory areas and (b) acknowledges that the differences observed at a particular point in time are contingent upon past experiences, as well as those currently prevailing;

3. to document the extent of social class differences in health during early adulthood.

The intention behind these aims was to broaden the conceptual framework from that commonly used to investigate explanations for differences in health between social groups, so that a more comprehensive view of the numerous underlying relationships might be achieved. Hence, the framework brought together several potential explanations that had been identified from the literature (Figure 1.4). These were grouped under five main headings: 'inheritance' at birth, socio-economic circumstances, education and attitudes, earlier health and individual behaviour.

Even though such models simplify many of the relationships that are involved, they invite criticisms that they are too complex. For example, Carr-Hill (1985) comments on his own efforts to provide a more sophisticated analysis of health differences that 'it and similar mental models are sufficiently complex to generate controversies and doubts about the correct interpretation of empirical studies'. While this might also apply to the work presented here, it has been demonstrated, nonetheless, that it is possible to extend beyond the confines of the restricted analyses that characterize much of the research in this field.

The conceptual framework provided a useful structure for the enquiry, but this structure is not fixed and modifications will be needed. As in other studies, some difficulties arose in operationalizing broad areas contained in the study framework (Chapter 5). It has not been possible to represent anything approaching the true interrelationships within particular areas. Combinations of events and circumstances are likely to be more powerful influences than any single factor, but in this study broad explanatory areas were represented usually by one, or at most three, variable(s).

Methods used to investigate the contribution of different explanatory variables to health differences were based on certain assumptions. As Thurnhurst (1984) stated:

'. . . statistical information is not a value-free instrument which somehow "speaks for itself"; it is socially constructed. Choice of data scrutinized, interpretation of information produced, and even the technical procedures employed necessarily reflect the ideological perspective of the analyst.'

So, however much effort is invested in impartiality, alternative methods and interpretation are possible. In the present work, for example, how do we determine what constitutes a substantial contribution towards class differences in health? Such issues are not always resolved by statistics. It is difficult, therefore, to decide when class differences in health have been 'explained' adequately. Also, while attempting to adhere to the timing of explanatory variables, some of the ordering was inevitably arbitrary. Even if this were not the case, a sequence does not overcome all difficulties of attributing cause and effect.

The study was limited to investigating health inequalities that had developed by early adulthood. This is a relatively healthy stage of life which inevitably influences the health outcomes that can be investigated. From the health measures available, only four were examined in detail and some important measures (such as disability and fitness) have not yet been considered. Other measures are appropriate for investigating health differences in early adulthood, and extending the analyses to include these measures would be desirable. Later – as the cohort ages, ill-health becomes more prevalent, and conditions are more limiting – there will be other possible health outcomes that can be considered.

The NCDS data were not collected specifically for the purpose of the present volume. Hence, there were some instances where additional explanatory variables would have been valuable. In general, however, this did not present a substantial problem. In the particular area of parents' health and health-related behaviour, the analyses have not yet been conducted even though the relationships are suggested in the framework for the study (Figure 1.4). Despite the large sample available initially, sample size becomes a constraint when several factors are investigated simultaneously, and this has consequences for the analysis (Chapter 11). So too does the sample representativeness (Appendix D), as this can influence the way in which factors are considered.

Against these constraints there are considerable advantages of the approach used in the present study. It is important to emphasize that the strengths – in particular, those relating to the breadth of explanatory variables and the temporal sequencing in the analysis – far outweigh the weaknesses described above. Hence, the data available in the NCDS were considered to be more than adequate for the task that was set in this volume. Also, this investigation was systematic in examining separately each of the broad areas identified in the framework. It could be argued, therefore, that this work goes beyond previous studies even before the final stage of analysis was used to integrate different explanations. Chapter 11 provided the crucial element, however, in assessing the cumulative effect of several explanatory variables and incorporating a time dimension into the analyses. Consequently, it has been possible to contribute to the health inequalities debate in many respects.

The main findings of the work can be summarized as follows.

First, in Chapter 3 it was shown that, in the study population of young adults born in 1958, there was a general trend of higher prevalence of reported disease, symptoms of illness and shorter stature in lower compared with higher classes; but the extent of differences depended on the health indicator. Of the numerous indicators examined, differences appeared to be most marked for malaise and for respiratory symptoms, as ascertained from the Medical Research Council (MRC) approved questions. However, for some reported conditions such as for migraine/recurrent sick headaches and fits/convulsions, the prevalence was similar in each social class, and for others – namely, hayfever and eczema – the gradient reversed. Social differences in selected health measures were demonstrated irrespective of the socio-economic measure used: social class, housing tenure, education or level of income.

Since early adulthood is a relatively healthy stage of life, social differences might not always be as pronounced as at older ages. In this group of young people, psychological problems were especially important, accounting for much of the morbidity. Two health measures (malaise and psychological morbidity) used in the detailed analyses were chosen to reflect this, while two other measures (self-rated health and height) were intended as general assessments of health.

Second, it was found that social mobility was not a major influence on class differences in these selected health measures (Chapter 4). It was particularly important to assess the effects of mobility in early adulthood because the change from class based on father's occupation to that based on own occupation is associated with a much higher degree of mobility than that occurring at older ages. The impact of selection might therefore be expected to be commensurate with this. A considerable amount of intergenerational mobility was indeed evident in the 1958 cohort study: it was found that young adults who were upwardly socially mobile were healthier than the group they had left and, conversely, those who were downwardly mobile were less healthy than the group they had left. Despite this, even for those health measures where the effect of mobility was greatest, the evidence from Chapter 4 suggests that mobility is not the only, nor indeed the major, influence on social differences in health at this stage of life.

Third, a systematic examination of other potential influences, organized under the headings identified in the study framework ('inheritance' at birth, socio-economic circumstances, education/attitudes, health of individual, and behaviour) produced many interesting findings, about which some general comments are needed. In particular, it was only rarely that social differences were largely explained (in a statistical sense) by any single variable. Even before undertaking the further analyses, it became apparent that there were usually several rather than a single cause for discrepant health experiences between social groups. This confirmed the necessity of a multivariate approach. However, before turning to the results from the multivariate analyses, some explanations were particularly prominent in the first (or area by area) stage.

'Inheritance' at birth, while defined for the purposes of the study framework as including both environmental and genetic characteristics, was operationalized with variables from the NCDS that were overwhelmingly environmental in their emphasis. The contribution of 'inheritance' was especially marked in relation to differences in adult short stature between social classes, but not as important for other health measures (Chapter 6). Socio-economic background was of more general significance for health differences at age 23, although again there were variations between the health measures. Both class and housing circumstances during childhood contributed to health differences, but later socio-economic circumstances were notable, especially for self-rated health and malaise (Chapter 7). Education was also important, which was not surprising given the role of qualifications in sorting individuals into occupations (Chapter 8). The contribution of individual behaviour was particularly notable in respect of smoking and social behaviour as rated by a teacher (Chapter 10). Childhood health was relevant to subsequent class differences in health only where it appeared that a similar dimension of health was being considered – namely, for height and for emotional health. Continuity in health problems inevitably plays a part in this. Otherwise, more diverse measures of health in childhood were less relevant to subsequent class differences in the particular health outcomes examined here (Chapter 9).

It is apparent from the above that there was considerable variation both in the extent to which all variables defining an explanatory area contributed to social class differences in health, as well as contrasts between areas. For example, the contribution of education was apparent, irrespective of the variable used to represent it, whereas that associated with individual behaviour was more dependent on the specific characteristic examined. This is not surprising, considering the different mechanisms through which particular events and circumstances are likely to influence social differences in health.

Fourth, the final stage of the work brought together the important variables identified from the earlier stage and incorporated these into a set of integrated analyses (Chapter 11). In doing so, it was possible to introduce time ordering into the investigation. Few studies adopt a multivariate approach (exceptions include the studies of Valkonen and Martelin, 1988, and Lundberg, 1991) and to our knowledge there have been no previous attempts to sequence events although Carr-Hill (1985) suggested that such analyses were needed in his examination of health and income.

For the selected health outcomes considered at age 23, class differences were largely 'explained' only after accounting for several variables. It is notable that a substantial part of differences between classes IV and V and classes I and II appeared to be explained by characteristics occurring by age 16. However, more immediate circumstances are likely to be relevant to all measures except adult height. For women a difference in odds of more than twofold existed between the extreme class groups even after allowing for several explanatory variables, mostly representing earlier circumstances. Further explanation of differences may be possible if current circumstances (such as employment, housing, behaviour) are taken into account.

Our multivariate analyses achieved two main results. First, they confirmed the impression gleaned from the separate investigations of the relative importance of particular factors; and, second, they demonstrated how the contribution of later events and circumstances, such as unemployment, could be understood in part by their association with earlier events and circumstances. This is not to imply that later circumstances are reflecting only the influence of earlier circumstances; and indeed they generally demonstrate an effect in addition to that already represented by the earlier measures. The multivariate analyses also emphasized that potential influences had to be related both to later health and social position in order to have an impact on health differences.

The foregoing illustrates how, in relation to the population studied and the health problems selected, the framework suggested in the opening chapter of this book has been justified in two notable respects – namely, in considering (i) a wide range of potential explanatory variables and (ii) the sequencing of events and circumstances. It is particularly in these respects, but also in others, that the work adds to that presented by the Black Report (DHSS, 1980) and subsequent reviews. Thus, while Black concentrated on mortality, a nationally representative sample has been used here to demonstrate the extent of differences in morbidity. Also, much of the previous evidence is piecemeal. Several explanatory factors have been assessed, but this is usually from separate studies with no opportunity to integrate factors in the analysis. By using a single study population (in this case a particular cohort) and multivariate analyses, the present work allows a more precise estimate of the relative influence of the different explanations. Further, as with several studies since Black which attempted to overcome static representations of health differences and their causes, the present study uses longitudinal data, although in relation to 'health' rather than, as has previously been the case, in relation to mortality.

We can agree with the Black Report, no doubt inevitably, that there are no simple explanations for class differences in health, but beyond this comparisons are difficult to make. Their conclusion that 'much of the evidence . . . can be adequately understood in terms of specific features of the socio-economic environment: features (such as work accidents, overcrowding, cigarette smoking) which are strongly class related in Britain and also have clear causal significance (p. 199)'

was based on an overview of class differences in mortality throughout the lifespan and from a variety of causes. In contrast, the present study provides a detailed enquiry into explanations for differences in four health outcome measures. It also concentrates on a specific stage of life. Influences in health differences that emerge by early adulthood could differ substantially from influences affecting health differences in later life. Certain factors, such as those associated with the working environment, have only begun to exert an effect on young adults, but there will be a cumulation of effects at older ages.

Thus, questions concerning the generalizability of the findings arise. These concern the extent to which it is possible to generalize about class differences:

1. across successive generations;
2. across different health outcome measures; and
3. over the life course.

1. By focusing on a particular cohort, time has been considered from a life-course perspective. But relationships observed for one cohort are not fixed. Previous and future generations will be exposed to a different mix of events and circumstances that will affect the relationships under consideration. To take an example relevant to the analyses described in previous chapters, unemployment has risen dramatically between 1974, when the cohort was age 16, and 1981, when age 23 (Figure 12.1). Previous post-war generations entered the labour market when rates were lower, and this is likely to affect the relationship between health and social position. The impact of unemployment on psychological health appears to vary not just with factors intrinsic to the individual but also with extrinsic factors such as the local unemployment rate (Jackson and Warr, 1987). There are other considerations, of course, since material support during periods of unemployment has varied even over a short timespan. Over a longer period still, there have been gross changes in welfare provision (Wilkinson, 1989). Given that it has been postulated that stability of home environment is associated with subsequent emotional well-being (Wadsworth, 1979), it is also relevant that family stability may have changed as a result, for example, of increasing divorce rates. Such changes not only affect the size of class differences in related health problems, but the balance of influences that are pertinent at any one time.

Trends of class differences in health over time are not constant. Some

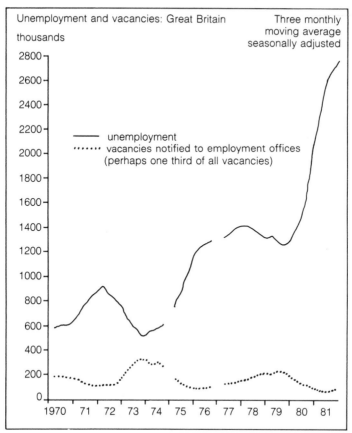

Fig. 12.1 Unemployment and vacancies between 1970 and 1981. *Source: Employment Gazette* (1982).

gradients appear to have reversed; for example, it has been suggested that heart disease was at one time more common in higher classes than, as now, in lower classes (Marmot *et al.*, 1978). Also, class differences in adult height have been studied over several generations and this is of particular relevance to the present work. One study used data from parents of the 1958 cohort study and their offspring pooled together with similar data from the 1946 birth cohort. Class differences in height were found (Kuh *et al.*, 1991) and, as in other studies based on the British Regional Heart Study (Walker *et al.*, 1988) and the OPCS national survey (Carr-Hill, 1988), the differences in height fluctuated over time. Hence, even for measures that are considered to have a substantial hereditary component, the evidence suggests that class differences are not inevitable.

Therefore, generalizing from the findings reported here to earlier and later generations is problematic because class differences in health can fluctuate over time, and it is likely that this reflects variations in contributory factors. Inter-cohort comparisons would provide further insight into the stability of relationships underlying class differences. The existence in Britain of three major birth cohort studies offers a valuable opportunity for such investigations.

2. Even though only a limited number of health outcome measures have been examined in any detail in this work, it is obvious and would have been expected that relationships depend upon the measure considered. The present study has shown similarities in the explanations for class differences in self-rated health, malaise and, to a lesser extent, psychological morbidity, but this is likely to reflect similarities in the measures rather than overarching explanations for differences in health in the age group studied. Also, there were discrepancies in the findings for these three measures, and those for height differed markedly. It is therefore difficult to generalize about causes of health differences in early adulthood, even at the level of broad areas of explanation. Several other health measures would need to be considered before an overall view could be put forward: for example, respiratory symptoms and obesity emerge as important health problems even at this relatively healthy stage.

Since evidence about the causes of class differences in health has been drawn from several studies using various health outcomes, it is perhaps inevitable that controversies are generated about the relative importance of different explanations. But when several health measures and alternative explanations for differences are considered together, it is more obvious that explanations for class differences depend upon the health measure used. Support for this conclusion is available from another study which examines the influence of different explanations for differences in mortality from ischaemic heart disease, although in relation to geographical rather than social differences. Data from the British Regional Heart Study were used to demonstrate how particular risk factors for IHD, such as height, were associated with place of birth, while others such as blood pressure were associated with place of residence in middle life (Elford *et al.*, 1989, 1990).

3. Finally, some of the findings from this work are relevant to the issue of whether generalizations about factors contributing to class differences in health can be made from one age to another. It was shown that an earlier measure of a particular health outcome accounted for a large part of class differences in the health outcome at age 23 (this was seen, for example, for height and emotional well-being). Thus, influences contributing to earlier differences in health are relevant to those seen later. Only for some health measures, such as adult height, will relationships be fixed after a particular age. For most health meas-

ures, there may be additional contributions from circumstances occurring at each stage of life. It will be important to assess the role of the work environment – not considered here, but which will be increasingly relevant beyond early adulthood. A follow-up investigation of a sample over a longer timespan will inform Figure 1.5, which speculates on the relative balance of influences at different ages.

Throughout this book it has become clear that the causes of class differences in health are far from simple. However, the complexity of the problem should not deter attempts to reduce health differences. This work points to some likely explanatory factors for class differences in four selected health measures. Many of these factors are amenable to change. The evidence suggests, for example, that the social distribution of birthweight contributes towards differences in adult stature and some of the influences on the former are already well known. In relation to the measures of emotional health considered, it is especially important to support those policies and services that attempt to prevent and intervene in cases of early problem behaviour, especially in lower classes. Unequal educational achievement and experiences of adverse circumstances, such as unemployment, further exacerbates health differences.

Evidence from the present work suggests that the foundations for tomorrow's social differences in health are already being laid. Circumstances prevailing at each stage of childhood and adolescence were relevant to health differences among young adults. Therefore action will need to be sustained across a wide spectrum of contributory factors and over a long period if social differences in health are to be reduced.

References

Acheson, D. (1987) Nutritional monitoring of the health of the nation. *J. Roy. Soc. Health*, **6**, 209–14.

Ajzen, I. and Fishbein, M. (1980) *Understanding Attitudes and Predicting Social Behaviour*, Prentice-Hall, Englewood Cliffs, NJ.

Alberman, E., Filakti, H., Williams, S., Evans, S. J. W. and Emanuel, I. (1991) Early influences on the secular trend in adult height between the parents and children of the 1958 birth cohort. *Annals Hum. Biol.*, **18**, 127–36.

Antonovsky, A. (1967) Social class life expectancy and overall mortality. *Millbank Mem. Fund. Q.*, **43**, 31–73.

Antonovsky, A. (1987) *Unravelling the Mystery of Health*, Jossey-Bass, San Francisco.

Antonovsky, A. (1989) Social inequalities in health: a complementary perspective, in *Health Inequalities in European Countries* (ed. A. J. Fox), Gower, Aldershot.

Arber, S. (1987) Social class, non-employment and chronic illness: continuing the inequalities in health debate. *Brit. Med. J.*, **294**(i), 1069–73.

Arber, S. (1989) Gender and class inequalities in health: understanding the differentials, in *Health Inequalities in European Countries* (ed. A. J. Fox), Gower, Aldershot.

Arber, S., Dale, A. and Gilbert, G. N. (1986) The limitations of existing classifications for women, in *The Measurement of Social Class* (ed. A. Jacoby), Social Research Association, Guildford.

Bagnall, G. (1991) *Educating Young Drinkers*, Routledge & Kegan Paul, London.

Baird, D. (1974) The epidemiology of low birth weight: changes in incidence in Aberdeen, 1948–72. *J. Biosoc. Sci.*, **6**, 323–41.

Baird, D. (1985) Changing problems and priorities in obstetrics. *Brit. J. Obstet. Gynaecol.*, **92**, 115–21.

Balarajan, R., Yuen, P. and Machin, D. (1987) Socio-economic differentials in the uptake of medical care in Great Britain. *J. Epid. Comm. Health*, **41**, 196–9.

Banks, M. H. and Jackson, P. R. (1982) Unemployment and risk of minor psychiatric disorder in young people: cross-sectional and longitudinal evidence. *Psychol. Med.*, **12**, 789–98.

Bartley, M. (1988) Unemployment and health: selection or causation – a false antithesis? *Sociol. Health Illness*, **10**, 41–67.

Beardmore, J. A. and Karimi-Booshehri, F. (1983) ABO genes are differentially distributed in socio-economic groups in England. *Nature*, **303**, 522–4.

Bebbington, P., Hurry, J., Tennant, C., Sturt, E. and Wing, J. K. (1981) Epidemiology of mental disorders in Camberwell. *Psychol. Med.*, **11**, 561–79.

Berkman, L. and Breslow, L. (1983) *Health and Ways of Living. The Alameda County Study*, Oxford Univ. Press, New York.

Berkman, L. F. and Syme, S. L. (1979) Social networks, host resistance and mortality: a nine year follow-up study of Alameda County residents. *Amer. J. Epidemiol.*, **109**, 186–204.

Bernstein, B. (1971) *Class, Codes and Control*, Routledge, London.

Blane, D. (1985) An assessment of the Black Report's explanations of health inequalities. *Sociol. Health Illness*, **7**, 421–5.

Blane, D., Power, C. and Bartley, M. (1990) *The measurement of morbidity in relation to social class*. Paper presented at the 3rd International meeting of the European Society of Medical Sociology, Marburg, Germany.

Blaxter, M. (1976) Social class and health inequalities, in *Equalities and Inequalities in Health* (eds C. O. Carter and J. Peel), Academic Press, London, pp. 111–25.

Blaxter, M. (1981) *The Health of Children: Studies in deprivation and disadvantage*, Heinemann, London.

Blaxter, M. (1983) Health services as a defence against the consequences of poverty in industrialised societies. *Soc. Sci. Med.*, **17**, 1139–48.

Blaxter, M. (1985) Self-definition of health status and consulting rates in primary care. *Q. J. Soc. Affairs*, **1(2)**, 133–71.

Blaxter, M. (1986) Longitudinal studies in Britain relevant to inequalities in health, in *Class and Health: Research and Longitudinal Data* (ed. R. G. Wilkinson), Tavistock, London.

Blaxter, M. (1987) Evidence on inequality in health from a national survey. *Lancet*, **i**, 30–3.

Blaxter, M. (1989) A comparison of measures of inequality in morbidity, in *Health Inequalities in European Countries* (ed. A. J. Fox), Gower, Aldershot.

Blaxter, M. (1990) *Health and Lifestyles*, Routledge and Chapman and Hall, London.

BMA (1987) *Deprivation and Ill-Health*, Board of Science and Education, British Medical Association.

BMDP (1985) *Statistical Software*, Univ. of California Press.

Brown, G. W. and Harris, T. O. (1978) *Social Origins of Depression: A Study of Psychiatric Disorder in Women*, Tavistock, London.

Brown, G. W., Harris, T. O. and Bifulco, A. (1986) Long-term effects of early loss of parent, in *Depression in Young People: Developmental and clinical perspectives* (eds M. L. Rutter, C. E. Lizard and P. B. Read), Guildford Press, New York, pp. 251–96.

Brown, M. and Madge, N. (1982) *Despite the Welfare State: Deprivation and Disadvantage*, Heinemann, London.

Bruch, H. (1974) *Eating Disorders; Obesity, Anorexia Nervosa and the Person Within*, Routledge & Kegan Paul, London, 396 pp.

Butler, N. R. and Alberman, E. D. (eds) (1969) *Perinatal Problems*, Livingstone, Edinburgh.

Butler, N. R. and Bonham, D. G. (1963) *Perinatal Mortality*, Livingstone, Edinburgh.

Butler, N. R. and Golding, J. (eds) (1986) *From Birth to Five: A study of the health and behaviour of a national cohort*, Pergamon, Oxford.

Calnan, M. and Rutter, D. R. (1986) Do health beliefs predict health behaviour? An analysis of breast self-examination. *Soc. Sci. Med.*, **22**, 673–8.

Carr-Hill, R. (1985) Health and Income: A longitudinal study of four hundred families. *Q. J. Soc. Affairs*, **1**, 295–307.

Carr-Hill, R. (1987) The inequalities in health debate: A critical review of the issues. *J. Soc. Policy*, **16**, 4, 509–42.

Carr-Hill, R. A. (1988) Time trends in inequalities in health. *J. Biosoc. Sci.*, **20**, 253–63.

Cartwright, A. and O'Brien, M. (1976) Social class variations in health care and in the nature of GP consultations, in *The Sociology of the NHS* (ed. M. Stacy), University of Keele, Keele, pp. 77–98.

Central Statistics Office, Sweden (1981) *Mortality Register 1961–1970*. Report 1981: 5, Stockholm.

Central Statistical Office Hungary (1988) *Studies in Mortality Differentials 4: Socio-economic and Occupational Mortality Differentials*, Vol. 1, Budapest.

Chalmers, I. (1985) Short, Black, Himsworth & social class differences in fetal and neonatal mortality rates. *Brit. Med. J.*, **291**, No. 6490, 231–2.

Chamberlain, R., Chamberlain, G., Howlett, B. and Claireaux, A. (1975) *British Births 1970, Vol. 1. The First Week of Life*, Heinemann Medical Books, London.

Charlton, A. and Blair, V. (1989) Absence from school related to children's and parental smoking habits. *Brit. Med. J.*, **298**, 90–2.

References

CICRED (Committee for International Cooperation in National Research in Demography) (1982, 1984, 1985) *Socio-economic Differential Mortality in Industrialized Countries*, Paris.

Cole, T. J., Donnet, M. L. and Stanfield, P. (1983) Unemployment, birthweight and growth in the first year. *Arch. Disease Child.*, **58**, 717–21.

Cole-Hamilton, I. and Lang, T. (1986) *Tightening Belts: a report on the impact of poverty on food*, The London Food Commission.

Colley, J. R. T., Douglas, J. W. B. and Reid, D. D. (1973) Respiratory disease in young adults. Influence of early childhood lower respiratory tract illness, social class, air pollution and smoking. *Brit. Med. J.*, **2**, 195–8.

Cox, B. D., Blexter, M., Buckle, A. J. L. *et al.* (1987) *The Health and Lifestyle Survey*, Health Promotion Research Trust, London.

Crisp, A. H. and McGuiness, B. (1975) Jolly Fat: relation between obesity and psychoneurosis in general population. *Brit. Med. J.*, **1**, 7–9.

Davie, R., Butler, N. R. and Goldstein, H. (1972) *From Birth to Seven*. Longman, London in association with National Children's Bureau.

Department of Health and Social Security (1980) *Inequalities in Health*. Report of a research working group. DHSS, London.

Desplanques, G. (1979) La mortalité des adultes suivant le milieu social: résultats de la periode 1955–1971. *Collection de l'INSEE*, Series D, No. 44.

Dohrenwend, B. P. and Dohrenwend, B. S. (1974) Social and cultural influences on psychopathology. *Ann. Rev. Psychol.*, **25**, 417–52.

Douglas, J. W. B. (1964) *The Home and the School*, MacGibbon & Kee, London.

Douglas, J. W. B. and Blomfield, J. M. (1958) *Children under Five*. George Allen & Unwin, London.

Douglas, J. W. B. and Simpson, H. (1964) Height in relation to puberty, family size and social class. *Millbank Memorial Fund Quarterly*, **42**, 20–35.

Douglas, J. W. B. and Waller, R. E. (1966) Air pollution and respiratory infection in children. *Brit. J. Prev. Soc. Med.*, **20**, 1–8.

Doyle, W., Crawford, M. A., Laurance, B. M. and Drury, P. (1982) Dietary survey during pregnancy in a low socio-economic group. *Human Nutr., Appl. Nutr.*, **36a**, 95–106.

Elford, J., Phillips, A. N., Thomson, A. G. and Shaper, A. G. (1989) Migration and geographical variations in ischaemic heart disease in Great Britain. *Lancet*, **i**, 343–6.

Elford, J., Phillips, A. N., Thomson, A. G. and Shaper, A. G. (1990) Migration and geographical variations in blood pressure in Britain. *Brit. Med. J.*, **300**, 291–5.

Emanuel, I. (1986) Maternal health during childhood and later reproductive performance. *Ann. N.Y. Acad. Sci.*, **477**, 27–39.

Employment Gazette (1982) Department of Employment, Vol. 90, No. 2, p. S5.

Essen, J. (1978) Living in one-parent families: income and expenditure. *Poverty*, **40**, 23–8.

Essen, J. and Lambert, L. (1977) Living in one-parent families: relationship and attitudes of 16 year-olds. *Child Care, Health Devel.*, **3**, 301–18.

Farr, W. (1839) Letter to the Registrar General, in *First Annual Report of the Registrar General of Births, Deaths and Marriages in England*, HMSO, London.

Farr, W. (1860) On the construction of life tables, illustrated by a new life table of the healthy districts of England. *J. Inst. Act.*, **IX**.

Ferri, E. (1976) *Growing up in a One-Parent Family*. NFER, Slough.

Fogelman, K. (ed.) (1983) *Growing up in Great Britain*, Macmillan, London.

Fogelman, K. (1985) *After School: the education and training experiences of the 1958 cohort*, NCDS Working Paper No. 3, Social Statistics Research Unit, City University, London.

Fogelman, K., Fox, A. J. and Power, C. (1989) Class and tenure mobility: do they explain social inequalities in health among young adults? in *Health Inequalities in European Countries* (ed. A. J. Fox), Gower, Aldershot.

Fogelman, K. and Manor, O. (1988) Smoking in pregnancy and development into early adulthood. *Brit. Med. J.*, **297**, 1233–6.

Fogelman, K., Power, C. and Fox, A. J. (1987) *Family Breakdown, Social Mobility and Health Inequalities*, NCDS Working Paper No. 25, Social Statistics Research Unit, City University, London.

Fogelman, K. and Richardson, K. (1974) School attendance: some results from the National Child Development Study, in *Truancy* (ed. B. Turner), Ward Lock Education, London.

Fogelman, K., Tibbenham, A. and Lambert, L. (1980) Absence from school: findings from the National Child Development Study, in *Out of School: Perspectives in Truancy and School Refusal* (eds I. Berg and L. Hersov), Wiley, London.

Forsdahl, A. (1977) Are poor living conditions in childhood and adolescence an important risk factor for arteriosclerotic heart disease? *Brit. J. Prev. Soc. Med.*, **31**, 91–5.

Forster, D. P. (1976), Social class differences in sickness and general practitioner consultations. *Health Trends*, **8**, 29–32.

Fox, A. J. (1980) Prospects for measuring changes in differential mortality. In *Proceedings of the Meeting on Socio-economic Determinants and Consequences of Mortality. Mexico City, June 1979*, UN/WHO.

Fox, A. J. (1988) Social network interaction: new jargon in health inequalities. *Brit. Med. J.*, **297**, 373–4.

Fox, A. J. (ed.) (1989) *Health Inequalities in European countries*, Gower, Aldershot.

Fox, A. J. and Collier, P. F. (1976) Low mortality in industrial cohort studies due to selection for work and survival in the industry. *Brit. J. Prev. Soc. Med.*, **30**, 225–30.

Fox, A. J. and Goldblatt, P. O. (1982) *Socio-demographic Mortality Differentials. Longitudinal Study 1971–1975*, LS No. 1, HMSO, London.

Fox, A. J., Goldblatt, P. O. and Jones, D. R. (1985) Social class mortality differentials: artefact, selection or life circumstances? *J. Epidemiol. Comm. Health*, **39**, 1–8.

Fox, A. J., Jones, D. R. and Goldblatt, P. O. (1984) Approaches to studying the effect of socio-economic circumstances on geographic differences in mortality in England and Wales. *Brit. Med. Bull.*, **40**, 309–14.

Fox, A. J. and Shewry M. (1988) New longitudinal insights into relationships between unemployment and mortality. *Stress Med.*, **4**, 11–19.

General Register Office, Scotland (1981) *Occupational Mortality 1969–73*, GRO(S), Edinburgh.

Ghodsian, M. (1977) Children's behaviour and the BSAG: some theoretical and statistical considerations. *Brit. J. Soc. Clin. Psychol.*, **16**, 23–8.

Ghodsian, M. and Fogelman, K. (1988) *A Longitudinal Study of Housing and Social Circumstances in Childhood and Early Adulthood*, NCDS Working Paper No. 29, Social Statistics Research Unit, City University, London.

Ghodsian, M., Fogelman, K., Lambert, L. and Tibbenham, A. (1980) Changes in behaviour ratings of a national sample of children. *Brit. J. Soc. Clin. Psychol.*, **19**, 247–56.

Glass, D. V. (ed.) (1954) *Social Mobility in Britain*, Routledge & Kegan Paul, London.

Goldberg, D. and Huxley, P. (1980) *Mental Illness in the Community*, Tavistock, London.

Goldblatt, P. (1987) *Mortality Differences at Working Ages: The Use of Generalised Linear Models to Compare Measures*, LS Working Paper No. 53, Social Statistics Research Unit, City University, London.

Goldblatt, P. (1988) Changes in social class between 1971 and 1981: could these affect mortality differences among men of working ages? *Pop. Trends*, **51**, 9–17.

Goldblatt, P. (1989) Mortality by social class 1971–1985. *Pop. Trends*, **56**, 6–15.

Goldblatt, P. (1990a) Social class mortality differences, in *The Biology of Social Class* (ed. N. Mascie-Taylor), Oxford Univ. Press, Oxford.

Goldblatt, P. (ed.) (1990b) *Longitudinal Study: Mortality and Social Organiz-ation, 1971–1981*, LS No. 6, HMSO, London.

Golding, J., Hicks, P. and Butler, N. R. (1984) Blood group and socio-economic class. *Nature*, **309**, 396–7.

Golding, J., Thomas, P. and Peters, T. (1986) Does father's unemploy-ment put the fetus at risk? *Brit. J. Obstet. Gynaecol.*, **93**, 704–10.

Goldstein, H. (1971) Factors influencing the height of seven-year-old children: results from the National Child Development Study. *Human Biol.*, **43**, 92–111.

Goldstein, H. (1983) A study of the response rates of 16-year-olds in the National Child Development Study, in *Growing up in Great Britain* (ed. K. Fogelman), Macmillan, London.

Goldthorpe, J. H. (1980) *Social Mobility and Class Structure in Modern Britain*, Clarendon Press, Oxford.

Goldthorpe, J. H. (1985) Epidemiology, genetics and sociology. *J. Biosoc. Sci.*, **17**, 373–5.

Gove, W. R. (1972) The relationship between sex roles, marital status and mental illness. *Soc. Forces*, **51**, 34.

Gove, W. R. and Tudor, J. (1973) Adult sex roles and mental illness, *Amer. J. Sociol.*, **78**, 812.

Graham, H. (1989) Women and smoking in the United Kingdom: The implications for health promotion. *Health Promotion*, **3**, 371–82.

Haberman, S. and Bloomfield, D. (1988) Social class differences in mor-tality in Great Britain around 1981. *J. Inst. Act.*, **115**, Pt III, 495–517.

Halsey, A. H., Heath, A. F. and Ridge, J. M. (1980) *Origins and Desti-nations: Family Class and Education in Modern Britain*, Clarendon Press, Oxford.

Hart, N. (1986) Inequalities in health: the individual versus the environ-ment. *J. Roy. Stat. Soc.*, Series A, **149**, 228–46.

Heath, A. (1981) *Social Mobility*, Fontana, Glasgow.

Hibbard, J. H. and Pope, C. R. (1983) Gender roles, illness orientation and use of medical services. *Soc. Sci. Med.*, **17**, 129–37.

Hibbett, A. and Fogelman, K. (1990) Occupational outcomes of truancy. *Brit. J. Educ. Psychol.*, **60**, 23–36.

Himsworth, H. (1984) Epidemiology, genetics and sociology. *J. Biosoc. Sci.*, **16**, 159–76.

Himsworth, H. (1986) Epidemiology, genetics and sociology: a reply. *J. Biosoc. Sci.*, **18**, 119–23.

Himsworth, H. (1989) Social class differences in infant mortality: a problem of competing hypotheses. *J. Biosoc. Sci.*, **21**, 497–500.

Hirst, M. (1983) Evaluating the malaise inventory: an item analysis. *Soc. Psychiatry*, **18**, 181–4.

Hirst, M. A. and Bradshaw, J. R. (1983) Evaluating the malaise inventory: a comparison of measures of stress. *J. Psychosomatic Res.*, **27**, 3, 193–9.

Holland, W. W., Rona, R. J. Chinn, S., Altman, D. G., Irwig, L. M., Cook, J. and Florey, C. du V. (1981) The National Study of Health and Growth. Surveillance of Primary School Children (1972–1976). In DHSS Report on Health and Social Subjects 21. Sub-committee on Nutritional Surveillance, 2nd Report, HMSO, London, Ch. 6, pp. 85–101.

Howe, G. R. and Lindsay, J. P. (1983) A follow-up study of a ten per cent sample of the Canadian labour force I: cancer mortality in males 1965–73. *J. Nat. Cancer Inst.*, **70**(1), 37–44.

Humphrey, C. and Elford, J. (1988) Social class differences in infant mortality: the problem of competing hypotheses, *J. Biosoc. Sci.*, **20**, 497–504.

Illsley, R. (1955) Social class selection and class differences in relation to stillbirths and infant deaths. *Brit. Med. J.*, **2**, 1520–4.

Illsley, R. (1986) Occupational class, selection and inequalities in health. *Q. J. Soc. Affairs*, **2**, 151–65.

Jackson, P. R. and Warr, P. (1987) Mental health of unemployed men in different parts of England and Wales. *Brit. Med. J.*, **295**, 525.

Joffe, M. (1989) Social inequalities in low birthweight: timing of effects and selective social mobility. *Soc. Sci. Med.*, **28**, 613–19.

Jones, D. R. and Sedgwick, P. (1991) Life events and accidents in the National Child Development Study (in preparation).

Kagamimori, S., Iibuchi, Y. and Fox, J. (1983) A comparison of socio-economic differences in mortality between Japan and England and Wales. *World Health Statist. Qly*, **36**, 119–28.

Kaplan, G. A. (1985) *Twenty years of health in Alameda County: the human population laboratory analyses.* Paper presented to the Society for Prospective Medical Annual meeting, San Francisco, 24 November 1985.

Kaplan, G. A. and Camacho, T. (1983) Perceived health and mortality: a nine year follow-up of the human population laboratory cohort. *Amer. J. Epidemiol.*, **117**, 292–304.

Kaplan, G. A., Roberts, R. E., Camacho, T. C. and Coyne, J. (1987) Psychosocial predictors of depression. *Amer. J. Epidemiol.*, **125**, 206–20.

Kelleher, C., Cooper, J. and Sadlier, D. (1990) ABO blood group and social class: a prospective study in a regional blood bank. *J. Epidemiol. Comm. Health*, **44**, 59–61.

Kiernan, K. E. (1986) Transitions in young adulthood, *Proceedings of British Society for Population Studies. Conference on Populations Research in Britain.*

Kiernan, K. E., Colley, J. R. T., Douglas, J. W. B. and Reid, D. D.

(1976) Chronic cough in young adults in relation to smoking habits, childhood environment and chest illness. *Respiration*, **33**, 236–44.

Kitagawa, E. M. and Hauser, P. H. M. (1973) *Differential Mortality in the United States. A Study in Socio-economic Epidemiology*, Harvard Univ. Press, Cambridge.

Knight, I. (1984) *The Heights and Weights of Adults in Great Britain*, HMSO, London.

Kogevinas, M. (1990) *Longitudinal Study: Socio-demographic Differences in Cancer Survival 1971–1983*, LS No. 5, HMSO, London.

Koskinen, S. (1985) Time trends in cause-specific mortality by occupational class in England and Wales, in *Proc. of 20th General Conference of the International Union for Scientific Study of Population*, Florence.

Kristofersen, L. (1979) *Yorke og Dodelighet*, Report No. 19, Central Statistics Office, Norway.

Kuh, D., Power, C. and Rodgers, B. (1991) Secular trends in social class and sex differences in height. *Int. J. Epidemiol.* (in press).

Kuh, D. and Wadsworth, M. (1989) Parental height: childhood environment and subsequent adult height in a national birth cohort. *Int. J. Epidemiol.*, **18**, 663–8.

Leete, R. and Fox, J. (1977) Registrar General's social classes: origins and uses. *Pop. Trends*, **8**, 1–7.

Leon, D. (1988) *The Social Distribution of Cancer. Longitudinal Study 5*, Series LS No. 3, HMSO, London.

Logan, W. P. D. (1960) *Morbidity Statistics from General Practice*, Vol. II (*Occupation*). *Studies on Medical and Population Subjects*, No. 14, HMSO, London.

Logan, W. P. D. and Brooke, E. M. (1957) *The Survey of Sickness 1943 to 1952. Studies on Medical and Population Subjects*, No. 12, HMSO, London.

Lundberg, O. (1991) Causal explanations for class inequality in health: An empirical analysis. *Soc. Sci. Med.*, **32**, 385–93.

Lynge, E. (1979) *Doedelighet og erhverv 1970–75*. Statistiske Undersoegelser nr. 37, Danmarks Statistic, Koebenhavn.

MacFarlane, A. and Cole, T. (1985) *From Depression to Recession – Evidence about the Effects of Unemployment on Mothers' and Babies' Health 1930s–1980s*, Maternity Alliance, London, pp. 38–57.

MacIntyre, S. (1986) The patterning of health by social position in contemporary Britain: directions for sociological research. *Soc. Sci. Med.*, **23**, 393–415.

MacIntyre, S. (1988) A review of social patterning and significance of measures of height, weight, blood pressure and respiratory function. *Soc. Sci. Med.*, **27**, 327–37.

Madge, N. and Marmot, M. (1987) Psychosocial factors and health. *Q. J. Soc. Affairs*, **3**(2), 81–134.

Marin, R. (1986) *Occupational Mortality 1971–80*, Study No. 129, Central Statistics Office of Finland, Helsinki.

Marmot, M. G., Adelstein, A., Robinson, N. and Rose, G. A. (1978) Changing social class distribution of heart disease. *Brit. Med. J.*, **2**, 1109–12.

Marmot, M. G. and Davey-Smith, G. (1989) Why are the Japanese living longer? *Brit. Med. J.*, **299**, 1545–51.

Marmot, M. G., Shipley, M. J. and Rose, G. (1984) Inequalities in death – specific explanations of a general pattern. *Lancet*, **1**, 1003–6.

Marsh, A. and Matheson, J. (1983) *Smoking Attitudes and Behaviour*, HMSO, London.

Martin, C. (1987) Responding to a public need: a study of housing and health. *Rad. Comm. Med.*, **30**, 28–34.

Martin, J. and White, A. (1988) *The Financial Circumstances of Disabled Adults Living in Private Households*, OPCS Disability Survey Report 2, HMSO, London.

Mascie-Taylor, C. G. N. and McManus, I. C. (1984) Blood group and socio-economic class. *Nature*, **309**, 395–6.

McCormick, A. and Rosenbaum, M. (1990) *Morbidity Statistics from General Practice 1981–1982, 3rd National Study: socio-economic analyses*, Series MB5. No. 2, HMSO, London.

Medical Research Council (1960) MRC committee on the aetiology of chronic bronchitis. *Brit. Med. J.*, **2**, 1665.

Mednick, S. A. and Baert, A. E. (1981) *Prospective Longitudinal Research: An empirical basis for the primary prevention of psycho-social disorders*, Oxford Medical Publications, Oxford.

Micklewright, J. (1986) *A Note on Household Income Data in NCDS3*, NCDS Working Paper No. 18, Social Statistics Research Unit, City University, London.

Minder, C. L. (1986) Socio-economic mortality differentials in Switzerland 1979–82. In *Socio-economic Differential Mortality*, Committee for International Cooperation in National Research in Demography, UN and WHO Report No. 6, Hungarian Central Statistics Office, Budapest.

Ministry of Health and Welfare, Japan (1973) *Occupational and Industrial Mortality in Japan* (Japanese), Health and Welfare Statistics Association, Tokyo (1959 report contains English summary).

Mitchell, J. R. A. (1977) An association between ABO blood group distribution and geographical differences in death rates. *Lancet*, **i**, 295–7.

Morton, A. D. and McManus, I. C. (1986) Attitudes to and knowledge about the acquired immune deficiency syndrome: lack of correlation. *Brit. Med. J.*, **293**, 1212.

Moser, K. A., Fox, A. J. and Jones, D. R. (1984) Unemployment and mortality in the OPCS Longitudinal Study. *Lancet*, **ii**, 1324–8.

Moser, K. A., Goldblatt, P. O., Fox, A. J. and Jones, D. R. (1987) Unemployment and mortality: comparison of the 1971 and 1981 Longitudinal Study Census Sample. *Brit. Med. J.*, **294**, 86–90.

Moser, K., Pugh, H. S. and Goldblatt, P. O. (1988) Inequalities in women's health: looking at mortality differentials using an alternative approach. *Brit. Med. J.*, **296**, 1221–4.

Mourant, A. E. & Kopec, A. C. (eds) (1978) *Blood Groups and Diseases*, Oxford Univ. Press, Oxford.

Nathanson, C. A. (1975) Illness and the feminine role: a theoretical review. *Soc. Sci. Med.*, **9**, 57–62.

Nathanson, C. A. (1977) Sex, illness and medical care. *Soc. Sci. Med.*, **11**, 13–25.

NCDS (1988) *NCDS News*, National Child Development Study Newsletter No. 3, Social Statistics Research Unit, City University, London.

Nordic Statistical Secretariat (1988) *Occupational Mortality in Nordic Countries 1971–80*, Statistical Reports of the Nordic Countries No. 49, Copenhagen.

OPCS (1973) *General Household Survey: Introductory Report*, HMSO, London.

OPCS (1978) *Occupational Mortality. Decennial Supplement 1970–1972*, DS No. 1, HMSO, London.

OPCS (1980) *Classification of Occupations 1980*, HMSO, London.

OPCS (1984a) *General Household Survey 1982*, HMSO, London.

OPCS (1984b) *Birthweight Statistics*, OPCS Monitor, Ref. DH3 85/5.

OPCS (1985) *Birthweight Statistics*, OPCS Monitor, Ref. DH3 86/2.

OPCS (1990) *Social Survey Division Annual Report, 1989/90*, HMSO, London.

Orth-Gomer, K. and Johnson, J. V. (1987) Social network interaction and mortality: a six year follow-up study of a random sample of the Swedish population. *J. Chron. Diseases*, **40**, 949–57.

Osborn, A. F., Butler, N. R. and Morris, A. C. (1984) *The Social Life of Britain's 5-Year-Olds*, Routledge & Kegan Paul, London.

Pagnanelli, F. (1986) Occupational and socio-economic mortality: the Italian first survey, in *Socio-economic Differential Mortality*, Committee for International Cooperation in National Research in Demography, UN and WHO Report No. 6, Hungarian Central Statistics Office, Budapest.

Palta, M., Prineas, R. J., Berman, R. and Hannan, P. (1982) Comparison of self-reported and measured height and weight. *Amer. J. Epidemiol.*, **115**, 223–30.

Park, A. T. (1966) Occupational mortality in Northern Ireland 1960–62.

References

Journal of the Statistical and Social Inquiry, Society of Ireland, **XXI**, Pt IV, 24–41.

Payne, J. (1983) *Summary Variables for Employment History Data*, NCDS4 Working Paper No. 16, Social Statistics Research Unit, City University, London.

Payne, R., Warr, P. and Hartley, J. (1984) Social class and psychological ill-health during unemployment. *Sociol. Health Illness*, **6**, 152–74.

Pearce, N. E., Davis, P. B., Smith, A. H. and Foster, F. H. (1983) Mortality and social class in New Zealand, I: Overall male mortality. *N.Z. Med. J.*, **96**, 281–5.

Peckham, C., Stark, O., Simonite, V. and Wolff, O. H. (1983) Prevalence of obesity in British children born in 1946 and 1958. *Brit. Med. J.*, **286**, 1237–42.

Peters. T. J., Butler, N. R., Fryer, J. G. and Chamberlain, G. V. P. (1983) Plus ça change: predictors of birth weight in two national studies. *Brit. J. Obstet. Gynaecol.*, **90**, 1040–5.

Plant, M. A., Peck, D. F. and Samuel, E. (1985) *Alcohol, Drugs and School-leavers*, Tavistock, London.

Pocock, S. J., Shaper, A. G., Cook, D. G., Phillips, A. N. and Walker, M. (1987) Social class differences in IHD in British men. *Lancet*, **ii**, 197–201.

Power, C., Fogelman, K. and Fox, A. J. (1986) Health and social mobility during the early years of life, *Q. J. Soc. Affairs*, **2** (4), 397–413.

Power, C., Manor, O., Fox, A. J. and Fogelman, K. (1988) *Health Selection: An Explanation for Inequalities in Health in Young Adults?* NCDS Working Paper No. 28, Social Statistics Research Unit, City Univ., London.

Power, C., Manor, O., Fox, A. J. and Fogelman, K. (1990) Health in childhood and social inequalities in health in young adults. *J. Roy. Statist. Soc.*, Series A, **153**, 17–28.

Power, C. and Peckham, C. (1988) *Childhood Morbidity and Adulthood Ill-Health*, NCDS Working Paper No. 32, Social Statistics Research Unit, City Univ., London.

Power, C. and Peckham, C. (1990) Childhood Morbidity and Adulthood Ill-Health. *J. Epidemiol. Comm. Health*, **44**, 69–74.

Preece, M. A. (1986) Growth measurements as indicators of health status, in *The Health and Development of Children* (eds H. B. Miles and E. Still), The Eugenics Society. Natterton Books Ltd, Humberside.

Preston, S. H. (ed.) (1980) *Biological and Social Aspects of Mortality and the Length of Life*, International Union for Scientific Study of Population, Ordina Publications, Belgium.

Preston, S., Haines, M. and Pamuk, E. (1981) Effects of industrialisation on mortality in developed countries, in *Solicited Papers*, Vol. 12, IUSSP 19th International Population Conference, Manilla, pp. 233–54.

Price, C. E., Rona, R. J. and Chinn, S. (1988) Height of primary school children and parents perceptions of food intolerance. *Brit. Med. J.*, **296**, 1696–9.

Pringle, M. L. K., Butler, N. R. and Davie, R. (1966) *11,000 Seven Year Olds*, Longman, London.

Prout, A. (1988) 'Off school sick': mothers accounts of school sickness absence. *Sociol. Rev.*, **36**, 765–89.

Pugh, H., Power, C., Goldblatt, P. and Arber, S. (1991) Women's Lung Cancer Mortality, Socio-economic status and changing smoking patterns. *Soc. Sci. Med.* (in press).

Raftery, J., Jones, D. R. and Rosato, M. (1990) The mortality of first and second generation Irish immigrants in the UK. *Soc. Sci. Med.*, **31**, 577–84.

RCGP, OPCS, DHSS (1982) Morbidity statistics from general practice, 1970–71; socio-economic analyses. *Studies on Medical and Population Subjects*, HMSO, London.

Registrar General (1857) *18th Annual Report of Births, Deaths and Marriages in England*, George Eyre and W. Spottiswoode, London.

Richman, N. (1978) Depression in mothers of young children. *J. Roy. Soc. Med.*, **71**, 489–93.

Roberts, H. and Barker, R. (1986) *The Social Classification of Women*, Social Statistics Research Unit, Working Paper No. 46, City Univ., London.

Robins, L. N. (1979) Follow-up studies, in *Psychopathological Disorders of Childhood* (eds H. C. Quay and J. S. Werry), 2nd edn, Wiley, New York, pp. 483–513.

Robins, L. N. (1986) The consequences of conduct disorder in girls, in *Development of Antisocial and Prosocial Behaviour: Research, Theories, and Issues* (eds D. Olweus, J. Block and M. Radke-Yarrow), Academic Press, Orlando., pp. 385–414.

Rodgers, B. (1990a) Behaviour and personality in childhood as predictors of adult psychiatric disorder. *J. Child Psychol. Psychiat.*, **31**, 393–414.

Rodgers, B. (1990b) Influences of early-life and recent factors on affective disorder in women: an exploration of vulnerability models, in *Straight and Devious Pathways from Childhood to Adulthood* (eds L. N. Robins and M. Rutter), Cambridge Univ. Press, New York.

Rodgers, B. (1990c) Adult affective disorder and early environment. *Brit. J. Psych.*, **157**, 539–50.

Rodgers, B. and Mann, S. A. (1986) The reliability and validity of PSE assessment by lay interviewers: a national population survey. *Psychol. Med.*, **16**, 689–700.

Rona, R. J. (1981) Genetic and environmental factors in the control of growth in childhood. *Brit. Med. Bull.*, **37**, 265–72.

Rona, R. J. and Chinn, S. (1982) National study of health and growth:

social and family factors and obesity in primary school children. *Ann. Human Biol.*, **9**, 147–56.

Rona, R. J., Swan, A. V. and Altman, D. G. (1978) Social factors and height of primary school children in England and Scotland. *J. Epidemiol. Comm. Health*, **32**, 147–54.

Rose, S., Lewontin, R. and Kamin, L. (1984) *Not in our Genes*, Penguin, Harmondsworth.

Royal College of Physicians (1983) Obesity. *J. Roy. Coll. Phys.*, **17**, 1.

Royal College of Physicians (1987) *A Great and Growing Evil*, Tavistock, London.

Rutter, M. (1967) A children's behaviour questionnaire for completion by teachers. *J. Child Psychol. Psychiat.*, **8**, 1–11.

Rutter, M. (1972) Relationships between child and adult psychiatric disorders. *Acta Psychiat. Scand.*, **48**, 3–21.

Rutter, M. and Garmezy, N. (1983) Developmental psychopathology, in *Socialization, Personality and Social Development* (ed. E. M. Hetherington), Vol. 4, Handbook of child psychology, Wiley, New York, pp. 775–911.

Rutter, M. and Madge, N. (1976) *Cycles of Disadvantage: a review of research*, Heinemann, London.

Rutter, M., Tizard, J. and Whitmore, K. (1970) *Education, Health and Behaviour*, Longman, London.

Rutter, M., Tizard, J., Yule, W. and Graham, P. (1976) Isle of Wight Studies: 1964–1974. *Psychol. Med.*, **6**, 313–32.

Shaper, A. G., Pocock, S. J., Walker, M., Cohen, N. M., Wale, C. J. and Thompson, A. G. (1981) British Regional Heart Study: cardiovascular risk factors in middle-aged men in 24 towns. *Brit. Med. J.*, **283**, 179–86.

Shepherd, P. (1985) *The National Child Development Study: an introduction to the background to the study and the methods of data collection*, NCDS Working Paper No. 1, Social Statistics Research Unit, City Univ., London.

Silman, A. J. (1987) Why do women live longer and is it worth it? *Brit. Med. J.*, **294**, 1311–12.

Sinclair, D. (1985) *Human Growth after Birth*, Oxford Medical Publications, Oxford.

Smith, P. B. and Mumford, D. M. (eds) (1980) *Adolescent Pregnancy: Perspectives for Health Professionals*, Hall & Co., Boston.

Smith, R. (1987) *Unemployment and Health*, Oxford Univ. Press, London.

Southgate, V. (1962) *Southgate Group Reading Tests: Manual of Instructions*, Univ. of London Press, London.

Sports Council (1984) *Exercise, Health and Medicine*. Proceedings of Symposium.

SPSS X (1986) *Users Guide*, 2nd edn, McGraw-Hill, New York.

Starfield, B., Katz, H., Gabriel, A., Livingstone, G., Benson, P. *et al.* (1984) Morbidity in childhood – a longitudinal view. *New England J. Med.*, **310**, 824–9.

Stark, O., Atkins, E. and Douglas, J. W. B. (1981) Longitudinal study of obesity in the National Survey of Health and Development. *Brit. Med. J.*, **283**, 13–17.

Stern, J. (1983) Social mobility and the interpretation of class mortality differentials. *J. Soc. Policy*, **12**, 27–49.

Stevenson, T. H. C. (1923) The social distribution of mortality from different causes in England and Wales. *Biometrika*, **XV**, 382–400.

Stevenson, T. H. C. (1927) *Decennial Supplement, England and Wales 1921, Part II: Occupation Mortality, Fertility and Infant Mortality*, HMSO, London.

Stevenson, T. H. C. (1928) The vital statistics of wealth and poverty (report of a paper to the Royal Statistical Society). *Brit. Med. J.*, **i**, 354.

Stewart, A. L. (1982) The reliability and validity of self-reported weight and height. *J. Chron. Diseases*, **35**, 295–309.

Stewart, A. L. and Brook, R. H. (1983) Effects of being overweight. *Amer. J. Public Health*, **73**, 171–8.

Stott, D. H. (1969) *The Social Adjustment of Children*, Univ. of London Press, London.

Strachan, D. P. (1988) Damp housing and childhood asthma: validation of reporting of symptoms. *Brit. Med. J.*, **297**, 1223–6.

Stunkard, A. J., Sorensen, T. I. A., Harris, C., Teasdale, T. W., Chakraborty, R., Schull, W. J. and Schulsinger, F. (1986) An adoption study of human obesity. *New England J. Med.*, **314**, 193–8.

Surtees, P. G., Dean, C., Ingham, J. G., Kreitman, N. B., Miller, P. McC. and Sashidharan, S. P. (1983) Psychiatric disorder in women from an Edinburgh community: associations with demographic factors. *Brit. J. Psychiat.*, **142**, 238–46.

Susser, M. and Susser, E. (1987) Indicators and designs in genetic epidemiology: separating heredity and environment. *Revue d'Epidemiol. de sante publ.*, **35**, 54–77.

Szreter, S. R. S. (1984) The genesis of the Registrar General's social classification of occupations. *Brit. J. Sociol.*, **XXXV**, 522–46.

Szreter, S. R. S. (1986) The first scientific social structure of modern Britain 1875–1883, in *The World We Have Gained* (eds L. Bonfield, R. M. Smith and K. Wrightson), Blackwell, Oxford.

Tanner, J. M. (1978) *Foetus into Man: Physical Growth from Conception to Maturity*, Open Books, London.

Tanner, J. M. (1986) Physical development. *Brit. Med. Bull.*, **42**, 131–8.

Tanner, J. M., Whitehouse, R. H. and Takaishi, M. (1966) Standards from birth to maturity for height, weight, height velocity and weight velocity: British Children 1965. *Arch. Diseases Child.*, **41**, 454–7, 613–35.

References

Tatham, J. (1908) *Supplement to the 65th Annual Report of the Registrar General of Births, Deaths and Marriages in England and Wales*, Part II, HMSO, London.

Taylor, B., Wadsworth, J., Wadsworth, M. E. J. and Peckham, C. (1984) Changes in the reported prevalence of childhood eczema since the 1939–45 war. *Lancet*, **ii**, 1255–7.

Taylor, C. B., Sallis, J. F. and Needle, R. (1985) The relationship of physical activity and exercise to mental health. *Public Health Reports*, **100**, 2, 195–202.

Tennant, C. (1985) Female vulnerability to depression. *Psychol. Med.*, **15**, 733–7.

Thurnhurst, C. (1984) Social inequalities in health – the medical empire strikes back. *Rad. Comm. Med.*, Sept., 35–7.

Tibbenham, A., Gorbach, P., Peckham, C. and Richardson, K. (1983) The influence of family size on height, in *Growing up in Great Britain* (ed. K. Fogelman), Macmillan, London.

Townsend, P. and Davidson, N. (1982) *Inequalities in Health: The Black Report*, Penguin, Harmondsworth.

UN/WHO (1980) *Proceedings of the Meeting on Socio-economic Determinants and Consequences of Mortality, Mexico City, June 1979*.

Vagero, D. and Persson, G. (1987) Cancer survival and social class in Sweden. *J. Epidemiol. Comm. Health*, **41**, 204–9.

Valkonen, T. (1987) Social inequality in the face of death, in *European Population Association Conference*, Central Statistics Office, Helsinki, pp. 201–60.

Valkonen, T. (1989) Adult mortality and level of education: a comparison of six countries, in *Health Inequalities in European Countries* (ed. J. Fox), Gower, Aldershot.

Valkonen, T. and Martelin, T. (1988) *Occupational Class and Suicide: An Example of the Elaboration of a Relationship*, Tutkimuksia Research Reports No. 222, Dept. of Sociology, University of Helsinki.

Verbrugge, L. M. and Wingard, D. L. (1987) Sex differentials in health and mortality. *Women and Health*, **12**(2), 103–45.

Waaler, H. T. H. (1984) Height, weight and mortality. The Norwegian Experience. *Acta. Med. Scand.*, Supp. 679.

Wadsworth, M. (1979) *Roots of Delinquency*, Robertson, Oxford.

Wadsworth, M. (1986) Serious illness in childhood and its association with later-life achievement, in *Class and Health* (ed. R. Wilkinson), Tavistock, London.

Walker, A. (1982) *Unqualified and Underemployed*, Macmillan, London.

Walker, M., Shaper, A. G. and Wannamethee, G. (1988) Height and social class in middle-aged British men. *J. Epidemiol. Comm. Health*, **42**, 299–303.

Warr, P. and Parry, G. (1982a) Paid employment and women's psychological well-being. *Psychol. Bull.*, **19**, 498–516.

Warr, P. and Parry, G. (1982b) Depressed mood in working class mothers with and without paid employment. *Soc. Psychiat.*, **17**, 161–5.

Weatherall, R. and Shaper, A. G. (1988) Overweight and obesity in middle-aged British men. *European J. Clin. Nutr.*, **42**, 221–31.

Webber, R. (1977) *The Classification of Residential Neighbourhoods: An Introduction to the Classification of Wards and Parishes*, Centre for Environmental Studies.

Weissman, M. M. (1987) Advances in psychiatric epidemiology. Rates and risks for major depression. *Amer. J. Public Health*, **77**, 445–51.

Weissman, M. M. and Klerman, G. L. (1977) Sex differences and the epidemiology of depression. *Arch. Gen. Psychiat.*, **34**, 98–111.

West, P. (1988) Inequalities? Social class differentials in health in British youth. *Soc. Sci. Med.*, **27**, 291–6.

Whichelow, M. J. (1988) Which foods contain dietary fibre? The beliefs of a random sample of the British population. *European J. Clin. Nutr.*, **42**, 945–51.

Whincup, P. H., Cook, D. G. and Shaper, A. G. (1988) Social class and height. *Brit. Med. J.*, **297**, 980–1.

Whitehead, M. (1988) The health divide, in *Inequalities in Health* (eds P. Townsend, N. Davidson and M. Whitehead), Penguin, Harmondsworth.

WHO (1977) *International Classification of Diseases*, 9th revision, WHO, Geneva.

WHO (1978) *Social and Biological Effects on Perinatal Mortality*, WHO, Geneva.

WHO (1984) *Report of the Working Group on Concepts and Principles of Health Promotion*, Copenhagen, 9–13 July 1984, World Health Organizations.

Wilkinson, R. G. (ed.) (1986) *Class and Health*, Tavistock, London.

Wilkinson, R. (1989) Class mortality differentials, income distribution and trends in poverty, 1921–1981. *J. Soc. Policy*, **18**, 307–35.

Appendix A

The NCDS questionnaire

Questionnaire at age 23 (limited to health questions only).

I want to talk now about your health.

Q1 How would you describe your health generally? Would you
say it is . . . READ OUT . . .

excellent.. 1
good.. 2
fair 3   (39)
or poor? 4
Don't know 8

Q2 Can I just check? Do you have any longstanding illness, disability or infirmity which *limits your activities* in any way compared with people of your own age?

Yes...	1	Ask Q3
No	2	Go to Q11
Don't know	8	Page 71

(40)

Q3 What is it? PROBE FOR: Name of condition. IF NOT KNOWN, OR
UNCLEAR, PROBE FOR DESCRIPTION OF CONDITION.

Q4 How old were you when you got this? IF DON'T KNOW, PROBE:
'When do you first remember knowing about it?'   (41) (42)

Age in years ....
From birth 00   (41–42)
Don't know 98

Q5 Are you under medical supervision for this/these condition/s?

Yes...	1	Ask Q6
No	2	Go to Q7

(43)

Q6 NAME AND ADDRESS OF DOCTOR OR HOSPITAL. TAKE NAME OF
SPECIALIST (NOT GP) IF SPECIALIST SEEN.

Q7 SHOWCARD T How much does your condition limit your activities? From this card, please tell me how much difficulty, if any, you have in . . . READ OUT IN TURN . . .

	No difficulty	Some difficulty	A great deal	Can't do at all	
. . . washing or dressing yourself?	1	2	3	4	(44)
. . . getting about the house?	1	2	3	4	(45)
. . . doing housework?	1	2	3	4	(46)
. . . getting out of the house on your own?	1	2	3	4	(47)
. . . leading your social life?	1	2	3	4	(48)

Q8 Does your condition mean you are unable to do the sort of work you would like to do?

Yes... 1
No 2   (49)
Don't know 8

Q9 Can I just check? Are you in paid employment at the present time?
(INCLUDE SHELTERED EMPLOYMENT)

Yes... | 1 Ask Q10 | (50)
No .... | 2 Go to Q11 |

Q10 SHOWCARD T   How much does your condition limit you in your job? From this card, please tell me how much difficulty, if any, you have in doing your job?

No difficulty 1
Some difficulty 2
A great deal.. 3   (51)
Can't do at all 4

ASK ALL
Q11 How tall are you without shoes?

(52)   (53) (54)
FEET [ ]   INCHES [ ][ ]   (52–54)
Don't know 998

Q12 What is your present weight without clothes on? (IF PREGNANT, WEIGHT BEFORE PREGNANCY)

178

STONES ☐☐ (55) (66)   LBS ☐☐ (57) (58)   (57–58)

Don't know 9998

Q13 Would you say you were . . . READ OUT . . .
. . . about the right weight? 1
. . . underweight?..2
. . . slightly overweight? 3   (59)
. . . or very overweight 4
(Don't know) 8

Q14 Do you wear glasses or contact lenses at all?

Yes, both glasses and contact lenses ..	1	Ask Q15
Yes, glasses only	2	Ask Q15	(60)
Yes, contact lenses only...................	3	Ask Q15
No, do not wear either....................	4	Go to Q16

Q15 Why do you need to wear them?

Code one only

Short sight (distant vision) 1
Long sight (near vision)..2
Both short and long sight 3   (61)
Astigmatism 4
Other (SPECIFY)...5
Don't know 8

Q16 Since your sixteenth birthday have you suffered from migraine or recurrent sick headaches?

| Yes................................... | 1 | Ask Q17 | (62) |
| No .... | 2 | Go to Q18 |

Q17 Have you had an attack in the last 12 months?
Yes...1
No 2   (63)
Don't know/Can't remember 8

Q18 Since your sixteenth birthday have you ever had any form of fit, convulsions, long faints or loss of consciousness?

Yes.............................	1	Ask Q19
No	2	Go to Q24	(64)
Don't know	8	Go to Q24

Q19 Have any of these attacks been called epileptic?
Yes...1
No 2   (65)
Don't know 8

Q20 How old were you when you had your most recent attack?
RING CODE 16 . . .17 . . . 18 . . . 19 . . . 20 . . . 21 . . .
22 . . . 23 . . .   (66–67)
Can't remember 98

Q21 Do you take any prescribed medicines to help control these
attacks?
Yes.. 1
No 2   (68)
Don't know 8

Q22 Are you under medical supervision for these attacks?
Yes... | 1 | Ask Q23 | (69)
No .... | 2 | Go to Q24 |

Q23 NAME AND ADDRESS OF DOCTOR OR HOSPITAL. TAKE NAME OF
SPECIALIST (NOT GP) IF SPECIALIST SEEN.

Q24 Since your sixteenth birthday have you had an attack of
asthma or wheezy bronchitis?
Yes... | 1 | Ask Q25 |
No .... | 2 | Go to Q29 | (70)
Don't know .... | 8 | Go to Q29 |

Q25 Have you had an attack in the last 12 months?
Yes.. 1
No 2   (71)

Q26 Do you take any prescribed medicines to help control these
attacks?
Yes.. 1
No 2   (72)
Don't know 8

Q27 Are you under medical supervison for any of these attacks?
Yes... | 1 | Ask Q28 | (73)
No .... | 2 | Go to Q29 |

Q28 NAME AND ADDRESS OF DOCTOR OR HOSPITAL. TAKE NAME OF
SPECIALIST (NOT GP) IF SPECIALIST SEEN.

Q29 Do you usually cough first thing in the morning in the winter?
COUNT A COUGH WITH FIRST SMOKE OR ON FIRST GOING OUT
OF DOORS. EXCLUDE CLEARING THROAT OR A SINGLE COUGH.
Yes.. 1
No 2   (74)

Q30 Do you usually cough during the day or at night in the
winter? IGNORE AN OCCASIONAL COUGH
Yes.. 1
No 2   (75)

Q31 Do you usually bring up any phlegm from your chest first thing in the morning in the winter? COUNT PHLEGM WITH THE FIRST SMOKE OR ON FIRST GOING OUT OF DOORS. EXCLUDE PHLEGM FROM THE NOSE. COUNT SWALLOWED PHLEGM.

Yes 1
No 2   (76)

Q32 Do you usually bring up any phlegm from the chest during the day or night in the winter?

Yes 1
No 2   (77)

Q33 In the last 12 months have you suffered from:
(a) Eczema?

Yes 1
No 2   (78)
Don't know 8

(b) Hay fever?

Yes 1
No 2   (79)
Don't know 8

REGULAR MEDICAL SUPERVISION

Q34 At the present time, do you have any *regular* medical supervision for *any condition other than the ones we have already spoken about*? (IF FEMALE: and apart from regular ante-natal care or post-natal care.)

NOTE: Regular = have consultations or check-ups with doctor/hospital at least once a year.

Yes	1	Ask Q35a
No	2	Go to Q36
Don't know	8	Go to Q36

(13)

Q35a What conditions are you under *regular* medical supervision for? LIST IN GRID BELOW. PROBE: 'Any other conditions?' UNTIL 'no'.

FOR EACH CONDITION LISTED
b) Are you under the regular supervision of someone at a hospital or clinic or is it just your GP you see regularly?

IF HOSPITAL OR CLINIC

c) OBTAIN NAME AND ADDRESS OF SPECIALIST AND
HOSPITAL/CLINIC.

(a) CONDITION	(b) WHO SUPERVISES	(c) NAME AND ADDRESS OF SPECIALIST AND HOSPITAL/CLINIC	
	(14) Hospital/Clinic 1 → GP only 2		(14)
	(15) Hospital/Clinic 1 → GP only 2		(15)
	(16) Hospital/Clinic 1 → GP only 2		(16)
	(17) Hospital/Clinic 1 → GP only 2		(17)

ACCIDENTS

Q36 Since your 16th birthday have you been admitted to hospital
or attended a hospital outpatient or casualty department as
a result of any kind of accident to *you*?

Yes...	1	Ask Q37
No	2	Go to Q41
Don't know	8	Go to Q41

(18)

Q37 Since your 16th birthday, how many accidents have you had
which involved going to hospital?

(19)   (20)

WRITE IN . . . ☐☐   (19–20)

Can't remember 98

Q38 COMPLETE GRID BELOW FOR EACH SUCH ACCIDENT. START WITH MOST RECENT AND WORK BACKWARDS.

FOR 'TYPE OF ACCIDENT' SHOWCARD U AND ASK:
'Which of these things on this card best describes your accident?' ENTER APPROPRIATE CODE IN GRID BELOW AS FOLLOWS:
1. Road accident as pedestrian
2. Road accident as driver/passenger in motor vehicle/pedal cycle, etc.
3. Accident at work
4. Accident at home
5. Sports accident
6. Other

	AGE WHEN ACCIDENT OCCURRED	TYPE OF ACCIDENT (CODE NUMBER FROM CARD)	Were you admited overnight or treated as an outpatient only? ADMITTED OUT-PATIENT ONLY	TYPE OF INJURY (WRITE IN)	
(21)			1 2(24)		(21–24)
(25)			1 2(28)		(25–28)
(29)			1 2(32)		(29–32)
(33)			1 2(36)		(33–36)
(37)			1 2(40)		(37–40)
(41)			1 2(44)		(41–44)
(45)			1 2(48)		(45–48)
(49)			1 2(52)		(49–52)

Q39 Has this (have any of these) accident(s) resulted in any permanent disability?

Yes.. | 1   Ask Q40 | (53)
No .... | 2   Go to Q41

Q40 What is this disability? WRITE IN DETAILS.

IN-PATIENT ADMISSION

Q41 Since your sixteenth birthday, *apart from any accidents*, have you been admitted to a hospital or clinic for an *overnight or longer stay* (IF FEMALE, apart from a routine childbirth)?

| EXCLUDE: School sick bays. |
| INCLUDE: All *complications* with childbirth |

Yes...	1	Ask Q42
No	2	Go to Q44
Can't remember	8	Go to Q44

(54)

Q42 Since your sixteenth birthday, on how many different occasions (IF FEMALE, apart from routine childbirth) have you been admitted to a hospital or clinic for an overnight or longer stay? RING CODE

NUMBER OF OCCASIONS: 1 2 3 4 5 6 7+   (55)

Can't remember 8

Q43 COMPLETE GRID BELOW FOR EACH ADMISSION. IF ADMITTED MORE THAN ONCE DURING PREGNANCY FOR SAME REASON, TAKE FIRST ADMISSION ONLY. START WITH MOST RECENT ADMISSION AND WORK BACKWARDS.

AGE WHEN ADMITTED (RING AGE CODE)	REASON FOR ADMISSION	NAME AND ADDRESS OF HOSPITAL/CLINIC	
16 . . . 17 . . . 18 . . . 19 . . .20 . . . 21 . . . 22 . . . 23 (56–57)			(56–57)
16 . . . 17 . . . 18 . . . 19 . . .20 . . . 21 . . . 22 . . . 23 (58–59)			(58–59)
16 . . . 17 . . . 18 . . . 19 . . .20 . . . 21 . . . 22 . . . 23 (60–61)			(60–61)
16 . . . 17 . . . 18 . . . 19 . . .20 . . . 21 . . . 22 . . . 23 (62–63)			(62–63)
16 . . . 17 . . . 18 . . . 19 . . . 20 . . . 21 . . . 22 . . . 23 (64–65)			(64–65)
16 . . . 17 . . . 18 . . . 19 . . .20 . . . 21 . . . 22 . . . 23 (66–67)			(66–67)
16 . . . 17 . . . 18 . . . 19 . . .20 . . . 21 . . . 22 . . . 23 (68–69)			(68–69)

EMOTIONAL PROBLEMS

Q44 Apart from anything you have already told me about, since
your sixteenth birthday have you seen a *specialist* for
depression or any other emotional or psychological problem?

Yes..	1	Ask Q45	
No	2	Go to Q48	(70)
Don't know	8	Go to Q48	
Refused.......................................	7	Go to Q48	

Q45 How old were you when you last saw a specialist for this
reason?
RING CODE 16 . . .17 . . . 18 . . . 19 . . . 20 . . . 21 . . .
22 . . . 23
Can't remember 98
Refused...97 (71–72)

Q46 On that occasion, what was the problem? RECORD DETAILS.

Q47 NAME AND ADDRESS OF SPECIALIST LAST CONSULTED.

ASK ALL

Q48 Do you have any other medical condition or problem
concerning your physical or mental health that hasn't
already been mentioned?

Yes..	1	Ask Q49	
No	2	Go to Q52	(73)

Q49 What is this? RECORD DETAILS.

Q50 Are you under medical supervision for this/these
condition(s)?

Yes..	1	Ask Q51	(74)
No	2	Go to Q52	

Q51 NAME AND ADDRESS OF DOCTOR OR HOSPITAL. TAKE NAME OF
SPECIALIST (NOT GP) IF SPECIALIST SEEN.

ASK ALL

Q52 When did you last consult a GP about *your own* health, apart
from having a check-up required for work or insurance or
for a vaccination?

CODE	. . . Less than 6 months ago? 1	(75)
FIRST	. . . 6 months, but less than 1 year ago?. 2	
THAT	. . . 1 year, but less than 5 years ago?....3	
APPLIES	. . . 5 years, but since your 16th birthday .	
	4	
	Not since 16th birthday 5	
	(Can't remember) 8	

185

Please read the questions set out below and TICK either 'Yes' or 'No' for each one.

1. Do you often have back-ache?	Yes	1	No	2	(16)
2. Do you feel tired most of the time?	Yes	1	No	2	(17)
3. Do you often feel miserable or depressed?	Yes	1	No	2	(18)
4. Do you often have bad headaches?	Yes	1	No	2	(19)
5. Do you often get worried about things?	Yes	1	No	2	(20)
6. Do you usually have great difficulty in falling or staying asleep	Yes	1	No	2	(21)
7. Do you usually wake unnecessarily early in the morning?	Yes	1	No	2	(22)
8. Do you wear youself out worrying about your health?	Yes	1	No	2	(23)
9. Do you often get into a violent rage?	Yes	1	No	2	(24)
10. Do people often annoy and irritate you?	Yes	1	No	2	(25)
11. Have you at times had a twitching of the face, head or shoulders?	Yes	1	No	2	(26)
12. Do you often suddenly become scared for no good reason?	Yes	1	No	2	(27)
13. Are you scared to be alone when there are no friends near you?	Yes	1	No	2	(28)
14. Are you easily upset or irritated?	Yes	1	No	2	(29)
15. Are you frightened of going out alone or of meeting people?	Yes	1	No	2	(30)
16. Are you constantly keyed up and jittery?	Yes	1	No	2	(31)
17. Do you suffer from indigestion?	Yes	1	No	2	(32)
18. Do you often suffer from an upset stomach?	Yes	1	No	2	(33)
19. Is your appetite poor?	Yes	1	No	2	(34)
20. Does every little thing get on your nerves and wear you out?	Yes	1	No	2	(35)
21. Does your heart often race like mad?	Yes	1	No	2	(36)
22. Do you often have bad pains in your eyes?	Yes	1	No	2	(37)
23. Are you troubled with rheumatism or fibrositis?	Yes	1	No	2	(38)
24. Have you ever had a nervous breakdown?	Yes	1	No	2	(39)

186

Supplementary tables

Table B.1 Major ICD categories* and respondents rating of their own health (percent in each ICD category)

Self-rating of health	No.	%	Infectious	Neoplasms	Endocrine, nutritional, metabolic and immunity	Blood and blood-forming organs	Mental disorders	Nervous and sense organs	Circulatory system	Respiratory	Digestive	Genito-urinary	Complications of pregnancy and birth	Skin and subcutaneous tissue	Musculoskeletal and connective tissue	Congenital anomalies	Poisoning	Operations and investigations	Symptoms	Inadequate	Healthy†
Men			(91)	(19)	(45)	(11)	(98)	(214)	(48)	(208)	(337)	(50)		(182)	(174)	(34)	(55)	(300)	(123)	(30)	(1475)
Excellent	(2999)	48	40	42	20	36	15	33	31	30	38	38		41	28	38	42	45	38	39	58
Good	(2736)	44	44	47	44	45	42	49	50	49	47	42		48	47	41	35	43	49	43	38
Fair	(476)	8	12	11	27	18	32	14	4	19	13	18		10	19	15	14	10	11	10	4
Poor	(51)	1	4	0	9	0	11	5	15	2	2	2		0	6	6	9	2	2	10	0
Women			(68)	(41)	(59)	(46)	(174)	(144)	(105)	(267)	(393)	(389)	(543)	(171)	(155)	(47)	(111)	(506)	(165)	(27)	(393)
Excellent	(2597)	41	26	32	24	20	13	23	24	27	31	27	33	30	25	17	31	36	27	22	58
Good	(2992)	48	54	54	49	37	41	46	42	55	47	52	50	50	44	45	40	45	46	56	38
Fair	(614)	10	19	12	27	35	38	26	30	17	20	18	14	18	27	34	28	17	21	22	4
Poor	(61)	1	0	2	0	9	9	5	5	1	3	3	3	2	4	4	2	3	6	0	0

Figures in brackets are actual numbers.

*Conditions were identified from reports of limiting longstanding illness, medically supervised conditions or hospital admissions.

†'Healthy' is defined as having no positive responses to any of the health questions in Appendix A.

Table B.2 Reported health problems at age 23

Condition or symptom	Men (n = 6290)		Women (n = 6268)		Both sexes (n = 12 538)	
	No.	(Rate)*	No.	(Rate)*	No.	(Rate)*
Longstanding illness, disability or infirmity which limits activities	319	(51)	256	(41)	575	(46)
Attack of migraine or recurrent sick headache since age 16	838	(133)	1812	(289)	2650	(211)
Fits, convulsions since age 16	227	(36)	324	(52)	551	(44)
Asthma or wheezy bronchitis since age 16	508	(81)	673	(107)	1181	(94)
Cough first thing in morning in winter	685	(109)	591	(94)	1276	(102)
Cough in day or night in winter	474	(76)	611	(97)	1085	(87)
Phlegm from chest in morning in winter	631	(101)	406	(65)	1037	(83)
Phlegm from chest during day or night in winter	453	(72)	335	(53)	788	(63)
Eczema in previous 12 months	227	(36)	436	(70)	663	(53)
Hayfever in previous 12 months	1037	(165)	1023	(163)	2060	(164)
Condition needing regular medical supervision at the time of the interview	324	(52)	568	(91)	892	(71)
Hospital admissions since age 16 (excluding routine childbirth)	1117	(178)	1883	(300)	3000	(239)
Depression, emotional, psychological problem, since age 16 for which specialist seen	149	(24)	313	(50)	462	(37)
Any other medical problem not covered by the above	408	(65)	483	(77)	891	(71)

*Per 1000 population.

Table B.3 The Malaise Inventory – percentages reporting symptoms

Malaise items	Men ($n = 6237$)*	Women ($n = 6248$)*
Do you often have back-ache?	14.7	23.2
Do you feel tired most of the time?	11.9	22.6
Do you often feel miserable or depressed?	10.2	18.7
Do you often have bad headaches?	6.0	19.8
Do you often get worried about things?	30.4	54.3
Do you usually have great difficulty in falling or staying asleep?	9.6	11.5
Do you usually wake unnecessarily early in the morning?	15.0	16.5
Do you wear yourself out worrying about your health?	1.8	3.1
Do you often get into a violent rage?	4.6	7.1
Do people often annoy and irritate you?	24.5	29.0
Have you at times had a twitching of the face, head or shoulders?	8.0	7.9
Do you often suddenly become scared for no good reason?	3.8	13.1
Are you scared to be alone when there are no friends near you?	2.2	16.8
Are you easily upset or irritated?	14.5	31.9
Are you frightened of going out alone or of meeting people?	3.3	12.1
Are you constantly keyed up and jittery?	3.3	4.4
Do you suffer from indigestion?	12.4	10.2
Do you often suffer from an upset stomach?	9.1	11.2
Is your appetite poor?	3.7	5.1
Does every little thing get on your nerves and wear you out?	1.4	3.3
Does your heart often race like mad?	6.0	8.2
Do you often have bad pains in your eyes?	4.7	5.3
Are you troubled with rheumatism or fibrositis?	2.7	5.1
Have you ever had a nervous breakdown?	1.2	2.1

*Numbers vary slightly for each item.

Table B.4 Prevalence ratios for major ICD categories* according to malaise

ICD category	Men		Women	
	Low malaise score ($n = 5889$)	High malaise score ($n = 381$)	Low malaise score ($n = 5281$)	High malaise score ($n = 987$)
Infectious	96	163	101	94
Neoplasms	107	0	101	38
Endocrine, nutritional, metabolic, immunity	92	219	90	151
Blood and blood-forming organs	87	300	77	221
Mental disorders	64	660	42	413
Nervous and sense organs	93	208	82	199
Circulatory system	96	171	81	200
Respiratory	95	189	98	109
Digestive	94	194	93	139
Genito-urinary	100	99	90	206
Complications of pregnancy and birth	–	–	91	151
Skin and subcutaneous tissue	97	143	91	149
Musculoskeletal and connective tissue	92	217	88	164
Congenital anomalies	97	145	98	108
Poisoning	80	420	78	218
Operations and investigations	100	115	98	113
Symptoms	92	227	79	212
Inadequate	89	275	88	165
'Healthy'†	105	33	113	28

Prevalence ratio = $\dfrac{\text{No. of observed cases per 1000 per malaise group}}{\text{No. of expected cases per 1000 (based on prevalence of malaise in the entire cohort)}} \times 100$

*Conditions were identified from reports of limiting longstanding illness, medically supervised conditions or hospital admissions.

†'Healthy' is defined as having no positive responses to any of the health questions in Appendix A.

Appendix B

Table B.5 Psychological and emotional problems, reported as receiving treatment between ages 16 and 23

	Men		Women	
Psychological problems*	(*n*)	(%)	(*n*)	(%)
Psychotic conditions	4	(0.1)	10	(0.2)
Non-psychotic disorders:				
Neurotic disorders	58	(0.9)	124	(2.0)
Depression	68	(1.1)	182	(2.9)
Personality disorders	12	(0.2)	5	(0.1)
Sexual deviations	4	(0.1)	–	–
Alcohol dependence	13	(0.2)	2	–
Drug dependence	8	(0.1)	3	–
Anorexia nervosa	1	–	14	(0.2)
Overdose	34	(0.5)	59	(0.9)
Other disorders (including post-natal depression)	42	(0.7)	59	(0.9)
Inadequate reply	9	(0.1)	12	(0.2)

*Excluding 13 mentally retarded young adults.

Table B.6 Final models, including significant variables in multivariate models shown in Tables 11.4 to 11.6; showing relative odds of poor health*

Selected variables†	Men‡			Women‡		
	'Poor' or 'fair' self-rated health	High malaise score	Psycho-logical morbidity	'Poor' or 'fair' self-rated health	High malaise score	Psycho-logical morbidity
Housing tenure at age 11 (renters versus owners)				1.31 (0.98, 1.75)	1.41 (1.06, 1.91)	
School absence through ill-health§ (>1 week versus <1 week)	2.29 (1.50, 3.49)			1.45 (1.11, 1.90)		
Smoking at 16 (smoking versus non-smoker)	1.80 (1.18, 2.75)				1.50 (1.14, 1.96)	
Behaviour score at 16 ('deviant' versus 'normal')	2.15 (1.19, 3.87)		3.18 (1.92, 5.26)	1.87 (1.23, 2.85)	2.09 (1.33, 3.06)	2.66 (1.67, 4.24)
End of school qualifications (none versus one or more)	1.65 (0.98, 2.76)			1.87 (1.38, 2.53)	1.77 (1.30, 2.41)	
Unemployment by age 23 (one or more periods versus none)			2.89 (1.51, 4.38)			1.73 (1.29, 2.33)
Social class at age 23 (classes IV and V versus I and II)	1.69 (0.79, 3.60)	1.14 (0.63, 2.05)		1.65 (1.03, 2.65)	2.85 (1.71, 4.76)	1.60 (0.99, 2.60)

*Relative odds of poor health adjusted for other variables indicated in the table; e.g. in women the relative odds of psychological morbidity associated with class at age 23 was 1.60, having adjusted for behaviour score at 16 and unemployment between ages 16 and 23.
†Indicated in Table 11.1.
‡Based on samples shown in Table 11.1.
§During preceding year.

Appendix C

Definition of measures

C.1 Income level

The measure of income used in Chapter 3 is net family income adjusted to allow for the size and composition of the family (i.e. NCDS subject and spouse or partner and any children in their care). It may be interpreted as a proxy measure for standard of living in that the effects are to adjust upwards the incomes of those with relatively low requirements (e.g. single adult families) and to adjust downward the incomes of those with relatively high needs (e.g. married and cohabiting couples, and those with children). The adjustments are based on the Supplementary Benefit scale rates applying in 1981. The measure was developed by Shepherd (1984), but for a discussion of similar measures see Van Slooten and Coverdale (1977) and Fiegehen *et al.* (1977).

C.2 Behaviour

The NCDS includes ratings of children's behaviour at ages 7, 11 and 16 from both their parents and teachers. All ratings of behaviour are screening techniques which, taken alone, do not indicate emotional maladjustment. This approach has limitations such as being unable to account for the context or transience of behaviour, or the different norms of behaviour adopted by the raters. Rutter *et al.* (1970) summarized the advantages and disadvantages of the statistical definition of 'deviant' behaviour thus:

> It avoids conceptual problems in definition, it is easy to handle statistically, and the use of questionnaires makes it easy to study very large numbers of children. . . . However, the method has serious disadvantages. It ignores the context of the behaviour, it allows no consideration of the extent to which the child is handicapped by his

difficulties, and it does not take into account the course or process of the child's overall development behaviour. . .

While the behaviour ratings might indicate deviance, therefore, this does not equate to a diagnosis of psychiatric disorder.

Although ratings of behaviour were available from both parents and teachers of children in the NCDS, only the latter were used in the present enquiry. Ratings for two of the three ages (11 and 16 years) were included and these are described below.

At age 11 teachers completed the Bristol Social Adjustment Guide (BSAG) which consists of 146 'items of behaviour' (Stott, 1969). These are designated to 12 separate syndromes:

1. Unforthcomingness
2. Withdrawal
3. Depression
4. Anxiety for acceptance by adults
5. Hostility towards adults
6. 'Writing off' adults
7. Anxiety for acceptance by children
8. Hostility towards children
9. Restlessness
10. 'Inconsequential' behaviour
11. Miscellaneous symptoms
12. Miscellaneous 'nervous' symptoms

A score is obtained for each of these syndromes and, in addition, a total score is derived. The latter was used in our analyses.

At age 16, teachers completed the Rutter School Behaviour Scale (Rutter, 1967) which consists of 26 items of behaviour rated as 'certainly applies', 'applies somewhat' or 'doesn't apply' to the study child (Table C.1). These were given a weight of 2, 1 and 0 respectively to produce a total score.

As described in earlier work on the cohort (Ghodsian *et al.*, 1980) the scores for both ages (BSAG at 11 and Rutter score at 16) were then transformed (square-root transformation) and divided into three categories:

1. 'High' scores were identified for approximately 13% of the sample; they are described here as 'deviant'. The cut-off used to define this group corresponds to that recommended by Rutter.
2. 'Low' scores were taken to be the lowest 50% of the distribution approximately, representing 'non-deviant' or 'normal' behaviour.
3. 'Intermediate' scores comprised the remaining children, approximately 35%.

Appendix C

Table C.1 Items in the Rutter score for age 16

Bold: Items from which 'emotional' subscore is derived.
Italic: Items from which 'conduct' disorder subscore is derived

Below is a series of descriptions of behaviour often shown by school children.

Please ring the appropriate number in each case to show the degree to which the study child exhibits the behaviour described.

Please complete on the basis of the child's behaviour in the past 12 months.

	Doesn't Apply	Applies Somewhat	Certainly Applies
i) Very restless, has difficulty staying seated for long	1	2	3
ii) Truants from school	1	2	3
iii) Squirmy, fidgety	1	2	3
iv) Often destroys or damages own or others' property	*1*	2	*3*
v) Frequently fights or is extremely quarrelsome with other children	*1*	*2*	*3*
vi) Not much liked by other children	1	2	3
vii) Often worries, worries about many things	**1**	**2**	**3**
viii) Tends to be on own – rather solitary	1	2	3
ix) Irritable, touchy, is quick to 'fly off the handle'	1	2	3
x) Often appears miserable, unhappy, tearful or distressed	**1**	**2**	**3**
xi) Has twitches, mannerisms or tics of the face or body	1	2	3
xii) Frequently sucks thumb or finger	1	2	3
xiii) Frequently bites nails or fingers	1	2	3
xiv) Tends to be absent from school for trivial reasons	1	2	3
xv) Is often disobedient	*1*	2	*3*
xvi) Cannot settle to anything for more than a few moments	1	2	3
xvii) Tends to be fearful or afraid of new situations and new things	**1**	**2**	**3**
xviii) Fussy or over particular	1	2	3
xix) Often tells lies	*1*	2	*3*
xx) Has stolen things on one or more occasions in the past 12 months	*1*	2	3
xxi) Unresponsive, inert or apathetic	1	2	3
xxii) Often complains of aches or pains	1	2	3
xxiii) Has had tears on arrival at school or has refused to come into the building in the past 12 months	**1**	**2**	**3**
xxiv) Has a stutter or stammer	1	2	3
xxv) Resentful or aggressive when corrected	1	2	3
xxvi) Bullies other children	*1*	2	*3*

These categories were used in the univariate and multivariate analyses presented in Chapters 10 and 11, but further subdivision of the 'deviant' group is described here in order to improve our understanding of the relationship between the rating and later health outcomes at age 23. This description is limited to behaviour as rated at age 16, which was selected for inclusion in the multivariate analyses.

Conventionally, deviant behaviour is differentiated according to propensity of the child to be anxious or depressed on the one hand and, on the other, aggressive. The two groups, usually referred to as neurotic or emotional behaviour and conduct or antisocial behaviour, overlap to a considerable extent (Rutter *et al.*, 1970). Subdivision of the deviant group into 'emotional' and 'conduct' (or antisocial) disorder was achieved by summing the items indicated in Table C.1. Children were designated as having 'emotional' disorder if their subscore exceeded that for 'conduct' and vice versa. The children with equal emotional and conduct subscores remain undifferentiated.

Table C.2 shows 15.6% of boys were rated as 'deviant' compared with 11.0% of girls, and this difference largely reflects sex differences in 'conduct' rather than 'emotional' disorder. Both subgroups were associated with significantly raised odds of poor self-rated health, malaise and psychological morbidity at age 23 compared with the low rating category (that is, those with 'normal' behaviour) although, in each case, it was for later malaise that the relative odds were especially notable (Table C.3).

Table C.2 Categories of behaviour ratings at age 16 (percentage in each category)

Behaviour rating at age 16	Boys ($n = 6415$)	Girls ($n = 6129$)	Both sexes ($n = 12\ 544$)
Low score	48.7	55.5	52.0
Intermediate score	35.7	33.5	34.6
High score	15.6	11.0	13.4
Emotional disorder	(5.6)	(6.0)	(5.8)
Conduct disorder	(7.3)	(3.2)	(5.3)
Other disorder*	(2.7)	(1.8)	(2.3)

*Not differentiated into emotional or conduct disorder.

Table C.3 Relative odds of poorer health at age 23 for those with 'deviant' behaviour ratings at age 16†

'Deviant' behaviour at age 16	'Poor' or 'fair' rating health		High malaise score		Psychological morbidity	
	Men	Women	Men	Women	Men	Women
Emotional disorder	4.92	3.62	6.59	4.98	2.93	2.91
Conduct disorder	1.95	1.94	4.19	4.50	1.72	2.44
Other*	2.67	3.31	8.79	3.45	4.47	2.06

*Not differentiated into emotional or conduct disorder.
†Compared with children, with low behaviour scores, that is 'normal' behaviour.

References

Fiegehen, G. C., Larnsley, P. S. and Smith, A. D. (1977) *Poverty and Progress in Britain 1953–1973*, Cambridge Univ. Press, Cambridge.

Ghodsian, M., Fogelman, K., Lambert, L. and Tibbenham, A. (1980) Changes in behaviour rating of a national sample of children. *Brit. J. Soc. Clin. Psychol.*, **19**, 247–56.

Rutter, M. (1967) A children's behaviour questionnaire for completion by teachers. *J. Child Psychol. Psychiat.*, **8**, 1–11.

Rutter, M., Tizard, J. and Whitmore, K. (1970) *Education, Health and Behaviour*, Longman, London.

Shepherd, P. (1984) *Earnings, Income and Other Aspects of the Financial Circumstances of the NCDS Cohort at 23*. NCDS Working Paper No., 19, City Univ., Social Statistics Research Unit.

Stott, D. H. (1969) *The Social Adjustment of Children*, Univ. of London Press, London.

Van Slooten, R. and Coverdale, A. G. (1977) The characteristics of low income households. *Social Trends*, **8**, 26–39.

Appendix D

Response rates at age 23

As described in Chapter 2, sample attrition had occurred after age 16 when response in the cohort was last examined (Goldstein, 1983). The previous investigation had concluded that while certain disadvantaged groups were less likely to provide information at age 16, for most purposes response biases were acceptably small. It is important to establish whether this still applied to the sample at age 23.

To this end, response at age 23 was compared primarily with birth characteristics, since birth is the point at which response rates are greatest. However, two separate response comparisons were necessary to allow for the stages of analysis described earlier in the book (Chapter 5), and these were performed for each sex and health outcome measure separately. In the initial stage, presented in Chapters 6 to 10, only a limited number of variables were needed for each analysis and response comparisons were undertaken to reflect this. Latterly, in the multivariate stage of analysis, data were required for several variables (Table 11.1) and these differed for each sex and health outcome, thereby defining different samples in each case. Response comparisons were conducted to assess the representativeness of the resultant smaller samples, which are referred to as multivariate samples.

Tables D.1 and D.2 show response patterns in terms of selected earlier characteristics (mainly at birth) for 23-year respondents and for samples used in the multivariate analysis of adult heights, for men and women separately. Since the results for height, self-rated health, malaise and psychological morbidity were similar, only one measure, namely height, is reported here.

Table D.1 Response samples for men† (shown in percentages)

Variables	23-year sample				χ^2 (df)		
	In multi–variate sample	Not in multi–variate sample	No data at age 23	Total	Multi-variate sample vs remainder	23-year sample vs remainder	
Social class at age 23	(2951)	(2974)	(3668)	(5925)			
(a) I and II	22.0	21.2		21.6	26.9***	–	(3)
(b) IIIN	18.2	15.9		17.0			
(c) IIIM	41.9	39.6		40.7			
(d) IV and V	18.0	23.3		20.7			
Social class at birth	(2894)	(2579)	(3280)	(8753)			
(a) No male HOH§	1.1	3.8	3.4	2.8	70.6***	12.2*	(4)
(b) I and II	14.9	19.5	17.0	17.0			
(c) IIIN	11.1	8.8	8.7	9.5			
(d) IIIM	52.1	46.3	49.8	49.5			
(e) IV and V	20.8	21.7	21.1	21.2			
Mothers smoking in pregnancy	(2928)	(2613)	(3337)	(8878)			
None	67.6	67.9	64.5	66.5	6.3 (N.S.)	15.5**	(3)
1–9 cigarettes/day	17.3	17.1	19.8	18.2			
10–19 cigarettes/day	13.2	12.8	12.9	13.0			
20+ cigarettes/day	1.8	2.2	2.7	2.3			
Age father left school	(2316)	(1942)	(1430)	(5688)			
14 years or less	65.1	56.5	56.3	59.9	66.1***	10.8**	(2)
15–17 years	26.9	27.9	31.3	28.4			
more than 17 years	8.0	15.6	12.4	11.7			
Age mother left school	(2342)	(2013)	(1498)	(5853)	27.9***	(N.S.)	(2)
14 years or less	50.7	48.7	47.5	49.2			
15–17 years	42.1	39.1	42.5	41.2			
more than 17 years	7.1	12.2	10.0	9.6			
Overall qualifications at leaving school	(2951)	(2184)	(2179)	(7314)			
None or CSE only	52.2	55.4	59.2	55.2	37.1***	28.3***	(3)
1–4 'O'-levels‡	25.0	21.9	19.1	22.3			
5 'O'-levels or better	11.6	9.6	8.9	10.2			
2+ 'A' levels	11.3	13.1	12.7	12.3			

Figures in brackets are numbers in the samples.
N.S. = Not significant.
†Relevant to 23-year height analyses.   ***$p < 0.001$
§HOH = Head of household.   **$0.001 < p < 0.01$
‡Grades A–C and CSE Grade 1.   *$0.01 < p < 0.05$
otherwise $0.05 < p$

D.1 Representativeness at age 23

The 23-year sample was found to be significantly different (at least at the 5% level) from the group without data for most of the characteristics

Table D.1 *continued*

					T-value (df)	
Variables	Response group	(*n*)	Mean	(SD)	Multivariate sample vs remainder	23-year sample vs remainder
Mothers height (in inches)	Total sample data at age 23	(8632)	63.37	(2.52)		
	in multivariate sample	(2951)	63.42	(2.47)	−1.25	−2.71** (8630)
	not in multivariate sample	(2450)	63.44	(2.55)		
	No data at age 23	(3231)	63.27	(2.53)		
Birthweight of cohort member (in ounces)	Total sample data at age 23	(8638)	118.6	(20.6)		
	in multivariate sample	(2856)	120.6	(18.1)	−6.58***	−9.49*** (8636)
	not in multivariate sample	(2547)	119.7	(18.8)		
	No data at age 23	(3235)	115.9	(23.5)		
Height at age 7 (in metres)	Total sample data at age 23	(7036)	1.228	(0.058)		
	in multivariate sample	(2951)	1.229	(0.055)	−1.24	−1.91 (7034)
	not in multivariate sample	(1921)	1.229	(0.060)		
	No data at age 23	(2164)	1.226	(0.061)		

Figures in brackets are numbers in the samples.
N.S. = Not significant.
†Relevant to 23-year height analyses.   ***$p < 0.001$
§HOH = Head of household.   **$0.001 < p < 0.01$
‡Grades A–C and CSE Grade 1.   *$0.01 < p < 0.05$
   otherwise $0.05 < p$

compared. An exception, applying to both sexes, was the age at which mothers completed full-time education. Further comparisons designed to assess the representativeness of subcategories of a particular variable can be expressed in percentage terms. So, for example, 2.68% of women with data at age 23 had had no male head of household at birth compared with 3.25% overall. This is an underestimation of 17.5% ((3.25 − 2.68) × 100 and divided by 3.25) which was the greatest percentage bias in the 23-year sample found in the selected categorical variables shown in the tables. Generally, however, the percentage bias was less than 10% and although Tables D.1 and D.2 suggest a continuation of a trend evident at earlier sweeps (that is the underrepresentation of certain disadvantaged groups, such as those with no male head of household at birth) the figures are reassuring. This is despite the number of relationships that achieve statistical significance, many of which are small differences only that are readily detected in such large samples. Furthermore, when analyses of response were extended to

Table D.2 Response samples for women† (shown in percentages)

Variable	23-year sample			Total	χ^2 (df)		
	In multivariate sample	Not in multivariate sample	No data at age 23		Multivariate sample vs remainder	23-year sample vs remainder	
Social class at age 23	(3073)	(3011)	(2876)	(6084)	11.9**	–	(3)
(a) I and II	20.9	21.3		21.1			
(b) IIIN	51.8	48.2		50.0			
(c) IIIM	9.2	9.2		9.2			
(d) IV and V	18.1	21.3		19.7			
Social class at birth	(3029)	(2639)	(2543)	(8211)	74.6***	27.3***	(4)
(a) No male HOH§	1.7	3.8	4.5	3.3			
(b) I and II	14.4	20.7	16.1	16.9			
(c) IIIN	10.5	8.4	8.6	9.2			
(d) IIIM	52.5	46.6	47.8	49.2			
(e) IV and V	20.9	20.5	23.0	21.4			
Mothers smoking in pregnancy	(3041)	(2678)	(2589)	(8308)	4.0 (N.S.)	4.9 (N.S.)	(3)
None	67.1	66.4	65.9	66.5			
1–9 cigarettes/day	18.5	18.7	18.2	18.5			
10–19 cigarettes/day	12.3	12.5	12.9	12.5			
20+ cigarettes/day	2.0	2.4	3.0	2.5			
Age father left school	(2431)	(1939)	(1034)	(5404)	34.0***	3.0 (N.S.)	(2)
14 years or less	61.0	54.2	56.2	57.6			
15–17 years	29.3	31.2	30.0	30.1			
more than 17 years	9.7	14.7	13.8	12.3			
Age mother left school	(2455)	(2034)	(1090)	(5579)	9.3**	2.5 (N.S.)	(2)
14 years or less	48.6	46.3	46.2	47.3			
15–17 years	42.0	41.8	41.6	41.8			
more than 17 years	9.5	11.8	12.2	10.9			
Overall qualifications at leaving school	(3073)	(2240)	(1704)	(7017)	24.8***	52.4***	(3)
None or CSE only	46.2	48.3	56.7	49.4			
1–4 'O'-levels‡	27.3	26.3	22.1	25.7			
5 'O'-levels or better	14.1	11.7	11.9	12.8			
2+ 'A' levels	12.5	13.8	9.3	12.1			

Figures in brackets are numbers in the samples.
N.S. = Not significant.

†Relevant to 23-year height analyses.   ***$p < 0.001$
§HOH = Head of household.   **$0.001 < p < 0.01$
‡Grades A–C and CSE Grade 1.   *$0.01 < p < 0.05$ otherwise $0.05 < p$

Table D.2 *continued*

Variables	Response group	(n)	Mean	(SD)	T-value (df) Multivariate sample vs remainder	T-value (df) 23-year sample vs remainder
Mothers height (in inches)	Total sample data at age 23	(8071)	63.39	(2.50)		
	in multivariate sample	(3073)	63.43	(2.50)	−1.06**	
	not in multivariate sample	(2506)	63.47	(2.47)		−2.92** (8069)
	No data at age 23	(2492)	63.27	(2.52)		
Birthweight of cohort member (in ounces)	Total sample data at age 23	(8144)	113.8	(20.0)		
	in multivariate sample	(2987)	115.6	(18.0)	−6.31***	
	not in multivariate sample	(2639)	114.7	(17.7)		−9.53*** (8142)
	No data at age 23	(2518)	110.6	(23.8)		
Height at age 7 (in metres)	Total sample data at age 23	(6598)	1.219	(0.061)		
	in multivariate sample	(3073)	1.220	(0.058)	−1.07*	
	not in multivariate sample	(1948)	1.220	(0.062)		−2.23* (6596)
	No data at age 23	(1577)	1.216	(0.063)		

Figures in brackets are numbers in the samples.
N.S. = Not significant.
†Relevant to 23-year height analyses.   ***$p < 0.001$
§HOH = Head of household.   **$0.001 < p < 0.01$
‡Grades A–C and CSE Grade 1.   *$0.01 < p < 0.05$
                                  otherwise $0.05 < p$

assess whether the *relationships* between social class at age 23 and selected earlier charactersitics (in particular childhood and adolescent health)
differed between 23-year samples and the remainder, the two groups
were not significantly different (Power *et al.*, 1990).

D.2 Representativeness of multivariate samples

As described above for 23-year response, multivariate samples differed
significantly from the remainder in several respects, although not for
mother's height and smoking behaviour during pregnancy, or for the
cohort member's height at age 7 (Tables D.1 and D.2). The categories
in which representativeness was poor (taken here as a percentage bias
of more than 10%) were: social classes I and II, IIIN and no male head
of household at birth; social class IV and V at age 23 (in men); mother
smoking 20+ cigarettes per day during pregnancy; mother's and
father's school leaving age greater than 17 years, and finally, qualifications of 5 'O' levels or better (in men). As pointed out by Goldstein
(1983) in earlier NCDS response comparisons, percentage bias depends
on the particular categorization adopted and biases, in turn, suggest
ways in which variables can be reclassified. The percentage biases
described above therefore aided the multivariate stage of analysis, in
which several variables had to be regrouped so that a greater number
of variables could be considered in a reduced sample. Table D.3 shows
the revised classification of variables that was adopted.

The next stage in the comparison of response was to establish as far
as possible what effects sample discrepancies might have in the main
analyses presented in this book. One way to achieve this is to examine
the relationship between social class at 23 and earlier characteristics (for
example, at birth) in multivariate samples compared with the remainder. All continuous variables in Tables D.1 and D.2 were examined in
this way, in addition to categorical variables identified as causing particular concern – that is, social class at birth and qualifications at the
end of schooling. Further analyses of parents' school-leaving age were
not conducted since these characteristics were less relevant to the multivariate analyses. Log–linear models and analysis of variance were used
(for categorical and continuous variables respectively) to test differences
between the multivariate samples and the remainder.

D.2.1 Categorical variables

Using the revised classification of variables shown in Table D.3, no
significant differences were found between the multivariate samples
and the remainderf, in terms of relationships between social class at

Table D.3 Variables included in multivariate analyses and their categorization

Area of explanation	Categorical variables	Continuous variables
'Inheritance' at birth	Social class 1. Non-manual 2. Manual (includes no male HOH‡) Mothers smoking during pregnancy 1. Non-smokers 2. Smokers	Midparent height† (in inches) Birthweight (in ounces)
Socio-economic circumstances	Unemployment between 16 and 23 1. None 2. One or more periods of unemployment Social class at age 7 1. Non-manual 2. Manual (includes no male HOH‡) Housing tenure at age 11 1. Owners 2. Renters Age at first child 1. No child by age 23 2. Child(ren) by age 23	
Education	Qualifications at end of schooling 1. No qualifications or CSEs up to Grade 4 only 2. Qualifications at CSE Grade 3 or higher	
Health in childhood and adolescence	School absence through ill-health* 1. One week or less 2. More than one week	Height at age 7 (in metres) Height at age 11 (in metres)
Behaviour	Teachers rating of behaviour** 1. 'Deviant' 2. 'Intermediate' 3. 'Normal' Smoking at age 16 1. Non-smoker 2. Smoker	

* During preceding year.
** See Appendix C, section C.2, for definitions.
† Average of mother's and father's heights
‡ HOH = Head of household.

birth and social class at age 23. This applied to both sexes. The same result was found for the relationship between qualifications achieved by the end of schooling and social class at age 23, in the multivariate samples compared with the remainder. However, these results were consistent for the samples used for analyses of self-rated health, malaise and psychological morbidity, but not for those used for adult height. Tables D.4 and D.5 compare the sample used for height with the remaining sample, in terms of class at birth and qualifications. For both men and women, there was a higher percentage of those in manual classes at birth who were subsequently classified as classes IV and V at age 23 in the remaining sample than in that used for multivariate analysis; while among men the no-qualifications group in classes IV and V at 23 was proportionately greater in the remaining sample compared with that used for multivariate analysis. Given such biases, it is

Table D.4 Response in the multivariate sample used for the analysis of height versus the remainder: a comparison of the relationship between social class at age 23 and class at birth (percentages of men and women)

Social class at age 23	Men				Women			
	Multivariate sample		Remaining sample		Multivariate sample		Remaining sample	
	Non-manual class at birth	Manual class at birth	Non-manual class at birth	Manual class at birth	Non-manual class at birth	Manual class at birth	Non-manual class at birth	Manual class at birth
	(751)	(2143)	(730)	(1849)	(754)	(2275)	(767)	(1872)
I and II	35.8	17.2	38.6	13.9	30.2	17.9	36.0	15.0
IIIN	24.6	15.9	23.0	12.9	54.0	51.0	49.0	48.1
IIIM	27.2	47.1	23.4	46.6	6.0	10.2	6.1	10.7
IV and V	12.4	19.9	14.9	26.6	9.8	20.9	8.9	26.2

Figures in brackets are actual numbers.

Table D.5 Response in the sample used for the multivariate analysis of height versus the remainder: a comparison of the relationship between social class at age 23 and qualifications at end of schooling (percentages of men only)

Social class at age 23	Men			
	Multivariate sample		Remaining sample	
	No qualifications	One or more qualifications	No qualifications	One or more qualifications
	(1540)	(1411)	(1209)	(975)
I and II	10.4	34.6	7.4	38.9
IIIN	9.7	27.4	11.0	22.3
IIIM	53.2	29.6	48.9	26.3
IV and V	26.7	8.4	32.7	12.5

Figures in brackets are actual numbers.

possible that the effect of class at birth is underestimated in multivariate analyses of short stature (Table 11.8).

D.2.2 Continuous variables

As stated above, the relationship between social class and continuous variables (mother's height, the birthweight of the cohort member and their height at age 7) in the multivariate sample versus the remainder, was tested using analysis of variance. No statistically significant differences were detected and therefore no further details are reported.

D.3 Conclusions

The comparison of response presented here has been conducted mainly, but not exclusively, to test the representativeness of data at age 23 in terms of birth characteristics. This comparison was not exhaustive but it has demonstrated the direction and extent of biases in the sample. Only a few of the categories examined were associated with serious bias at age 23, to the extent that they were under- or overrepresented by 10% or more. This is reassuring for the initial phase of analysis in our investigation of class differences in health (presented in Chapters 6 to 10) although there is evidence here from the poor representation of those with no male head of household at birth that, as at age 16, the 'largest biases of all are found among certain groups of disadvantaged children' (Goldstein, 1983).

In the more restricted samples in the multivariate phase of the study, response was more problematic given the degree of sample attrition that occurred, and some biases had become more pronounced. While this did not affect class comparisons of self-rated health, malaise and psychological morbidity, the effect of class at birth may be underestimated in analyses of adult height.

References

Goldstein, H. (1983) A study of the response rates of 16-year-olds in the National Child Development Study, in *Growing up in Great Britain* (ed. K. Fogelman), Macmillan, London.

Power, C., Manor, O., Fox, A. J. and Fogelman, K. (1990) Health in childhood and social inequalities in health in young adults. *J. Roy. Statist. Soc.*, Series A, **153**, 17–28.

Appendix E

Statistics

E.1 Odds ratio

The odds ratio is defined for a single 2×2 contingency table or as a summary statistic for S 2×2 contingency tables where S is the number of strata. A single 2×2 contingency table may be formed by two independent populations where each is characterized by a random variable with a dichotomous response. For example, populations can be defined according to the presence or absence of a certain factor while the response variable indicates the presence or absence of a certain disease as illustrated below:

		Disease		Total
		+	−	
	+	p_1	$1-p_1$	1
Factor				
	−	p_2	$1-p_2$	1

In this table p_1 is the probability of having the disease in one population while p_2 is the probability of having the disease in the other population. The odds in favour of having the disease when the factor is present are $p_1 /(1 - p_1)$ and the odds in favour of having the disease when the factor is absent are $p_2 /(1 - p_2)$. The odds ratio (OR) is the ratio of these two odds:

$$\text{OR} = \frac{p_1/(1 - p_1)}{p_2/(1 - p_2)} = \frac{p_1 (1 - p_2)}{p_2 (1 - p_1)}$$

A single 2×2 contingency table may also be formed by considering a pair of random variables with dichotomous response as illustrated below:

		B		Total
		1	2	
A	1	p_{11}	p_{12}	$p_{11} + p_{12}$
	2	p_{21}	p_{22}	$p_{21} + p_{22}$
Total		$p_{11} + p_{21}$	$p_{12} + p_{22}$	1

In this table p_{ij} represents the probability of an observation falling in cell i,j ($i=1,2$; $j=1,2$) and

$$p_{11} + p_{12} + p_{21} + p_{22} = 1.$$

In this situation the odds ratio, which is defined in the same way, that is OR $= p_{11} p_{22}/p_{21} p_{12}$, is thought of as a measure of association between the two random variables A and B. (It is also referred to as cross-product ratio.)

Cornfield (1951) first used the odds ratio as a measure of relative risk. An estimate of the odds ratio for a 2×2 table is

$$\widehat{OR} = n_{11} n_{22}/n_{21} n_{12}$$

where n_{ij} represents the number of observations falling in cell i,j. The odds ratio plays a central role in logistic models. For further reading concerning the odds ratio the reader is referred to Fleiss (1981).

E.2 Logistic models

As mentioned in Chapter 5, logistic models were used to estimate odds of poor health, both before and after adjusting for several explanatory variables. Logistic regression procedures available in SPSS X (1986) and BMDP (1985) were used for the simple analyses in Chapters 6 to 10, while only the BMDP procedure was used for multivariate analyses in Chapter 11. A description of the model is given below, but further details are given by Bishop *et al.* (1975).

The basic model is a regression model used for the analysis of a dichotomous response variable and one or more independent variables. If Y is a dichotomous random variable that takes the value 1 whenever a certain event takes place (for example, if an individual has poor health at age 23, $Y=1$; otherwise $Y=0$), the linear logistic model is formulated by

$$P(Y=1) = \frac{\exp(U)}{1 + \exp(U)}$$

or equivalently by the log-odds representation

Appendix E

$$\ln\left(\frac{P(Y=1)}{1-P(Y=1)}\right) = U$$

where U is a linear function of the independent variables and $P(Y=1)$ represents the probability that Y takes the value 1.

For the estimation of the unadjusted odds ratio, U has the form

$$b_0 + b_1 \text{ CLASS AT } 23$$

where the b's are unknown parameters.

In Chapters 6 to 10 the unadjusted odds ratios were compared with the adjusted ratios, where the adjustment was carried out separately for each explanatory variable. Consider, for example, the adjustment for PARENTS' HEIGHT: in this case, U has the form

$$b_0 + b_1 \text{ CLASS AT } 23 + b_2 \text{ PARENTS' HEIGHT}$$

In the multivariate analyses in Chapter 11 several models were examined. Starting with one independent variable in addition to class at 23 (as shown above for adult short stature), another independent variable was then included, for example:

$$U = b_0 + b_1 \text{ CLASS AT } 23 + b_2 \text{ PARENTS' HEIGHT} + b_3 \text{ CLASS AT } 7$$

followed by

$$U = b_0 + b_1 \text{ CLASS AT } 23 + b_2 \text{ PARENTS' HEIGHT} + b_3 \text{ CLASS AT } 7 +$$
$$b_4 \text{ HEIGHT AT } 7$$

and then

$$U = b_0 + b_1 \text{ CLASS AT } 23 + b_2 \text{ PARENTS' HEIGHT} + b_3 \text{ CLASS AT } 7 +$$
$$b_4 \text{ HEIGHT AT } 7 + b_5 \text{ HEIGHT AT } 11$$

until the last model:

$$U = b_0 + b_1 \text{ CLASS AT } 23 + b_2 \text{ PARENTS' HEIGHT} + b_3 \text{ CLASS AT } 7 +$$
$$b_4 \text{ HEIGHT AT } 7 + b_5 \text{ HEIGHT AT } 11 + b_6 \text{ QUALIFICATIONS}$$

when all of the explanatory variables in Table 11.7 had been included. Parameter estimates derived from the different models shown above were used to indicate the effect of additional explanatory variables.

Two test statistics were used to assess the fit of the logistic models, the Hosmer statistic and the C. C. Brown statistic (BMDP, 1983). Hosmer and Lemeshow (1980) proposed a chi-squared test based on dividing the data into groups on the basis of the logistic estimate of their response rate and then comparing the observed and expected number of responses in each group. Brown (1982) suggests a test that is based on the adequacy of the fit for the logistic model as a special case of a more general family of models. In almost all the logistic models presented in Chapter 11 both tests indicate that the fit of the model is adequate. The availability of these two statistics and the treatment of independent continuous variables motivated the use of BMDP for the multivariate analyses.

For further explanation of logistic models the reader is referred, for example, to Armitage (1971) or Bishop *et al.* (1975).

References

Armitage, P. (1971) *Statistical Methods in Medical Research*, Blackwell Scientific Publications, Oxford.

Bishop, Y. M. M., Fienberg, S. E. and Holland, P. W. (1975) *Discrete Multivariate Analysis, Theory and Practice*, MIT Press, Cambridge, Mass.

BMDP (1985) *Statistical Software*, Univ. of California Press.

Brown, C. C. (1982) On a goodness of fit test for logistic model based on score statistics. *Commun. Statist., Theory and Methods*, **11**, 1087–105.

Cornfield, J. (1951) A method of estimating comparative rates from clinical data. Applications to cancer of the lung, breast and cervix. *J. Natl Cancer Inst.*, **11**, 1269–75.

Fleiss, J. L. (1981) *Statistical Methods for Rates and Proportions*, 2nd edn, Wiley, New York.

Hosmer, D. W. and Lemeshow, S. (1980) Goodness of fit tests for multiple logistic regression model. *Commun. Statist., Theory and Methods*, **9**, 1043–69.

SPSS X (1986) *Users Guide*, 2nd edn, McGraw-Hill, New York.

Index

Page numbers in bold are for figures, those in italic are for tables.